The Black Seminoles

UNIVERSITY PRESS OF FLORIDA

Gainesville Tallahassee Tampa Boca Raton Pensacola Orlando Miami Jacksonville

The Black Seminoles

HISTORY OF A FREEDOM-SEEKING PEOPLE

Kenneth W. Porter

Revised and edited by

Alcione M. Amos

and Thomas P. Senter

Copyright 1996 by the Board of Regents of the State of Florida
Printed in the United States of America on acid-free paper

01 00 99 98 97 96 6 5 4 3 2 1

Library of Congress Cataloging-in-Publication Data
Porter, Kenneth Wiggins, 1905–1981.
  The Black Seminoles: history of a freedom-seeking people / Kenneth W.
Porter; revised and edited by Alcione M. Amos and Thomas P. Senter.
      p. cm.
Includes bibliographical references and index.
ISBN 0-8130-1451-4
  1. Black Seminoles—History. 2. Black Seminoles—Government relations.
3. Black Seminoles—Social conditions. 4. Seminole Indians—African
influences. 5. Afro-Americans—Relations with Indians. I. Amos, Alcione M.
II. Senter, Thomas P. III. Title.
E99.S28P67   1996
973'.04043—dc 20   96-11055

The University Press of Florida is the scholarly publishing agency for the
State University System of Florida, comprised of Florida A & M University,
Florida Atlantic University, Florida International University, Florida State
University, University of Central Florida, University of Florida, University of
North Florida, University of South Florida, and University of West Florida.

University Press of Florida
15 Northwest 15th Street
Gainesville, FL 32611

To our children and to Professor Porter

▧ Contents

Illustrations follow page 134.

⊠ Preface

Kenneth W. Porter wrote the first draft of this book in 1947 and intermittently worked on it until his death in 1981. The original manuscript was a product of his extensive research on the Black Seminoles, which he began in the early 1940s. During lengthy visits to Brackettville and Del Rio, in Texas, and Nacimiento de los Negros in Coahuila, Mexico, Porter interviewed about twenty-six elderly members of the communities. The wealth of information he obtained through the rich, vivid oral history of the Black Seminoles was supplemented and often confirmed by his methodical and exhaustive work in archives and libraries in both the United States and Mexico. The result was an outstanding history of the Black Seminole people and their able and charismatic nineteenth-century leader, John Horse. After Porter's death, the original manuscript, about seven hundred pages long with detailed footnotes, was placed in the Schomburg Center for Research in Black History in New York City. William Loren Katz was instrumental in depositing Porter's collection of papers there and became its curator.

In June 1991, Thomas P. Senter, then contemplating work on a biography of General John L. Bullis (who as a young lieutenant had commanded the detachment of Black Seminole scouts in Texas), contacted Alcione M. Amos, who had been researching Black Seminole history for close to fifteen years. Together we decided to edit Porter's unpublished work.

The task took the next three years. The text had to be extensively revised to bring it up to date historically, for much information about John Horse and the Black Seminoles had come to light after Porter had finished the manuscript. Twenty-six chapters were condensed into seventeen, hundreds of footnotes and sources had to be checked, and new facts were woven into the narrative. We made every effort to verify all references. We were, in general, successful. Only in very few cases (mostly relating to material from Mexican archives) was it impossible to check the sources. In such instances, we trusted that Porter's notes—which are filed among his papers at the Schomburg Center—were correct. Parenthetically, our verification of the footnotes proved that Porter was a most accurate researcher. We found virtually no errors in his work. Thus, the final manuscript is a product of the coeditors' partnership. We take full responsibility for any mistakes or omissions.

Although many individuals helped make our book possible, it would be impossible to acknowledge every one of them, from the anonymous clerical staff at the Library of Congress to the courteous National Archives personnel. But a few people must be specifically cited and thanked. First and foremost is Annette Porter, who kindly gave us permission to edit the original manuscript. Without her trust and confidence, we could not have undertaken the project.

Ian Hancock of the University of Texas at Austin reviewed parts of the manuscript and encouraged us throughout its development. He also arranged for his student, Michael Aceto, to research extensively the newspaper holdings of the university library. Frank Laumer directed us to the unpublished diary of Lieutenant Henry Prince, which added many details to the book's Florida section. Charles Neal, Jr., carefully investigated the Adam Payne assassination episode and other obscure aspects of Black Seminole history in Texas. He was extremely generous in sharing his findings. Sergio Velasco from the Texas State Archives supplied copies of several letters from the Governor's Papers collection, which were essential to clarify an important episode in John Horse's life. George A. Miles of the Beinecke Library at Yale University provided access to the Muzquiz Records even though they were being recataloged at the time. Alfonso Vasquez Sotelo, director of the Archivo General del Estado de Coahuila; Martha Rodrigues Garcia, a researcher from Saltillo, Coahuila; and Maria Carmen Onate, of the Acervo Historico Diplomatico of the Secretaria de Relaciones Exteriores in Mexico City, furnished numerous copies of letters about the Black Seminoles in Mexico.

Miss Charles Emily Wilson, William "Dub" Warrior, and Ethel Warrior (leaders of the Black Seminole communities in Brackettville and Del Rio) also provided continuous support and valuable information. Texans Donald

Swanson, Charles Downing, and Dick Thompson contributed a myriad of facts that enriched the manuscript. Don was especially helpful despite the recent loss of his wife. Ben Pingenot generously made available the original of John T. Sprague's journal, which added precious detail to the Black Seminole crossing into Mexico. Diana Bruce at the Institute of Texan Cultures; Diana Lachatanere of the Schomburg Center for Research in Black History; and Dolores Raney, county clerk of Kinney County, all facilitated our research.

We also thank Tom Hood, who helped verify citations; Roland Wood, who created our book's maps; Shirley H. K. Bennett, who provided expert legal advice; Doyle Crane, who read and reviewed the last draft; and Cindy Bartholomay, who word-processed the text.

Other individuals who either encouraged us or provided information that strengthened the manuscript include Lou and Carl Green, Alice Fay Lozano, Happy Shahan, Larry Berger, Woody Myers, General Colin Powell, Ernie Blackburn, Art Gomez, Jim Kenney, Tom Dunlay, Lucia St. Clair Robson, Kevin Mulroy, Ken Perry, Mike Musick, Bill Haenn, and General Bullis's descendants: Bill Halcomb (his grandson) and Paul Schaffer (his grandnephew).

We also thank our families, especially our children: Katie, Sam, and Jessie Senter and Sandy Amos. We dedicate this book to them.

Finally, we must honor the memory of Kenneth W. Porter, who was interested in black history long before it became fashionable. His outstanding research and writing skills made this book possible.

Our people lived in Texas for over one hundred years. Before that we were in Mexico, where some of us still live, and before that we were in Oklahoma, and even earlier than that in Florida. And before that, we came from Africa. . . . In all our travels we have never lost an awareness of our identity and a pride in our freedom, because it is our freedom that makes us different.

Miss Charles Emily Wilson, Black Seminole, Texas, 1992

PART ONE

War and Peace,
Florida, 1812–1842

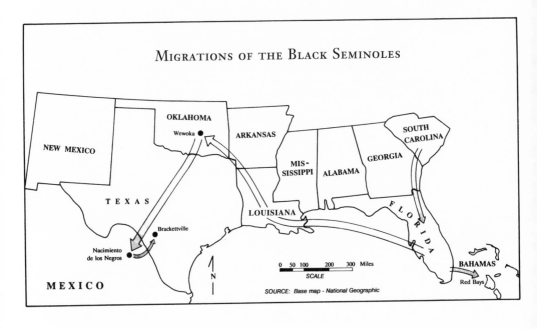

MIGRATIONS OF THE BLACK SEMINOLES

NEW MEXICO

OKLAHOMA
Wewoka

ARKANSAS

TEXAS

Brackettville

Nacimiento
de los Negros

MEXICO

N

MIS-
SISSIPPI

LOUISIANA

ALABAMA

GEORGIA

SOUTH
CAROLINA

FLORIDA

BAHAMAS

Red Bays

0 50 100   200   300 Miles
SCALE

SOURCE: Base map - National Geographic

CHAPTER ONE

⌧ Their Best Soldiers Are Black

Every negro found in arms will be put to death without mercy.
BRIGADIER GENERAL THOMAS FLOURNOY

The year 1812 was a difficult one for American citizens. They had to defend their hard-won independence, once again fighting the British. It was not a good time to be born. But during that tumultuous year, a young black woman living among the Seminole Indians gave birth to a son in the wilds of the Florida Alachua savanna west of St. Augustine. She named him John. Her identity is unknown, as is the baby's father. Perhaps he was the Seminole tribesman, Charles Cavallo, who may have owned her. This child of obscure origins would later become a man of many names and varied roles. From Florida to Texas, through the Indian Territory and Mexico, John would doggedly pursue one goal: freedom for himself and his people. This is their story.[1]

Right before John's birth, south of the American border, in the territory still precariously held by Spain, a net of international intrigue was entangling the blacks and tribespeople of East Florida. The United States had coveted that area since the turn of the century. With Spain bled dry by Napoleon's armies, Spanish officials in East Florida were virtually powerless to resist American expansionism. Thus, on January 15, 1811, Congress secretly authorized President Madison to seize all or any part of Florida if the "local authorities" agreed or a foreign government tried to occupy any portion of the region.

General George Mathews, former governor of Georgia, was sent to East Florida to annex it to the United States. During the summer of 1811, he actively encouraged American settlers in the area to create their own government. U.S. border troops were expected to assist them. Obviously, "local authorities" was an elastic term. Then, on March 14, 1812, the so-called "Patriots," mainly Georgians, hoisted their flag. Bolstered by federal gunboats, they moved swiftly. On March 18 they seized Amelia Island (northeast of modern Jacksonville) and presented it to General Mathews.

The Patriots then marched south. Within a month, they had besieged St. Augustine, capital of East Florida. The city's capitulation—and with it, the whole Spanish province—seemed inevitable. Although the entire garrison consisted of only about four hundred men, mostly untrained local militia, the Spaniards still possessed two potential sources of military strength: Florida's Seminole Indians and blacks.

But the Patriots were so contemptuous of the Seminoles that they coolly began apportioning their lands as bounties to one another. General Mathews reportedly told the principal Seminole chief, King Payne, that "he intended to drive him from his land." John H. McIntosh, a leading Patriot, warned Bowlegs, another chief, that "he intended to make him . . . a waiting man." But cut off from St. Augustine and its munitions by the blockading force of Patriots and U.S. troops at Picolata on the St. Johns River, the Seminoles took no immediate action.[2]

Although the tribespeople faced losing their homes to the land-hungry American settlers who would subsequently stream into Florida, blacks were confronted by a far more serious menace. Those held as vassals by the Seminoles dreaded returning to the strict slavery of the South, and the numerous free and fugitive blacks who lived among the Indians—many of them slaves from Georgia and South Carolina or their descendants—felt just as threatened.

Except for twenty years of British rule just before and during the American Revolution, Florida had been under Spanish authority for nearly a century. The territory had been a natural, sometimes even official, refuge for runaways. As early as 1687, the Spaniards bedeviled rival English settlements by offering freedom and land, in return for military service, to British slaves who fled to them.[3] But when Spain ceded Florida to Great Britain in 1763 in exchange for Cuba, most of the black military colonists were evacuated to Havana. A few opted to remain and settled among Indians who were friendly to the Spanish. In 1725, an English agent visited the Lower Creeks, who were loosely allied with the Spaniards. He found fugitive blacks among them, protected by some of the chiefs. In addition, some runaways probably had always preferred to stay with the tribespeople rather than subject themselves to supervision and discipline in St. Augustine. Thus, after the British acquired Florida, escaped slaves were no longer officially welcomed, although they probably continued to be received by some of the Indians. With the outbreak of war between England and its former colonies in 1775, fugitive blacks from Georgia and South Carolina found Florida a safe haven once again.

Meanwhile, bands of Lower Creeks had constantly drifted into Florida during the 1700s. Some groups wanted to avoid the English, but others were their allies and fought the Spanish and their tribal partners. Because the immigrants had separated from the main body of Lower Creeks, they were sometimes known as "Seminoles," or seceders.[4] Their principal town was Cuscowilla, on the Alachua savanna west of St. Augustine. It was founded by Cowkeeper, a chief of the Oconee band. Because he staunchly supported England, it is unlikely that he protected blacks fleeing from British plantations.[5]

During the two decades of English rule, some Seminole chiefs began to buy blacks. They and their Lower Creek kin noted the prestige that both the Spanish and English attached to owning slaves. Additionally, British officials had given blacks to some Indian leaders as reward for services—"King's gifts."[6]

The Seminoles were somewhat perplexed about how to use their new property best. They apparently had no intention of devoting their lives to managing slaves. Soon, however, they solved their dilemma by supplying the blacks with tools to cut down trees, build houses for themselves, and raise corn. When the crop was harvested, their masters received a reasonable proportion of it as a kind of tribute. One observer reported that no more than ten bushels of corn were ever demanded. The remainder was kept by the so-called slaves. The blacks soon acquired livestock, which their Seminole patrons never meddled with. At slaughtering time, they supplied the tribespeople with a fat hog or a side of beef. It was a mutually beneficial relationship. The "owner" provided protection, and the "slave" paid a modest amount in return. This arrangement was, obviously, quite different from traditional plantation bondage.

Georgia and South Carolina blacks soon learned of the advantageous position enjoyed by the Seminole slaves. Thus, during both war and peace, runaways fled through the wilderness to the Seminole villages. They would put themselves under the care of various chiefs, such as King Payne, who had succeeded Cowkeeper about 1785. Unlike his pro-British predecessor, King Payne became reconciled to the Spanish government and followed its lenient policy toward fugitive blacks. Indian patrons probably asserted ownership of their slaves if they were claimed by a former master or any other white man. But whites generally did not understand this unusual arrangement. They perceived it as only what they knew, conventional bondage.

The blacks lived apart from the Seminoles in their own villages, prized evidence of their independence. Additionally, their patrons did not supervise them, and the blacks would share the "sofkee" pot (sofkee is a gruel made of corn) with their owners whenever they visited their homes. They also habitually carried arms. Thus, except for their annual tribute, the blacks were no more subordinate to the chiefs than the Seminoles themselves.[7]

Soon the distinction between purchased slaves and runaways—if it ever existed—blurred and essentially vanished. Indeed, the relationship between the blacks and the tribespeople might be described as primitive democratic feudalism, with basically no personal inequality between the two groups. Years later, General Edmund P. Gaines spoke with approximate accuracy of "the Seminole Indians with their black vassals and allies."[8]

The Seminoles eventually found the blacks useful in areas besides agriculture. They all spoke some European language, usually English or Spanish, and soon learned their patrons' Muskogean dialect. Therefore, they became the Indians' principal interpreters. Furthermore, those who fled to Florida as adults knew the ways of the whites, so they were often able to predict their behavior in a particular situation.

Given these attributes, the transition from interpreters and unofficial advisers to tribal counselors was easy. In one case, Juan, a former slave of King Payne, served as an interpreter for the Seminoles and had their "utmost confidence." Thus, an association originally limited to mutual material advantage became cemented by reciprocal respect and affection. Intermarriage inevitably occurred, although probably not often because the blacks lived independently and separately.[9]

The contrast between the Black Seminoles' situation and Southern slavery was striking.[10] Their everyday life was idyllic compared to that of plantation slaves. They built houses in their own villages, Indian style, with palmetto planks lashed to upright posts and thatched with palmetto leaves; and their dwellings were usually better constructed than the tribespeople's. Furthermore, Black Seminoles were not bound to the hoe. They spent part of their time hunting and fishing. During war, men and youths armed themselves and assembled under their own captains. Their leader, in turn, obeyed the Seminole chief to whom the blacks owed allegiance.

They thrived amazingly well under this regime. A traveler in the early 1820s, a time when the Seminoles—both the tribespeople and the blacks—were not particularly prosperous, declared: "The Negroes . . . both men and women [are] . . . the finest looking people I have ever seen. . . . They are . . . much more intelligent than their owners."[11] Another observer stated that "the Indian Negroes are a fine formed athletic race, [and] speak English as well as Indian & feel satisfied with their situation."[12]

Thus, there was no group in Florida that would resist annexation more than the Black Seminoles. The Spaniards would forfeit self-rule and the tribespeople their land. But the Black Seminoles would simultaneously lose their independence, their homes, and their freedom.

Not all the free blacks in Florida lived among the Seminoles. Many owed their emancipation to lenient Spanish laws. Others had escaped to the British during the turmoil of the American Revolution or to the Spaniards after the retrocession. But the Black Seminoles were the boldest, the best trained to arms, and the most strategically located to bring themselves and the Indians into the struggle. Therefore, they were the most effective allies to whom the St. Augustine authorities could now turn.

Meanwhile, the Spanish received a brief reprieve. The U.S. government, under Federalist and Northern pressure, decided that General Mathews had proceeded too openly. In early April 1812, President Madison summarily dismissed him. This action, however, was largely a subterfuge. Madison wanted to avoid open hostilities with Spain because war with England was imminent. Secretary of State James Monroe soon ordered Georgia Governor David B. Mitchell to assume command in East Florida. Mitchell was assigned to restore the original situation but only if the Patriots were granted amnesty. This allowed him to keep troops in Florida. As governor, Mitchell could also call on his state militia. He immediately mobilized part of it. The militia commander hoped that the Seminoles would "take up the cudgels" for the Spaniards. This would "afford a desirable pretext for the Georgians to penetrate their country, and Break up a Negroe Town: an important Evil growing under their patronage."[13]

But Mathews's dismissal somewhat discouraged the Patriots and gave the Spanish authorities a momentary respite. They wisely used it to bolster their forces. The St. Augustine garrison now consisted of four hundred whites and five hundred blacks.

In July 1812, Governor Mitchell complained indignantly that the Spaniards had armed all the able-bodied black men they could find. He also denounced the arrival of black troops from Havana. His major concern was that reinforcements would encourage American slaves to revolt. Mitchell wrote to the Spanish governor: "Your certain knowledge of the peculiar situation of the southern section of the union . . . [regarding] (Negroes) . . . [should] have induced you to abstain from introducing them into the province, or from organizing such as were already in it."[14]

Meanwhile, St. Augustine was still closely besieged by land and cut off from further supply. Help was necessary; otherwise, the city would fall from starvation if not by military means. In July, a black man from St. Augustine had arrived at Payne's town. He warned its inhabitants, the residents of nearby Alligator Hole, and those of the neighboring black villages about the whites' plans to seize their lands and conquer them. The man confirmed what Payne's people had feared for so long and tipped the balance in favor of war. Two hundred Seminole warriors from the Alachua towns and Alligator Hole, along with forty black fighters, prepared to resist the invaders.[15] On July 25 a joint force of tribesmen and blacks struck the plantations along the St. Johns River, which were owned by settlers cooperating with the Patriots. The attacks prompted panic in the nearby militia camp, causing many desertions.

At this time, U.S. Army Colonel Thomas A. Smith was commanding troops at Point Petre, near the mouth of the St. Marys River about two miles from Amelia Island. He observed that "the blacks assisted by the Indians have become very daring & from the want of a proper knowledge of the country the parties which I have sent out have always been unsuccessful."[16] Despite the August 15 arrival of Colonel Daniel Newnan, adjutant general of Georgia, with 250 militiamen, the position of the Patriots and U.S. regulars further deteriorated. Besides the strengthened Spanish garrison and the costly raids at their rear, the Americans now faced a different type of Georgia volunteer:

escaped slaves. Taking advantage of the confusion, the slaves deserted their plantations and joined the allied Indian and black forces. Colonel Smith reported on July 30: "They [the Seminoles] have . . . several hundred fugitive [*sic*] slaves from the Carolinas & Georgia at present in their Towns & unless they are checked soon they will be so strengthened by [more] desertions from Georgia & Florida. . . . [I]t will be found troublesome to reduce them."[17]

But not all the runaways joined the tribespeople. Some preferred to enlist with the Spanish. As Governor Mitchell complained, "[the Spanish] governour has proclaimed freedom to every negro who will join his standard. . . . Indeed the principal strength of the garrison at St. Augustine consists of negroes." The influx of slaves who escaped from Georgia into East Florida to assist the Spanish continued until November 1813.[18]

The blockade of St. Augustine ended abruptly and disastrously for the besiegers. On the evening of September 12, two wagons—escorted by twenty-two U.S. Marines and Georgia volunteers—laboriously proceeded west from the Patriot camp near St. Augustine. They were headed for the American depot at Davis Creek on the St. Johns River. In Twelve Mile Swamp, so-called because of its distance from the St. Johns, a group of about fifty blacks and a few tribesmen waited for the column. A free black named Prince Witen led them.

As the soldiers drew near, Witen's men opened fire at point-blank range. Marine Captain John Williams, commanding the unit, was hit eight times. Captain Tomlinson Fort of the Georgia militia and six privates were also wounded. As the troops fell back, a sergeant was shot and scalped in front of his horrified companions. Then the ambushers closed in for the kill. Although gravely wounded, Captain Williams gamely rallied his remaining men. They mounted such a fierce bayonet charge that their attackers withdrew, allowing the survivors to escape with their casualties but abandoning the wagons.[19]

The sharp action, which lasted for about twenty-five minutes, proved decisive because it cut the American supply route. Shortly thereafter, Colonel Smith frantically summoned the Georgia militia. With their support, his command retreated from St. Augustine to the provision camp at Davis Creek (near present-day Bayard). Federal gunboats could protect his soldiers there.

Although the blockade was temporarily interrupted, it could still be resumed if the foe in the besiegers' rear were crushed. In fact, on August 21, Colonel Newnan and his Georgia volunteers had been ordered to find the hostiles and destroy their villages. But difficulty obtaining horses and supplies, as well as illness, delayed their departure. Moreover, the Georgians had less than a week to serve. Although Newnan asked them to extend their enlistments, only eighty-four responded. A few Patriots and militiamen from other detachments were added, bringing the total to 116. On September 24, with this force, twelve horses, and four days' rations, Newnan marched west for the Alachua towns.

The morning of the fourth day, about six or seven miles from their destination, near present-day Windsor in Alachua County, Newnan's troops encountered about one hundred warriors led by King Payne, mounted on a white horse, and his brother (or half-brother) Bowlegs, the war leader. Upon sighting their enemy, the Seminoles threw down their packs. They prepared their weapons, formed a line of battle, and began shooting. King Payne rode back and forth encouraging his men, but the borderers' return fire was intense. Soon the white horse ran riderless.

The warriors, infuriated that their chief was gravely wounded, fought desperately for two and a half more hours. They constantly tried to outflank the soldiers. The Georgians, however, eventually drove them back into the swamp. During the fighting, nine of Newnan's men were wounded, two mortally. Seven Seminoles had fallen.[20]

Huddled behind hastily erected barricades, the Georgians waited for the next clash, which began just before sunset. It was heralded by a furious yelling—the deep-chested shouts of blacks blended with harsh Indian cries. The attackers now numbered about two hundred. The battle continued until eight o'clock. The blacks fought so bravely that Colonel Newnan later stated: "Negroes . . . were their best soldiers." Finally, the Seminoles had to retire as darkness fell; but they maintained a desultory, harassing sniping during the night.[21]

After a week of siege, many invaders had succumbed to wounds, disease, or starvation. More than half were out of action. Newnan, in desperation, ordered a night withdrawal. Carrying their casualties on stretchers, his command set out for the St. Johns River on Sunday evening, October 4. The next day, they were ambushed and lost some men. The soldiers struggled through the wilderness for several more days, subsisting on "gophers, alligators, and palmetto stocks." Eventually they reached Colonel Smith's base camp. In all, the Georgians had eighteen killed, nine wounded, and another eight missing.

Newnan estimated Seminole losses at fifty but specified only fourteen times when warriors had actually fallen. Thus, what started as a punitive expedition ended as a ragged retreat. Nevertheless, repulsing Newnan would give the Seminoles only four months' respite.[22]

Meanwhile, the Florida settlers' fears of slave insurrection were intensified by the many blacks reportedly fighting with the Indians. On January 14, Patriot leader John McIntosh, complained to Secretary of State James Monroe that "[the] slaves are excited to rebel, and we have an army of negroes raked up in this country, and brought from Cuba to contend with. . . . St. Augustine, the whole province will be the refuge of fugitive slaves; and . . . bring about a revolt of the black population in the United States."

The federal government did not ignore McIntosh's appeals. Authorities again prepared their forces in Florida to suppress the Seminoles and ultimately seize the territory.[23] By now, the citizens of Tennessee were also consumed with battle fever. Ever since America had declared war against England on June 18, 1812, western Tennesseans had prepared to march under General Andrew Jackson against British-held Mobile and Spanish Pensacola. Eastern Tennesseans had also organized a regiment of volunteer cavalry. On learning of Newnan's defeat, they acted immediately. More than two hundred horsemen rode out early in December. On January 7, 1813, they arrived at Colerain on the St. Marys River and reported to Brigadier General Thomas Flournoy, commander of the Georgia militia.

The Indians, meanwhile, alarmed about these developments, sued for peace through Creek agent Benjamin Hawkins. But Major General Thomas Pinckney, who had replaced Governor Mitchell, ordered the expedition to proceed. The volunteers were to link up with Colonel Smith's two hundred regulars. In February, the Tennesseans and a few Georgians rode for the Alachua towns. Smith was to join them near the first Seminole settlement.

The two forces united on February 7 and quickly moved on the Alachua villages. According to Brigadier General Flournoy, "every negro found in arms [would] be put to death without mercy."[24] The warriors, who had mustered about two hundred men against Newnan's Georgians, knew they were unable to resist an army nearly four times as large. So they hurried their families into the swamps.

On February 9 the column reached Payne's deserted town. Bowlegs's village was several miles to the southwest; and a body of volunteers under Colonel John Williams, the Tennessee commander, marched for it on the next day. But the Indians and blacks, at heavy cost, delayed the advance. Thus, the troops did not reach their destination until February 12.

The soldiers began plundering and destroying the enemy's possessions in the two settlements, but the warriors harassed them so much that the invaders decided not to head for a third, more distant town. Nevertheless, the troops were satisfied after leveling the two principal villages, announcing, "the balance of the Seminole Nation is completely in waste." Fifty or sixty hostiles, they declared, had been killed, while the Americans had only one dead and seven wounded. The Alachua region was now open to settlers. In addition, almost the entire Seminole food supply was destroyed, and by spring the survivors were reportedly starving. The strength of the Seminoles east of the Suwannee River was, for all practical purposes, broken.[25]

One victory, however, does not necessarily win a war. Tribal and black resistance enabled Northern and Federalist opposition in Congress, once again, to halt temporarily the occupation attempt. By May 15, 1813, the Patriots, who had scornfully repudiated an amnesty offer on March 30, were now on their own when federal troops withdrew. Some of them soon returned to the United States, but those who remained confiscated their former comrades' property and sold free blacks unlucky enough to fall into their hands.[26]

The more intransigent Patriots, led by Buckner Harris, invaded the recently pacified Alachua region. In addition to his rather tenuous title as president of the legislative council of East Florida, Harris was a Georgia militia brigadier general. His men built a fort, surveyed the land for settlement, and requested annexation to the United States. But on April 19, 1814, their petition was firmly rejected. This rebuff was followed by Harris's death: on May 5 he was "waylaid and killed." The Americans believed the attackers were blacks who presumably received the reward that the Spanish governor had reputedly offered for Harris's head. Not surprisingly, the leaderless Patriot movement soon fell apart; and the group eventually accepted peace terms from the Spaniards in 1816.

Thus ended, temporarily, the U.S. attempt to seize Spanish-owned East Florida, which had failed largely due to black-instigated resistance. An uneasy peace prevailed in Florida for the next five years.[27]

CHAPTER TWO

☒ This Savage and Black War

The next enemy . . . engaged were the negroes at Sawannee.
GOVERNOR D. B. MITCHELL

The blacks and tribespeople had cautiously emerged from the swamps after the Tennesseans withdrew in early 1813. Subsisting on koonti (a root from which the Seminoles made flour), they gradually drifted west from the fertile Alachua savanna to the banks of the Suwannee River. The storm of war had receded temporarily from their land. For the next year, however, it would rage furiously to the north and west among the Upper Creeks and eventually wheel down and engulf the Seminoles again.

The Upper Creeks, dwelling in the heart of present-day Alabama, had been less exposed to white influence than the Lower Creeks on the Chattahoochee River along the Georgia border. Therefore, they were more susceptible to the propaganda of Tecumseh and his prophets, who advocated an economy based upon hunting and trading rather than agriculture. Civil war soon erupted between the militant Creek traditionalists—called Red Sticks because of their scarlet war clubs—and the more conciliatory prowhite faction. Before long, two thousand warriors were also fighting the Americans.

Peter McQueen, a principal Red Stick leader who was part white, led the first large attack against U.S. forces. Using arms obtained in Spanish Pensacola, they routed about 180 Mississippi territorial militia and their mixed-blood allies on July 27, 1813. The battle occurred at Burnt Corn Creek, about eighty miles north of Pensacola.

On August 30 the Red Sticks struck Fort Mims just north of Mobile, where several hundred people, including whites, their slaves, and mixed bloods, had taken refuge. The hostiles overwhelmed them and slaughtered almost the entire garrison. Blacks, who then occupied a position among the Upper Creeks somewhat similar to their Seminole counterparts, were conspicuous in the war party. Significantly, the Red Sticks spared most of the slaves in the post because "the Master of Breath has ordered [us] . . . not to kill any but white people and half-breeds."

For a time, the warriors had everything their own way. But the Fort Mims massacre enraged the Americans. By October 12, 1813, General Andrew Jackson and 3,500 Tennessee militia had entered the fray, and nearly a thousand Georgian volunteers crossed the Chattahoochee River to the east on November 24. A third column marched north from Mobile.

The Red Sticks fanatically resisted the troops. The blacks among them, dreading a return to harsh plantation slavery, fought alongside their masters at least once after the Fort Mims attack. They were also accompanied by newly arrived runaways. At the Battle of the Holy Ground (near present-day Montgomery), twenty-one Creeks and twelve blacks were killed on December 23, 1813.

Nevertheless, despite fierce resistance, supply problems, insubordinate civilian soldiers, and incompetent officers, Jackson's will ultimately triumphed over every obstacle. On March 27, 1814, his men shattered a force of about nine hundred Red Sticks in the Battle of Horseshoe Bend, breaking the back of the Creek resistance. Most of the warriors not involved in the fight soon fled into Florida. The tide of war was rolling closer to the Seminoles.[1]

In May 1814, His Majesty's warship *Orpheus*, commanded by Captain Hugh Pigot, anchored at the mouth of the Apalachicola River. Lieutenant George Woodbine, with the brevet (honorary) rank of captain, went ashore with a small command. He had been commissioned to recruit the area's many fugitive Creeks and blacks for British service by providing them with food and weapons. On shore, Woodbine operated from Prospect Bluff, fifteen miles up the river. In early June, Captain Pigot departed, leaving Woodbine in charge. The lieutenant soon went to Pensacola to obtain more supplies and organize the Red Sticks who had taken refuge there. He also began recruiting more runaway slaves.

Meanwhile, the English were planning a major diversion in the Gulf of Mexico region to distract U.S. forces. Initially, their goal was to relieve pressure on the Canadian front. Royal Marine Brevet Major Edward Nicolls, with the local rank of lieutenant colonel, headed the effort. Nicolls first distributed handbills among the black population in Mobile, offering them land in the British West Indies when the fighting ended and guaranteeing their freedom. He then proceeded to Pensacola. Late in August, he hoisted the Union Jack beside the Spanish flag and had himself declared commander of the city by the war-weary Spaniards. He also issued a proclamation to the people of Louisiana, urging them to join him in liberating their territory. Additionally, he and Woodbine continued arming the local Red Sticks and fugitive slaves.

General Jackson, now commanding the Seventh Military District, which Nicolls was busily attempting to overthrow, was well aware of his seditious activities. Because Old Hickory had been intending to seize Pensacola all along, the English presence probably moved up his timetable. But after arriving in Mobile on August 15, Jackson had to await fresh troops before marching on Pensacola. A month later, he was further delayed by an abortive British attack in which Nicolls and several Red Sticks participated. Finally, bolstered by reinforcements, Jackson marched east on November 3. Five days later, after capturing Pensacola, he forced the English, including Nicolls and Woodbine, to evacuate nearby Fort Barrancas. The triumphant Americans returned to Mobile on November 11.

In the interim, Nicolls and Woodbine had sailed from Pensacola for the Apalachicola River, about 150 miles to the east, accompanied by their Indian and black allies, including approximately one hundred fugitive slaves. Some of the runaways had left their Spanish owners and joined the royal forces when promised freedom. At Prospect Bluff, on the Apalachicola's eastern bank, Nicolls completed the building of a fort. Called British Post, it was the headquarters for his negotiations with the Seminoles, former Red Stick Creeks, and the region's many runaway slaves.[2]

Nicolls stayed at the fort after peace was declared and the Treaty of Ghent, formally ending the War of 1812, was signed on December 24, 1814. He had made a pact with the Seminole chief, Bowlegs, in whose name he frequently wrote to Indian agent Benjamin Hawkins. Nicolls also trained and armed about three thousand Indians and three hundred blacks while at the fort.

Early the following summer, he sailed for London to arrange an agreement making the Creek Nation His Majesty's military partner, a deal that would also include the Seminoles. He took the Creek prophet, Francis, and a few other prominent Red Sticks to help him negotiate. But the effort failed, ending his dream of becoming Indian superintendent for the two tribes.

Meanwhile, most of the other Creeks and all the blacks had remained at the post on Prospect Bluff, and the warriors had kept the many weapons that the English had abandoned. They included four pieces of heavy artillery, six light cannons, thousands of small arms, and vast quantities of ammunition. Eventually, the tribespeople drifted eastward under their various chiefs to establish their own villages. But the blacks stayed behind under the strict discipline of a black leader named Garson. Little is known about him except for his name and two or three episodes in his career, which suggest that he was cunning, courageous, and cruel.

The Negro Fort, as it became known, was a beacon that drew restless slaves from miles around. At that time there were reportedly about a thousand runaways in Florida. Welcomed by the blacks at the post, they settled under the protection of its ramparts. Eventually, their fields and pastures extended fifty miles along the Apalachicola River.

But the fortress was vulnerable to raids from slave-hunting Indians friendly to the whites and from posses of planters seeking their own runaways. In turn, the post's inhabitants allegedly harried the border, drove off cattle, fired on boats, and caused great anxiety among the region's slaveholders. The Spanish governor soon received protests about the Negro Fort from the newly appointed southern division commander, Andrew Jackson. Although the Spaniard professed his willingness to suppress the "lawless banditti," he said that he could not do the job. So Jackson ordered General Edmund P. Gaines to destroy the stronghold and return the blacks to their owners.

Gaines soon established a base in Georgia—eventually called Fort Scott—at the junction of the Flint and Chattahoochee rivers, just before they joined and formed the Apalachicola. He located it close to the Florida border to intimidate the Negro Fort garrison. To supply the new post, two transports loaded with ordnance and provisions left New Orleans escorted by two gunboats. The vessels arrived at the mouth of the Apalachicola on July 10, 1816, where they received a message from General Gaines stating that he had sent Lieutenant Colonel Duncan Clinch down the river with regular troops. If fired on from the Negro Fort, Clinch was authorized to destroy it. The small fleet was ordered not to enter the Apalachicola until Clinch's men were in position.

Gaines obviously wanted to provoke an attack to justify the stronghold's destruction. The blacks obliged and fired the first shots on July 17. They ambushed and annihilated a crew that had gone out in a rowboat to seek drinking water. Only one sailor escaped by swimming, and another was captured.

Meanwhile, Clinch's command started down the river toward the Negro Fort and soon encountered a large party of slave-hunting Lower Creeks led by Captain William McIntosh. Clinch quickly recruited them. For helping in the attack, the Creeks would receive the powder, small arms, and clothing seized at the fortress. They also would be paid fifty dollars for each American-owned slave they seized.[3] Before long, McIntosh's men intercepted a black courier from Garson carrying a white man's scalp on his belt. The messenger, sent to summon the Seminoles for aid, described the boat party's fate.

Clinch swiftly pushed on. Presently, his troops surrounded the fort and ordered the garrison to surrender. The defenders jeered derisively and hoisted the Union Jack accompanied by a red battle flag of death. After the blacks fired their cannon, the Creek contingent became less enthusiastic about the task at hand. Clinch's men, however, settled down for a siege and ordered up the gunboats, prompting the runaway slaves living along the river to abandon their villages and run into the forest.

Early on July 27, the American vessels came within range of the Negro Fort. After being shelled, the sailors returned fire; but the shots from their light weapons sank harmlessly into the post's thick walls. In turn, balls from the blacks' heavy cannons, manned by inexperienced artillerists, whistled harmlessly overhead or splashed into the muddy Apalachicola.

Then the ninth round from one of the gunboats, heated red-hot in the cook's galley, penetrated the fort's magazine and exploded spectacularly. Most of those inside the post were killed instantly. There were only about fifty survivors, many of whom died later of severe injuries. Those who lived were eventually returned to their owners.

By some freak of fate, the black leader Garson and his Choctaw counterpart survived the explosion. When the troops learned that the sailor captured ten days before had been "tarred and burned alive," they turned the two men over to the Creeks. After scalping the Choctaw, they stabbed him to death and then shot Garson. With the Negro Fort destroyed, the fugitives who had taken refuge into the surrounding forest fled further east to the Suwannee River.[4]

Stunned by the catastrophe on the Apalachicola, the Indians and blacks remained quiet for several months. The blacks found refuge on the Suwannee and began reorganizing. They built villages, near the tribespeople, that extended down the coast as far as Tampa Bay. But as both groups saw the white settlers buffeting their borders, their hostility rose. Within six months, they were planning revenge for past injustices and resistance to future aggressions.

Early in 1817, reports claimed that six hundred armed blacks (their number probably greatly exaggerated) were drilling and marching to drumbeats. They were commanded by officers, selected from within their own ranks, and under strict military discipline. The blacks were accompanied by the same number of tribesmen, and new recruits constantly joined them.

By now, the blacks had chosen Bowlegs as their king and his chief "slave," Nero, as their commander. They agreed to serve with the Seminole warriors but in their own companies and under their own captains. The men swore revenge for the Negro Fort's destruction and were said to be "in complete fix for fighting." They wanted nothing better than to battle the Americans or William McIntosh's mixed-blood Lower Creeks to "let them know they had something more to do than . . . at Appalachicola."[5]

In 1817 Alexander Arbuthnot, a Scottish trader from the Bahamas, arrived on the Suwannee aboard his schooner *Chance*. He soon opened a trading house near the river close to the Seminoles. Apparently, Spanish officials had authorized him to operate in the area. Arbuthnot seemed genuinely concerned about the Indians, believing that they had been mistreated by the Americans and deceived by the British; so he frequently wrote to U.S. authorities on behalf of Bowlegs and his followers. He also asked the English to aid the Seminoles against American encroachment. But his friendship with the inhabitants of Bowlegs's town was to prove his downfall.[6]

Early in the autumn of 1817, Arbuthnot's schooner returned to the Suwannee from a trip to the West Indies. Two white men were on board. The older of the pair was British Captain Woodbine, who had helped train the Negro Fort defenders. Probably some of the blacks on the Suwannee knew him. The younger man was Robert C. Ambrister, who soon took charge of the warriors' drilling and training.

Meanwhile, in August 1817 General Gaines had sent an ungrammatical and confused message to Chief Kenhadjo, who led the Mikasuki band and lived at the town and near the lake named after the tribe. The officer probably thought that the letter made good "Indian talk." Still, his concluding sentences were stark: "You harbor a great many of my black people among you at Sahwahnee. If you give me leave to go by you against them, I shall not hurt any thing belonging to you."

Kenhadjo's reply was brief: "I harbor no negroes. When the Englishmen were at war with America, some took shelter among them. . . . [I]t is for you white people to settle these things among yourselves. . . . I shall use force to stop any armed Americans from passing my towns or my lands." A U.S. general had demanded, from a Seminole chief, the right to go slave hunting in Spanish territory and been refused. Kenhadjo, previously uninvolved in the hostilities surrounding him, was now an enemy.[7]

The next clash between American troops and blacks or Indians took place in Fowl Town, a village in Georgia located fifteen miles from Fort Scott near the Florida line. About forty-five Mikasuki Seminole warriors and their families lived in the village. Neamathla, Fowl Town's chief, had warned Major David E. Twiggs at Fort Scott "not to cross or cut a stick of wood on the east side of the Flint River."[8] In response, detachments from the post attacked the village late in October and again in November. They drove the people into the swamps, killing a score or so in the process. The troops then plundered and finally burned the town. The entire countryside immediately arose, and the First Seminole War began.

The Indians were estimated at "more than two thousand, besides the blacks, amounting to near four hundred men, and increasing by runaways from Georgia." Their revenge for Fowl Town was swift and bloody. The Americans had barely finished sacking Neamathla's village when a large open boat moved slowly up the Apalachicola toward Fort Scott. Commanded by Lieutenant R. W. Scott, it carried forty soldiers—half of whom were ill—seven women, and four children. On November 30 an ambush killed nearly all on board. Only six men escaped by swimming, and one woman was taken prisoner.

A few days later, a fleet of five vessels was trapped on the Apalachicola by Indians and blacks strategically placed on both sides of the river. During the four-day siege, two whites died and thirteen were wounded. The convoy was finally rescued by troops from Fort Scott.[9]

On December 13, 1817, Fowl Town warriors seized William Hambly and Edward Doyle, agents of Forbes and Company, a British trading firm on the Apalachicola. The men had received the runaway slaves, belonging to the Spanish, who were captured after the Negro Fort disaster. Hambly and Doyle were first taken to Mikasuki and then to the black towns on the Suwannee. There the pair was tried for alleged complicity in the Negro Fort destruction. Many suggested that they should be turned over to the few Choctaw survivors of the catastrophe for punishment.

But the black chief Nero intervened. He sent the men to St. Marks, where the Spanish commandant kept them in "protective custody." Apparently, the Spaniard was either unable or unwilling to prevent the Seminoles from using his fort at their convenience, whether as arsenal, prison, or headquarters.[10]

The border war continued, with the hostiles raiding plantations and killing settlers. They also seized livestock and slaves. Resupply up the Apalachicola to Fort Scott was "impossible . . . the shore being lined on both sides of the river, with Indians and negroes, who keep up a constant fire." Meanwhile, General Gaines was transferred; and Andrew Jackson, scourge of the Red Sticks, was selected to replace him.[11]

In January 1818 Old Hickory mustered two regiments of mounted volunteers, marched for Fort Scott, and reached it on March 9. Reinforced by the post's regulars, the troops went down the Apalachicola's east bank. At Prospect Bluff, after the arrival of provision ships under convoy, they built a new fortification, which Jackson named Fort Gadsden after his engineer, Captain James Gadsden. The new post was constructed exactly where the Negro Fort had stood.[12]

Jackson heard that Peter McQueen, the prominent Red Stick who had led the Burnt Corn attackers, and the prophet Francis, who had gone to England with Edward Nicolls, were at St. Marks accompanied by British adventurer George Woodbine, merchant Alexander Arbuthnot, and a "motley crew" of hostiles who were mostly fugitive slaves. Jackson feared that the Seminoles would turn the coastal town into a stronghold, so he ordered the fleet to proceed down the Apalachicola to the Gulf of Mexico, sail east to St. Marks, and blockade the town. Jackson would follow them overland.

In April a Tennessee regiment operating with William McIntosh's Creeks sacked the Mikasuki and other nearby Indian villages. They killed one black man, captured three tribespeople, and burned three hundred houses. There was little opposition. Jackson, meanwhile, pushed on to St. Marks. He arrived on April 6 and seized it without resistance. There were no Indians or blacks there, but Jackson found and imprisoned Arbuthnot to await court martial. He also located two Red Stick chiefs—Imala Mico and the prophet Francis—on an American vessel in the harbor. Lured aboard by the display of a British flag, the two men were summarily hanged.

After two days at St. Marks, Jackson's force headed toward Bowlegs's town and the black villages on the Suwannee, one hundred difficult miles to the east. Word of their movement preceded them. After hearing about Jackson's expedition, Alexander Arbuthnot had sent a messenger to his son on April 2. The younger Arbuthnot was commanding a schooner on the Suwannee River just below Bowlegs's town. "The main drift of the Americans," the Scottish trader wrote, "is to destroy the black population of Swany. Tell my friend, Boleck [Bowlegs], that it is throwing away his people to attempt to resist such a powerful force."[13] Alexander Arbuthnot knew that, despite all exaggerations, only a thousand warriors would be able to face Jackson, including a few hundred blacks. In contrast, Jackson had 3,500 men, including 2,000 Creeks.

By now, Robert C. Ambrister, the former Royal Marine lieutenant, had operated with the blacks on the Suwannee for about six months. Ambrister "stated he had come to the country on Woodbine's business to see the negroes righted." Woodbine had received a land grant from the Florida tribespeople that would be worthless if the United States seized the region. Thus, whether for patriotism, love of adventure, sympathy for the blacks, or less laudable motives (a share in Woodbine's land grant?), Ambrister became fatally involved in the Suwannee inhabitants' affairs.[14]

During the winter of 1817–18, Alexander Arbuthnot sold ammunition, as usual, to the Seminoles. But Ambrister was apparently not satisfied with the amount. So on March 20, leading twenty-four armed blacks, he seized Arbuthnot's schooner and took nine kegs of powder and five hundred pounds of lead. Three days later, he plundered the Scottish merchant's store and distributed the spoils to the warriors.

On April 5 or 6 a black woman who had escaped from the devastated Mikasuki towns reached the Suwannee. After hearing her report of the attacks, Ambrister quickly sent out a party of blacks against the Americans. But the men encountered so many fleeing Mikasukis that the extent of the disaster overwhelmed them. They swiftly returned to the Suwannee settlement for further council.

Meanwhile, a black man had brought Arbuthnot's warning letter, which he claimed came from an Indian courier; and Ambrister read it to his followers. At first, the Black Seminoles considered the messenger an enemy spy sent to sow alarm and confusion in their ranks. Eventually, however, they became convinced of his good faith. The blacks accordingly prepared to send their families and possessions across the river. (Their villages were on the western bank and the Indians' on the eastern.) Then they made ready to meet the enemy.

But as Jackson drew nearer, Ambrister's enthusiasm waned. He was, after all, a former British officer and a gentleman. It was one thing to command Indians and blacks under His Majesty's commission. It was quite another—as Ambrister would soon discover—for a private citizen to arm, direct, and encourage such insurgents against the United States. To lead them personally into battle was too much; so he withdrew to his headquarters on Arbuthnot's schooner, leaving Nero to reassume the command over the blacks.

Unaware that the foe was alerted, Jackson's army struggled through the swampy wilderness. On April 16, about 3 P.M., Jackson reached a large pond that, according to his Indian guides, was just six miles from the Suwannee. He had hoped to reach the river by midday and have the whole afternoon for the attack, so he considered camping for the night. But after six mounted Seminoles were spotted in the distance, the only course was to push on.

Jackson divided his force into three columns. Sensing the possibility of crushing their enemy, the troops marched as rapidly as possible. But as fast as they moved, the half-dozen scouts were quicker. They galloped into the black village, which extended three miles along the river, shouting that soldiers were coming and Creeks were in the vanguard.

Bowlegs had already recognized the wisdom of Arbuthnot's advice to withdraw. With the Suwannee between him and the enemy, he and his people swiftly disappeared into the swamp. The blacks were less fortunate. Because some of their families were still on the western side of the river, they frantically began ferrying those not already evacuated across the Suwannee. Suddenly, Jackson's army appeared as if out of the sunset. Some black warriors had remained behind to cover the withdrawal; a few Indians joined them.

The blacks had vowed to give the Americans "something more to do than they had had at Appalachicola."[15] But they had not expected so many soldiers. Moreover, Bowlegs and most of his men were across the river. Nevertheless, the blacks would protect their families as best as possible.

In the deepening twilight, the few hundred defenders prepared to fight. Although greatly outnumbered by the Tennesseeans and Creeks on Jackson's left wing and with their smoothbore British muskets outranged by the American weapons, the men desperately held their ground. But the gathering darkness soon told them that they had prevented pursuit for the night. It was now time to withdraw. Two blacks, their escape cut off by the rapidly advancing troops, were captured. Nine others and two Indians lay dead. The rest fled to the Suwannee. They plunged in and swam for the eastern shore where their families had gone.

Years later, a black participant in the fight said that he and his comrades had fought as long as they dared. But the soldiers and Creeks "came too hot upon them and they all ran to save their lives."[16] It was later estimated, perhaps with exaggeration, that the battle at the Suwannee cost the defeated warriors one-fourth to one-half their number. They were either dead on the field or at the bottom of the river. In contrast, only thirteen of Jackson's army had wounds that needed attention. These men were largely Creeks, who had experienced most of the action. Still, none of the victors doubted that the blacks had been those that they had met on the Suwannee. Thus, despite a defeat, Nero's fighting men partly fulfilled their proud boast of a year earlier—to avenge the Negro Fort destruction.

Andrew Jackson now possessed a deserted town, a few stray livestock, and some corn. The pillaging would take a day or two, and his men needed rest; so the army camped next to the Suwannee. They spent days searching the region for refugees left behind in the general flight. On April 28, Creek scouts, scouring the swamps for six miles beyond the river, flushed out and killed three warriors. They also captured five blacks and nine Indian women and children but attempted no further pursuit because the Seminoles had scattered so widely. By far, the greater prize was the white man who had blundered into Jackson's camp at midnight while returning to the Suwannee. His name was Ambrister.

Jackson took Ambrister to St. Marks where he and Arbuthnot were swiftly court-martialed. On the morning of April 29 the Scottish trader was hanged on his own schooner's masthead. A few minutes later, a firing squad executed Ambrister. Jackson had already returned to Fort Gadsden. On May 5 he wrote that the two men had been "tried . . . by a special court of selected officers; legally convicted as exciters of this savage and negro war; legally condemned, and most justly punished."

In late May 1818, Jackson heard that several hundred tribespeople were at Pensacola being fed by the Spanish governor. Using the town as headquarters, the warriors had made murderous forays into the United States. Jackson marched on Pensacola and entered it on May 24. After some resistance, he forced the garrison to surrender. Five days later, leaving behind a small occupying force, he started homeward. Although he was severely criticized by important American government officials for his audacious invasion and seizure of Spanish Florida, Andrew Jackson was the military's idol and lionized more than ever by the people of the frontier.[17]

John Horse was now five or six years old. He and his mother undoubtedly were among those evacuated from the Black Seminole villages on the Suwannee's west side when Jackson's men appeared. That wearisome experience was to be repeated in later years.

CHAPTER THREE

⬚ The Gathering Storm

These negroes . . . [are] intelligent . . . and they have great influence over . . . the Indians whom they, in fact, govern.

JEAN A. PÉNIÈRES

For months after Andrew Jackson's punitive 1818 expedition, which broke Seminole power west of the Suwannee River, Florida's Indians and blacks were constantly moving. The Red Stick Creeks, who had been fighting and fleeing for five years; the Mikasuki and Alachua Seminole bands; the blacks who lived among them; and newly arrived fugitive slaves—all were seeking new homes.

Most of the stubborn Mikasukis, who had fired the first shots in the First Seminole War, did not journey far. In November 1818 Chief Kenhadjo reportedly intended to "go back to his old situation" and reside in what was called New Mikasuki, about thirty miles west of the upper Suwannee River. But some bands went as far south as the Alachua savanna where King Payne's and Bowlegs's people had lived before being dislodged during the Patriot invasion six years earlier. The distance that the Red Sticks traveled indicated how strongly they felt the whites' hatred. Within a few years, most of the villages around Tampa Bay reportedly belonged to these refugee Creeks.

Bowlegs's Alachuas, meanwhile, traveled about 120 miles south of their old location. Their principal town, Okihumpky, was just west of Lake Harris. The Alachua blacks stayed, as before, in separate villages near the tribe. Peliklakaha was their main community, and other black settlements were probably located farther west. An 1819 report stated that "the negroes of Sahwanne fled with the Indians of Bowleg's Town toward Chuckachatte [Chocachatti]," north of Tampa Bay and sixty or seventy miles southeast of the Suwannee villages.[1]

The unattached blacks, including Captain Woodbine's and Major Nicolls's former soldiers as well as runaways, settled near Tampa Bay. Woodbine had already moved some of their former comrades there. Eventually, they likely assumed the same type of vassalage with Indian patrons to which the Black Seminoles were accustomed. Many blacks, however, "went from Tampa Bay, & Charlotte Harbour, in boats to the Florida Keys." From there, they were "taken to the Bahamas by the Providence wreckers." Still others, distrusting the wrecking captains, put to sea in great dugout canoes. In all, perhaps two hundred made the perilous journey to Andros Island in the Bahamas. Descendants of the original settlers, some of them named Bowlegs, currently live there in a small village named Red Bays.[2]

Andrew Jackson had marched, largely unopposed, through much of East Florida, sacking Indian and black villages, court-martialing and executing British subjects, as well as capturing Spanish forts and deposing their commanders. His ease of action clearly demonstrated Spain's inability to keep Florida. Although President Monroe had returned Jackson's conquests to the Spaniards in August 1818, they realized that eventually their possession would be lost again.

Thus, in February 1819 the Adams-Onis Treaty was signed, providing for Florida's cession to the United States at a price of 5 million dollars and the release of American claims to Texas, although formal transfer did not occur until 1821. Andrew Jackson was named the first territorial governor but only served a few months before leaving. His replacement was William Pope DuVal.[3]

Initially, the warriors did not resist continued U.S. expansionism. They finally realized that Spain could not, and England would not, assist them any longer. Useful only when furthering both Spanish and British diplomatic goals, the tribespeople were now discarded. Jackson's ruthlessness also convinced them, at least temporarily, that they could not effectively fight the Americans.

New leaders soon appeared in the Indian and black settlements. Bowlegs died shortly after Jackson's Suwannee raid. By 1821, he was succeeded, according to Seminole custom, by his sister's son, Micanopy. Fat, vain, unaggressive, and indolently good-natured, the new chief was notably kind to the blacks attached to him. In fact, they made him so comfortable at Peliklakaha that Micanopy preferred it to his official residence in Okihumpky.

A new black chief also emerged, as Nero apparently died during Jackson's attacks on the Suwannee settlements. By 1826 (at the latest) Abraham appeared. He was a full-blooded black born around 1790. Formerly owned by a Dr. Sierra of Pensacola, Abraham probably was one of Major Nicolls's recruits and survived the 1816 Negro Fort disaster. Tall and sparely built, he had a courtly manner and a clear, fluent, genteel style of speech. His smiling, intelligent face was somewhat marred by a badly crossed right eye. Abraham's favorite roles were politician and diplomat. He was called "a perfect Talleyrand of the Savage Court" and had "the crouch and the spring of the panther."[4]

Abraham gained Micanopy's complete confidence and became his interpreter. In 1826, he accompanied a Seminole delegation to Washington in that capacity. After they returned to Florida, Micanopy freed him for his faithful services. Abraham was also a religious enthusiast and somewhat of an exhorter, traits that won him the name "the Prophet." Although he was occasionally accused of ambition, avarice, deceit, drunkenness, and even cowardice, no one ever doubted Abraham's intelligence or his hold on Micanopy. Thus, he exemplified the Black Seminoles in the eyes of white contemporaries.

From 1812 to 1818, the blacks among the tribespeople had been recognized for their military prowess and aggressiveness. But after 1821, when they were more closely scrutinized, their intellect and the power they wielded over their Seminole "lords" were now emphasized. One observer said: "The negroes, who dwell among these people as their slaves, are intelligent, speak the English language, . . . and . . . have a great influence over . . . the Indians. . . . They fear being again made slaves, under the American government, and will omit nothing to increase or keep alive mistrust among the Indians, whom they in fact govern. If it should be necessary to use force with them, it is to be feared the Indians would take their part. It will, however, be necessary to remove from the Floridas this group of lawless freebooters, among whom runaway negroes will always find refuge."[5]

Soon after U.S. authority in Florida was confirmed by fort construction at strategic locations, settlement was encouraged. In 1823, the dispirited tribes did not resist efforts to seize their best land, including the fertile Alachua savanna where the descendants of Cowkeeper, founder of the Seminole Nation, had lived for more than two generations. On September 18, 1823, at Moultrie Creek just south of St. Augustine, the major Seminole leaders signed a treaty ceding their claims to all of Florida except for a reservation, far to the south, cut off from the sea. In return for this cession and a pledge to apprehend runaway slaves, the Indians were promised a little property and some money.

Interestingly, during the Moultrie Creek negotiations, Neamathla, the Mikasuki chief and principal Seminole spokesman, refused to enumerate the blacks among his people. But a rough census taken the previous year estimated the number of "slaves," "Maroon Negroes," or "half slaves" (as they were variously called) at about eight hundred, including 150 men. Neamathla did submit the names of thirty-seven Indian towns with a total of 4,883 inhabitants but did not list Peliklakaha, the main Black Seminole community.

As signers of the Moultrie Creek agreement, the names of "Miconope, or Pond Governor," and his two brothers-in-law appear for the first time. One was "Onselmatche, or Jumper," an old Red Stick Creek. He was Micanopy's principal counselor and "sense keeper." The other was "Philip," the St. Johns River chief, second in the nation only to Micanopy. Their names should be remembered.[6]

The Moultrie Creek treaty proved immediately disastrous. Although the Seminoles were promised government rations for a year during their removal south, food was woefully inadequate. Some reluctant tribespeople were slow to leave their homes. Others, more prompt, still found it difficult to find new locations in which to settle and grow crops. The government had not investigated the land assigned to them before determining its boundaries.

Two years later, Governor DuVal finally examined the reservation. He declared it was not "worth cultivation. The best of the Indian lands are worth but little, [and it] . . . is by far the poorest and the most miserable region I ever beheld." A drought came as a final catastrophe. On December 20, 1825, Lieutenant Colonel George M. Brooke wrote from Cantonment Brooke, Tampa Bay, to Colonel George Gibson: "The major part of the [Seminole] nation are . . . suffering . . . unless the government assists them, many of them must starve, and others will depredate on the property of the whites." Brooke soon began distributing food to the famished people on his own.[7]

Thus, the difficulties that developed from the compulsory removal—forcing the Seminoles on government rations—gave whites the upper hand both economically and militarily. The return of runaway slaves could now be compelled merely by threatening to withhold provisions. Not surprisingly, early in 1826, the Indians reportedly surrendered so many fugitive blacks that only about twenty were still at large. But this roundup undoubtedly did not include the long-established Black Seminole "slaves," who numbered about eight hundred in 1822. The twenty runaways left in the Seminole Nation probably established remote camps, which might explain the failure to apprehend them. On September 23, 1823, an observer wrote about one such colony on Pine Island in Charlotte Harbor: "They are well armed and refuse to allow Americans to visit the island."[8]

As the hungry Seminoles compliantly returned fugitive slaves, unscrupulous Americans sometimes arbitrarily seized blacks living among the tribespeople. In 1829 John Hicks, the pro-white Mikasuki chief who had replaced Neamathla, complained that some whites even sold blacks to his people and then reclaimed them as runaways.[9]

So apparently for the third time in his young life, John Horse and his mother had been forced to seek a new home, knowing hunger and hardship in the process. First, they went from the Alachua region to the Suwannee. Then they had to go to another location farther south, only to be dislodged by the Treaty of Moultrie Creek. The only difference between the final move and the previous two was that gunfire had not accompanied it. By 1826, if not earlier, John was living in a village on Thlonoto-sassa Lake twelve miles from Camp Brooke on Hillsborough (Tampa) Bay.

It is not known whether he lived with the Seminole tribesman Charles Cavallo, the chief of Thlonoto-sassa (and probably also his father), or in a black stepfather's household. The only close kin about whom there is specific knowledge was a half-sister named Juana. Light complected with Indian looks, she reportedly had the same mother as John but a different father.

John's interracial heritage had one obvious advantage: he could speak English, which his mother had taught him, and was thus able to communicate with the soldiers at Camp Brooke. This ability was beyond the powers of his Indian playmates, whom he undoubtedly spoke to in whatever variety of Hitchiti—perhaps influenced by the Muskogee of his Upper Creek neighbors—seemed appropriate. Nevertheless, his bilingualism was sometimes impaired by a tendency to stammer.[10]

Until his family moved to the Tampa Bay area near Camp Brooke or until the post was established near John's village (whatever the actual sequence was), he had not observed many whites. Eventually, curiosity must have overcome his initial mistrust. He soon discovered that the military camp was an interesting and instructive place. He also found he could make small change by running errands for the officers and supplying them with fish and game.

One autumn morning in 1826, Andrew, the black cook of Lieutenant Colonel George M. Brooke, commander of the cantonment, appeared at the officer's door. Andrew told him there was a young Black Seminole wanting an interview. He also said the youth had some "gophers" (land turtles) for sale. Since arriving in Florida, Brooke had developed a taste for their succulent meat and owned a pen of rails for keeping them.

Presently, between his quarters and the kitchen, the colonel met a "long-legged, lathy negro boy of some fourteen years." His long, crinkly hair and copper complexion indicated some Indian blood. The officer's main interest, however, was in the youngster's large fiber bag. Brooke asked to see the terrapins, and John tumbled out two unusually fine specimens. The officer eyed them covetously and asked their price. After a moment's hesitation, the youth said "about two bits." Brooke took a coin from his pocket and gave it to the boy. Then he turned toward the kitchen and told his cook to put the reptiles inside the pen. After learning the young salesman's name, the colonel asked John for a steady supply in the future. If possible, he wanted more brought tomorrow. For the next few days, John returned with more gophers for sale. Colonel Brooke gladly paid a quarter for each new acquisition. Then he began planning a great feast for the post's officers. Terrapin would be the main course.

Days later, and shortly after one of John's visits, Brooke finalized his plans for the menu and asked Andrew to count the turtles in the pen. He was stunned when informed that there were only two; the same pair John had delivered that morning. Upon reflection, the officer realized that the youngster had repeatedly sold him the same ones.

Enraged, Brooke commanded his orderly to go immediately to Thlonotosassa and fetch John. The soldier soon reappeared, shoving the ashen-faced lad before him. The officer, barely containing his fury, confronted John. Desperately searching for words while trying to conquer his nervous stammer, John mumbled that his only intent was to not disappoint the colonel.

The ingenious excuse deflated Brooke's anger. Rather than punishing him, he ordered the youngster to provide, eventually, the turtles already purchased. The officer then nicknamed him Gopher John lest he forget his dishonesty. This sobriquet stayed with him for life.[11]

The next several years were fairly peaceful and pleasant for the Seminoles. John soon acquired a rifle and became noted for his ability to supply wild game. He probably was a popular hunting guide. While a teenager, John also raised livestock. In his mid-twenties, he owned at least ninety head of cattle. Finally, by his late teens, he married and started a family. He was supposedly the brother-in-law of Holatochee, a close kinsman of head chief Micanopy.[12]

When John was about twenty, a menace appeared that would cause greater hardship for the Seminoles than all their previous problems—from the Patriot invasion in 1812 to the Treaty of Moultrie Creek. It was the Indian Removal Act, which President Andrew Jackson signed on May 28, 1830. The law stated that most tribes east of the Mississippi should be transported to an Indian Territory west of the great river where Oklahoma and Kansas are now located. The Seminoles were included, although their land was so poor that white settlers did not want it.

There were other reasons for their removal. Some tribespeople had stayed at their old locations, refusing to occupy the barren treaty land; and fugitive slaves continued to join them. These blacks were not always returned to their rightful owners, who then used this situation to justify penetrating the tribal reservation. Supposedly searching for their own runaways, they sometimes seized blacks belonging to the Seminoles and those freed under Spanish law. Unscrupulous frontiersmen also stole Seminole cattle.[13]

All these provocations fanned flames that could ignite a border war, and applying the relocation policy to the Seminoles might prevent such a conflict. Nevertheless, because they were not directly in the settlers' path, they might have been allowed to stay on their lands if not for the many blacks among them. These people were considered a threat to the "peculiar institution" of slavery in the South, so the Indians were encouraged to go to more fertile lands in the West.

In 1832, Colonel James Gadsden arrived to negotiate an emigration treaty. He came at an opportune time. The previous year's drought had devastated the Seminoles' meager crops. "Most of them had been for three months subsisting on roots and the cabbage of the palmetto tree." Gadsden's offer of food if they agreed to leave was very appealing.

But less than a decade before—against their better judgment—the Seminoles had consented to move to a barren area. Therefore, they initially refused to consider relocating. Instead, the tribespeople demanded that a special delegation investigate the land that the government offered them. "Should they be satisfied," the nation would leave within three years. Under these conditions, the Treaty of Payne's Landing, on the Oklawaha River, was negotiated on May 9, 1832.

The inspection party sent to the Indian Territory was composed of seven chiefs, including Jumper. Interpreters were Abraham and Cudjo. After arriving at Little Rock on November 3, 1832, the group proceeded overland to Fort Gibson. There they were intimidated for a month and then cajoled into signing a treaty on March 28, 1833. It declared that the "special delegation . . . have expressed themselves satisfied" with the Creek country, set aside for the Seminoles, between the Canadian and the North Fork rivers. The delegates also agreed to merge their tribe with the Creeks. The government immediately insisted that the Fort Gibson agreement rendered the Payne's Landing treaty fully operative. The tribespeople must prepare to leave within three years.

Most Seminole leaders, however, had no intention of ever allowing themselves or their people to be relocated. As Jumper put it, "those of us who went to the West consented; but the rest of the nation do not. The popular sentiment rejects it." Despite their satisfaction on paper, the Seminoles soon rejected their proposed new home.[14]

Because these treaties were read by government agents to illiterate black interpreters, who then translated what they heard into the Seminole language, misunderstandings could easily occur, even if the framers or their representatives ensured that the documents were presented accurately and attempted in good faith to make their meaning clear. But it is unlikely that these conditions were fulfilled. In fact, Indian agent John Phagan, who manipulated the delegation into accepting the Fort Gibson agreement, was so unscrupulous that he was later removed from office for embezzlement. General Wiley Thompson replaced him. Furthermore, a provision in the Treaty of Payne's Landing for paying two hundred dollars to the two black interpreters, Abraham and Cudjo, upon their removal to the Indian Territory, was alleged a bribe. Although it may have influenced Cudjo, the money failed to win over Abraham, as his subsequent actions proved.[15]

The government insisted that the Seminoles were to reside among, and join, the powerful Creek Nation. The annexation was likely intended, indirectly, to maintain order among the resentful Red Sticks and bellicose Mikasukis. Therefore, a large military presence to control them might be less necessary. But the "Old Seminoles," such as those of the Alachua band, had not been part of the Creek Nation for a hundred years and refused to yield to them now. Additionally, the Upper Creek refugees in Florida detested the Confederacy's Lower Creeks because of their alliance with the whites during the Red Stick War. The Alachuas also remembered that McIntosh's Lower Creeks had helped destroy the Suwannee settlements in 1818. Finally, the Seminoles did not want to forfeit their independence by becoming a despised minority among the Creeks.

The Black Seminoles probably knew that the Creeks had a dubious claim to them. The tribe had been held responsible for the slaves who escaped to the Seminoles when they were still considered Lower Creeks. Therefore, the blacks feared that the Indians might seize them and use superior numbers to subject the blacks unlawfully to real servitude or sell them to the whites.

So when (and if) the Seminoles assembled to be transported West, both those with legal title and unscrupulous slavers with no valid claims could demand that the authorities return the blacks. Or they could just kidnap them. The Black Seminoles were resolved not to submit to this danger. Indeed, they were *the* determining factor in the Seminole opposition to removal.

The blacks fortunately enjoyed a great advantage in Abraham's influence over Micanopy, who apparently never did anything against his interpreter's advice. One officer wrote that the chief "owned many negroes. . . . His principal slave Abraham . . . dictated to those of his own color, who [in turn] to a great degree controlled their [Seminole] masters. They were a most cruel and malignant enemy. For them to surrender would be servitude to the whites; but to retain an open warfare, secured to them plunder, liberty, and importance." In fact, Abraham had cunningly made secret war preparations while pretending he was committed to the relocation effort. He also communicated with Florida plantation slaves, urging them to join the Seminoles when the fighting began.

Another prominent Black Seminole leader was John Caesar. A close associate of King Philip, he was described as active and smart. Considered next to Abraham in importance, John Caesar worked the St. Augustine area where he recruited runaways and free blacks to the cause.[16]

The government's view, expressed through the new Seminole agent, Wiley Thompson, was that the Treaty of Payne's Landing had the force of law. The

Seminoles must remove within three years. Thompson rejected their demands for a council to consider further the special delegation's report, and most tribespeople still refused to consider emigrating.[17]

Then Osceola emerged. He was the lighting rod that attracted and directed Seminole rage. The young leader was present when Thompson met the chiefs on October 23, 1834, and April 24, 1835. As Cudjo interpreted, Osceola whispered vigorously in Micanopy's ear and shouted defiantly. Occasionally he drew and furiously brandished his knife. Osceola reportedly disrupted the October meeting by plunging his blade into the agent's table, some say through a document lying upon it. He then declared, "The only treaty I will ever execute will be with this!"[18]

After October 1834, the Seminoles began buying ammunition in unusually large quantities, so at the April 1835 talk Thompson prohibited its sale. The ban precipitated one of Osceola's infamous demonstrations of "insolence." Knowing the law forbade the selling of powder and lead to slaves, Osceola acidly proclaimed: "Am I a Negro? . . . a slave? My skin is dark, but not black." Then, ominously, he added: "I will make the white man red with blood; and then blacken him in the sun and rain, where the wolf shall smell his bones and buzzards liven upon his flesh."[19]

The conference broke up in disarray. Only eight chiefs and the same number of subchiefs agreed, under the agent's threats, to leave Florida. The principal headmen—Micanopy, Jumper, Alligator, and others—flatly refused to comply. Their names were immediately stricken from the chiefs' list.

Meanwhile, Osceola and some of his men continued to frequent Fort King, where the Seminole agency was located; and Osceola repeatedly cursed Wiley Thompson. In early June he became so insulting that he was arrested and imprisoned.[20] But after six days of confinement, he contritely offered to emigrate and induce others to do so. Soon after he was released, some of his followers came in and said they would relocate, too. Thompson was so pleased that he presented Osceola with an unusually fine rifle. The Seminole accepted it with a gleam in his eyes, which the agent took for gratitude. Thompson was confident that, with Osceola as an ally, few obstacles to removal remained.

The government declared that January 8, 1836, was the date when the Seminoles must be at Tampa Bay ready to be loaded onto transports. Otherwise, the U.S. Army would hunt them down. But skirmishes during the summer of 1835, in which lives were lost on both sides, revealed the rancor between Indians and whites. Osceola now showed his real feelings, threatening to kill the chiefs who were selling off their livestock in preparation for leaving.

On November 28 a large party of warriors headed by Osceola, Holata Mico, and Abraham executed Charley Emathla, leader of the emigration faction, reputedly over Abraham's protests. Osceola contemptuously scattered the gold the dead man had received for his cattle, exclaiming, "See! It is the price of your blood!" The group had considered killing Coa Hadjo (Mad Panther), second chief of the St. Johns River band. But they spared him, after warning that if he ever mentioned removal, he would die.

Meanwhile, the few other emigration chiefs—Holata Emathla, Fuche Luste Hadjo (Crazy Black Dirt), and elderly Econchatomico (Red Ground Chief)—with some five hundred people fled to Tampa Bay on November 14 seeking military protection. Shortly thereafter, slavers attacked Econchatomico's settlement, seized some blacks, and carried them off to Georgia. Among the captives was Econchatomico's part-black granddaughter. This raid proved what the less compliant chiefs and their black followers had always feared. Their misgivings were now completely confirmed. Other clashes, with several killed and wounded, occurred early in December; but some people still believed that the Seminoles would ultimately depart with little resistance.[21]

Just before the Second Seminole War began, and during its first two years, certain leaders were prominent. Although Micanopy was tacitly acknowledged as head chief, his position was more titular than personal, more nominal than actual. A number of able men surrounded him. They were primarily his kinsmen by blood or marriage and greatly surpassed him in ability. Their names included Jumper, Alligator, King Philip, Coacoochee, Arpeika, and Osceola.

Jumper, sometimes called "the Lawyer" (due to his role as sense bearer or advocate for Micanopy), and whose busk or Indian name was Ote Emathla (Island Leader), was an old Red Stick Creek. In 1813, he was reportedly second in command of the Fort Mims attackers. He had married one of Micanopy's sisters. Jumper was in late middle age, six feet tall, and gaunt from tuberculosis. He had "small and deadly eyes, contracted forehead, . . . [and a] very prominent nose." He was also described as "cunning, intelligent, deceitful, . . . active and brave."

Alligator, or Halpatter Tustenuggee, of the Alachua band was Micanopy's principal war leader and probably his kinsman. He was in his forties. Although very short, Alligator was "well built, with a good countenance, and a Roman nose . . . a great warrior and a great talker; . . . the most shrewd, crafty, politic, and intelligent chief. . . . [He also spoke] English."

Other relatives of Micanopy lived in the St. Johns Valley. King Philip (Emathla), principal leader of the St. Johns River band, was also the second chief of the Seminole Nation. He was said to have "royal blood," which probably meant he was related to Cowkeeper. About sixty years old, King Philip had married one of Micanopy's sisters. He was hostile to the whites but "wished to avoid . . . rather than to resist them." His favorite son was Wild Cat (Coacoochee).

Although inconspicuous during the first year of the war, Wild Cat eventually became "by far the most dangerous chieftain in the field." Born about 1810, he was slight, active, and well proportioned. Endowed with a bright "countenance," he was "playful and attractive" with "a dark fierce eye beaming with intelligence." His voice was "clear and soft, speech fluent, gestures rapid and violent." Wild Cat was also highly imaginative, with a touch of mysticism. After Osceola's death in 1838, he became the principal Seminole war leader.

The Mikasukis also firmly resisted emigration. Their headman was Arpeika. Better known as Sam Jones, he was "a well set, neatly formed and perfectly finished small man with locks white as driven snow." Nearly seventy years old, Arpeika was described as "active as a hind, and intrepid as a lion." Unlike the pro-white Mikasuki chief, John Hicks (now dead), he greatly opposed removal.[22]

An estimated two-thirds of the Florida tribespeople were, by 1821, Upper Creek refugees—Red Sticks. Although not a distinct element in the resistance, they produced the war leader whose name is most linked to the Second Seminole War: Osceola, or more properly, Asi Yahola. Also known as Powell, after an English father (or stepfather), he derived one-fourth of his ancestry from a Scottish grandfather. Born in Alabama of a Creek woman in about 1804, he came with his mother to Florida at an early age. Six feet tall and sparely built, he was spirited, strong willed, eloquent, and courageous. Because he had no hereditary claim to leadership, his charisma primarily attracted some of the most hostile warriors—principally Mikasuki and Black Seminoles.

Before the fighting began, John knew most of the chiefs, probably including Osceola. During the conflict, he greatly strengthened those relationships; but nothing is known about his activities before the war started or even during its first year. A description of John at age thirty, in 1842, most likely approximates his appearance in 1835. From "a long-legged, lathy . . . boy," he had grown into "a fine-looking fellow of six feet, as straight as an Indian, with just a smile of red blood mantling to his forehead . . . a jaunty air that would fix your attention at sight." Powerfully built, John was fond of the silver armlets, rich sashes, and elaborate plumed head shawls of the Seminole dandy. His long hair was always well groomed.[23]

Some of John's more formidable traits now included his marksmanship, coolness, courage, and cunning—foreshadowed by the youthful exploit recalled in the nickname Gopher John. Combined, these attributes marked him as a potential leader among those of his own age—both tribespeople and black—and among the Seminole chiefs. To the Seminoles, he was not known as Gopher John but by his personal name coupled with some form of his master's surname: John Cavallo, or Cowaya. Cowaya seems to have been a corruption of the Hitchiti word *kaway* (horse). Later, he would be called John Horse or Juan Caballo.[24]

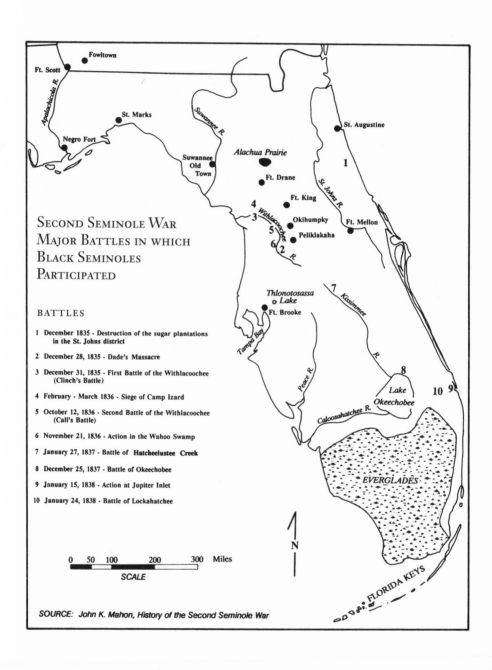

Fowltown

Ft. Scott

Apalachicola R.

St. Marks

Negro Fort

Suwannee R.

Suwannee
Old
Town

Alachua Prairie

St. Augustine

Ft. Drane

St. Johns R.

1

Ft. King

**SECOND SEMINOLE WAR
MAJOR BATTLES IN WHICH
BLACK SEMINOLES
PARTICIPATED**

4
3 Withlacoochee
5
6 2 R.

Okihumpky

Ft. Mellon

Peliklakaha

7 Kissimmee R.

BATTLES

Thlonotosassa
Lake

Ft. Brooke

1 December 1835 - Destruction of the sugar plantations
   in the St. Johns district

2 December 28, 1835 - Dade's Massacre

3 December 31, 1835 - First Battle of the Withlacoochee
   (Clinch's Battle)

4 February - March 1836 - Siege of Camp Izard

5 October 12, 1836 - Second Battle of the Withlacoochee
   (Call's Battle)

6 November 21, 1836 - Action in the Wahoo Swamp

7 January 27, 1837 - Battle of Hatcheelustee Creek

8 December 25, 1837 - Battle of Okeechobee

9 January 15, 1838 - Action at Jupiter Inlet

10 January 24, 1838 - Battle of Lockahatchee

Tampa Bay

Peace R.

Caloosahatchee R.

8

Lake
Okeechobee

10 9

EVERGLADES

N

0   50   100   200   300   Miles

SCALE

FLORIDA KEYS

SOURCE: John K. Mahon, History of the Second Seminole War

CHAPTER FOUR

⊠ From Dade's Massacre to the Siege of Camp Izard

The negroes . . . from the commencement of the Florida War . . . formed the most active, vindictive, and incorrigible portion of the foe arrayed against our troops.

CAPTAIN JOHN T. SPRAGUE

Near the end of December 1835, the long-smoldering conflict between the Seminoles and the whites burst into flames.[1] Seizing the initiative in late December, the Indians and their black allies attacked widely dispersed targets in carefully organized and coordinated raids.

King Philip and John Caesar, with the St. Johns warriors, struck first. They hit the region's plantations near Christmastime, destroying five over two days. Local slaves, prepared for the campaign by John Caesar's propaganda, swarmed to the Seminoles by the hundreds, painting their faces to symbolize their new allegiance and participating in the plunder and destruction. The fertile sugar-growing area on the St. Johns River, south of St. Augustine, was devastated. In panic, the local settlers fled into nearby towns.[2]

Nevertheless, during the mayhem the marauders were occasionally merciful. A woman named Mary Godfrey, fleeing with her four young daughters from her home late one evening, was confronted by a black with an upraised ax. He hesitated a moment, then lowered his weapon and bade them not to fear, leading them to where they could see the lights of a military camp. The black said that he had two children still enslaved by the whites. He hoped God would protect them wherever they were, just as he had preserved his enemies when they were within his power. Then he quickly slipped into the night to rejoin his comrades.[3]

Preparations were being made at Tampa Bay's Fort Brooke to reinforce the more vulnerable Fort King (near present-day Ocala) where the Seminole agency was located. But a guide for the relief column was needed. Luis Pacheco, a slave belonging to Mrs. Antonio Pacheco, knew the country well and spoke the Indian language. So he was hired on December 23 for twenty-five dollars a month.

The relief unit, under Brevet Major Francis L. Dade, left Fort Brooke for Fort King earlier on the same day. The unit included five line officers, a surgeon, one hundred enlisted men, and a six-pound cannon on a wagon. Dade had assumed command of the column on the morning they departed, replacing Captain George Gardiner who reluctantly remained behind to care for his sick wife. After Gardiner quickly arranged her transfer to a more sophisticated medical facility at Key West, he and Luis Pacheco, who had just arrived from Sarasota, galloped north after Dade. "There was," Pacheco remembered many years later, "a whole 'passel' of hound dogs in the troop"—possibly a sign that slave hunting was anticipated.[4]

About this time, an Indian runner reached Osceola's stronghold in the Cove of the Withlacoochee River, saying that the Seminoles intended to attack the soldiers en route. But Osceola had unfinished business at the Seminole agency.

General Wiley Thompson, the agent, was honest and conscientious. He tried to do the best for his wards within the limits of the law and his orders. Still, the Seminoles bitterly hated him. Abraham had predicted that he "would be killed by Indians while walking about his place."[5] This prophecy was probably received seriously by tribespeople and blacks alike. Moreover, Osceola never forgave Agent Thompson for jailing him after one of the warrior's outbreaks of insulting and violent language.

The vengeful Osceola and forty or fifty Mikasuki warriors hid themselves near Fort King, where Osceola planned to settle accounts with Thompson. On December 28 the agent dined with Lieutenant Constantine Smith. As the pair went for a postprandial walk, Osceola's band ambushed them, riddling the two men with bullets. Thompson was hit fifteen times. After scalping the corpses, they attacked the house of the sutler, Erastus Rogers, killing him and his two clerks. Although the warriors returned quickly to the Wahoo Swamp, they arrived too late for the battle with Major Dade.

The Seminoles may have learned of the Dade expedition's size and mission from Luis Pacheco, but more than a half century later he still vehemently denied it. In any case, word had gone out among the Indians to intercept Dade before he joined General Clinch at Fort King. The attack was delayed, however, because of Osceola's absence and Micanopy's desire to resist removal using inertia rather than militancy. Although Jumper finally won him over, Micanopy reportedly had to be carried to the battleground on the shoulders of some young warriors. Nonetheless, he would play his part as head chief by firing the first shot.

On the night of December 27 a group of Indians and blacks lay waiting in the Wahoo Swamp. Dade's men, who had been shadowed daily, camped an hour down the trail. The Seminoles intended to ambush them in open country where the soldiers would not expect it and have little cover. If the warriors were defeated, they could retreat into the nearby marshy wilderness.

The attackers, primarily members of the Alachua band, emerged from the swamp at daybreak and hid among the grass and scrub palmetto of an islandlike pine barren near the left (west) side of the road to Fort King. Although the Seminoles numbered, according to their own account, only 180, the whites, as usual, later exaggerated the total to between eight hundred and a thousand men.

The Seminoles had not been involved in a war since Andrew Jackson's 1818 expedition, when nearly all the fighting was done by the Red Sticks and the blacks, with some skirmishing by the Mikasukis. Most of the Alachuas had avoided being drawn into that engagement and had not seen serious action since the 1812–13 raids of the Georgia Patriots and the Tennesseans. Few of the Seminoles had ever been in battle; but a handful of hardened veterans such as Jumper and Alligator, and possibly some blacks who had fought at the Suwannee, helped inspire the others.

The ambushers watched the trail where they expected Dade's column to pass. When the soldiers finally appeared close to 8:00 A.M., Major Dade rode ahead with Luis Pacheco walking at his side. There were no flankers. The officer and the guide drew even with the nearest concealed Seminoles, moved along their line, and then were beyond it. The troops followed marching in columns of two, overcoats buttoned over their cartridge boxes and muskets against the damp December chill. They looked straight ahead, oblivious of danger.

Dade checked his mount and turned to Luis, who pointed down the trail at a gray horse. The animal, perhaps deliberately placed there by the hostiles, had just wandered onto the path. As the two men conversed, the attackers each singled out a soldier. Micanopy aimed at Major Dade's breast. With a choking cry of "My God!" the dying officer slumped in his saddle.

Luis dropped to the ground so quickly that observers thought he had been shot through the brain. His sudden move later caused suspicion that he had expected the ambush. Dade's men, however, certainly did not. Before they could assume a defensive posture, the Seminole battle cry rang out and the warriors poured tremendous fire into the massed ranks. The officers were specifically targeted.

When the smoke lifted, the jubilant blacks and tribesmen howled wildly. It seemed to them—and the stunned troops—that nearly the entire left side of the column, one-half of the total force, had gone down with the first volley. The surviving soldiers tore at their overcoats to free their cartridge boxes and weapons while frantically searching for someone to shoot. The attackers, rising from prone positions to their knees, plied ramrods furiously as they reloaded and fired at the struggling whites. Then two of the three uninjured officers began rallying their men, deploying them as skirmishers and directing each to get behind a tree. Captain Gardiner was especially conspicuous in organizing the defense. Alligator remembered him later as "a great brave."

Lieutenant William E. Bassinger and a squad hurriedly readied the cannon. Suddenly a puff of smoke streaked with flame burst from its muzzle. The six-pounder initially frightened the ambushers, who retreated over a little hill, giving the soldiers time to fell trees to erect a crude breastworks. Soon, however, the Seminoles recognized the delay between the shots. They began targeting the exposed artillerists in the intervals between firings. Since the cannonballs were striking far more palmetto trees than Indians and blacks, the warriors began jeering each discharge and pressed the attack.

They advanced toward the hastily constructed, knee-high, triangular barricade and kept shooting. The troops responded, both with muskets and the six-pounder. But presently the cannon ran out of ammunition and fell silent. Lieutenant Bassinger, the only officer left alive, was severely wounded. After many hours, gunfire from the breastworks began to slacken. Finally, about 2:00 P.M., it ceased.

The besiegers, pondering this turn of events, heard the pounding of hooves. They turned around and saw about fifty mounted black warriors. The newcomers, knives and axes in hand, rushed in for the kill. Unopposed, they swarmed over the barricade and cut down the few defenders still alive. Systematically stabbing and axing the wounded, the blacks made "obscene and taunting derisions, and . . . frequent cries of 'what have you got to sell?'"—a question that lounging soldiers often asked blacks when they visited military posts.[6]

Only three wounded men survived the carnage. They feigned death and then slipped away after the attackers left. Among the Seminoles, three were reported killed and five wounded. It was later said that the warriors plundered, stripped, and horribly mutilated the enemy corpses. But Luis Pacheco denied this assertion. According to him, Jumper had forbidden such action. Two months later, a relief force found the slain men lying in regular order. Although most had their weapons and equipment removed, they were otherwise undisturbed, with personal effects untouched.[7]

In a single stroke the Seminoles had eliminated more than one hundred troops, but the struggle to stay in Florida had just begun. Still, they now had Luis Pacheco, a new source of information about their enemy's specific plans. The black guide remained hidden behind a tree until the attackers surrounded him. Years later, Luis claimed that, although he was threatened several times, someone always intervened for him. Finally Jumper's son placed Pacheco under his protection, explaining, "That's a black man. He is not his own master. Don't kill him!" The guide repaid his captors' clemency by reading the letters and dispatches found on the officers' bodies, thus giving the Seminoles valuable details of military strategy. Luis remained with Jumper, allegedly participating in hostile actions until the chief's surrender. In 1838 he was shipped with other prisoners to Indian Territory.[8]

Exultant over their success, especially with so few casualties, the allied Indians and blacks returned to the Wahoo Swamp camp with their war prizes. They erected a pole and arrayed the scalps upon it. Osceola and his band arrived later that evening, laden with plunder from the sutler's store. A scalp dance and victory feast began, with singing, boasting, and jesting at the whites' expense. Liquor was abundant. General Thompson's scalp was given a prominent place on the pole. The wittier celebrants began to address it, mimicking the tone he had used when lecturing them. The blacks, with their superior knowledge of English, probably distinguished themselves in this mockery. The drunken revelry continued most of the night until they all collapsed from exhaustion and intoxication.[9]

The next morning, when the revelers had scarcely recuperated from the exertions of battle and their victory party, scouts arrived. They announced that a large column was advancing from Fort Drane toward the Withlacoochee. General Duncan L. Clinch, on whose plantation the fort was located, led the troops, which included about 250 U.S. Army regulars commanded by Lieutenant Colonel Alexander Fanning and several hundred Florida militiamen under Brigadier General and Territorial Governor Richard K. Call. The soldiers, who were making a show of force to impress the Seminoles, were completely unaware of Major Dade's fate.

The warriors knew the troops had to be met, but they had no supreme commander capable of planning battle strategy and leading them. Osceola and his Mikasukis were anxious to fight because they had missed the action against Dade. But Micanopy was gone. He had returned to Peliklakaha with many of his men, including the blacks.

Eventually, the Seminoles organized a band of 200–250 warriors, which included between thirty and fifty blacks. With Osceola and Alligator as principal leaders, they set out for a well-known ford on the Withlacoochee, about twenty miles from its mouth. They thought their enemy might try to cross at that spot because the water was only about two feet deep at that point.

The Seminoles lay near the ford all night in preparation for an ambush the next day, December 31. In the morning, their scouts reported that about one-third of the force, the regular soldiers, had already crossed downstream because General Clinch had inadvertently missed the ford. After finding a leaky canoe, he had had his men ferried across the fifty-yard-wide river a few at a time. But the mounted Florida volunteers had tried to swim their horses across the flood-swollen waters, and their noisy efforts had attracted the attention of prowling scouts.

The chiefs decided to move their forces downstream. About noon, the warriors slipped into a densely wooded hammock where they could observe the enemy through the brush. Many regulars, as oblivious to danger as Dade's men had been, lounged on the bank. They watched the militia struggling in the river and occasionally offered sardonic advice. Very few volunteers were able to cross. Those who did left their arms and accoutrements to be transported by the lone canoe.

The attackers roughly equaled the number of troops on the same side of the Withlacoochee. A decisive blow might annihilate them before more militiamen could ford the river to bolster the ranks. Emerging stealthily from the dense hammock, the warriors crept forward through the brush to move within better range, remaining undetected by the sentries posted in the tall grass. Then Osceola's piercing war cry rose for the first time on a battlefield, and his men unleashed a crashing volley upon the unwary regulars.

This action was not like the fusillade that mowed down half of Major Dade's command. The Americans were scattered about rather than marching in a solid column down a trail. So, although some of the soldiers were hit and fell where they stood, others seized their weapons and returned fire. General Clinch quickly ordered a counterattack until more Florida volunteers could cross the Withlacoochee to support them. But the warriors had cleverly posted some of their best marksmen to target the militia on the opposite bank, and Governor Call's Floridians concluded that they were being attacked by an enemy on their side of the water. With their backs to the river, the volunteers formed a line to defend themselves; and most did not cross the Withlacoochee to aid the regulars. Only a few militiamen swam over to anchor Clinch's left flank. Because there were not enough men on his side of the river, General Clinch ordered a fighting withdrawal.

The Seminole sharpshooters continued to snipe effectively at the troops, but the soldiers could only fire randomly at the muzzle flashes winking in the thickets. The attackers began following a pattern: they marked their targets, fired, threw themselves down to avoid the return volley, and shifted positions before reloading and shooting again. Osceola stood several paces in front of his foremost warrior, deliberately wiping out his rifle before reloading. He periodically ordered, "Take away the wounded, never mind the dead!"[10]

But even Osceola did not stand his ground when the regulars suddenly charged through the swamp and scrub with fixed bayonets as Indians and blacks scattered before them. They rushed them two more times, but the warriors retreated just enough to return easily to their previous locations after the troops withdrew. When Clinch's men fell back to the riverbank and prepared to cross, the Seminoles rallied. They deliberately glided forward again, firing with murderous effect, while skillfully avoiding the return volleys.

Suddenly, Osceola's battle cry was silenced: a musket ball had hit him in the arm. He withdrew, cradling one arm with the other. Once again the long line of bayonets rose and surged forward, and this time the ambushers fled. As soon as a log bridge across the river was complete, the troops recrossed to the other side.

General Clinch and the battered regulars withdrew to Fort Drane. Most of the militia, their enlistments expired, went home. Four soldiers died and fifty-nine were wounded during the fighting. Still, as one officer wrote, the losses could have been worse. He recalled, "[The] firing was heavy, and the bushes literally cut up around us, how it was that more were not shot I cannot tell."[11]

A prisoner at Fort Brooke later reported that "Abram was . . . at With-lacoochee but made off on the first fire." If he actually left the battle, however, his retreat apparently did not discourage his followers. Of the three Seminoles killed and five wounded at the river, two of the dead and three of the injured were black. The blacks had constituted, at most, one-fourth of the attackers but suffered more than half the casualties. The two who died were members of Micanopy's household, which grieved the head chief. He ordered that in future his black dependents should not expose themselves so recklessly.

One month after the Withlacoochee battle, Osceola sent a terse, prophetic letter to Clinch: "You have guns and so have we . . . you have powder and lead, and so have we . . . your men will fight, and so will ours, till the last drop of the Seminole's blood has moistened the dust of his hunting ground."[12]

For nearly two months after Clinch's repulse, the Seminoles controlled the Withlacoochee region. If the enemy approached the wilderness, the families of the warriors could hide. Another refuge lay in the Cove of the Withlacoochee: the Wahoo Swamp, a "vast Place—secluded from the world . . . [a] world in itself."[13] Meanwhile, in the valley of the St. Johns, King Philip's Indians and John Caesar's blacks continued their work of devastation, destroying sixteen large plantations in January and recruiting hundreds of fugitive slaves.[14] The Seminoles near Okihumpky and Peliklakaha continued to monitor the garrisons at Forts King and Drane and constantly watched the road between Forts Brooke and King.

In late February 1836, scouts saw a large army marching north from Fort Brooke to Fort King. The soldiers were retracing the route of Major Dade's doomed command but were too many to be ambushed and annihilated. While the Indian villages along the route were abandoned and families hurried into the swamps, the warriors hastened to the Withlacoochee crossing or shadowed the column's flank.

The troop commander was Brevet Major General Edmund P. Gaines. A leathery veteran of the First Seminole War and leader of the Negro Fort campaign, he was in New Orleans on an inspection tour when word of the Dade disaster arrived. As head of the western department of the army, he had jurisdiction over the Tampa Bay area. Gaines immediately collected all available men and sailed to Fort Brooke in early February. He led six companies of the Fourth Infantry and a regiment of Louisiana volunteers.[15]

On February 6 Gaines learned that Brevet Major General Winfield Scott, his counterpart in the army's eastern department, had been selected to lead the Florida campaign. Gaines ignored the directive and pushed on. By snubbing his old rival, he further estranged himself from the prickly Scott.

On February 13 Gaines's command left Tampa. Guided by seventy-seven friendly Indians but with only ten days' provisions, the troops set out for Fort King. Although they encountered no hostiles on the way, the soldiers must have been constantly shadowed.[16] On February 20 the column reached Dade's battleground and buried the dead. Two days later, they finally arrived at Fort King, and General Gaines sent for fresh supplies from Fort Drane. On February 26, with just nine days' rations, he marched southwest for the Withlacoochee, hoping that his thousand men would be enough to find and defeat the Seminoles.[17]

On the afternoon of February 27 they reached the river. Their guides—"the friendly Indians"—promptly declared that they had reached the ford that General Clinch had sought and missed. But the Withlacoochee was thirty yards wide and looked deep and swift, and the opposite bank was six feet high. Still, no signs of hostiles had been detected, so General Gaines ordered that the waters be sounded to determine if the river could be crossed.

In the underbrush across the Withlacoochee, a group of tribesmen and blacks lay concealed. They watched as a squad of unarmed soldiers cautiously waded into the water while their companions lined the shore. The Seminoles took careful aim. As their leader's war cry disrupted the afternoon stillness, they fired. The wounded cried out and sank, while others tried to return to the riverbank. While the troops fired at the thickets across the Withlacoochee, some men plunged into the water to drag out their beleaguered comrades. As the whites frantically sought shelter, the attackers coolly reloaded and fired again. After one hour of skirmishing, General Gaines ordered a withdrawal. He left behind some outposts and camped nearby. Several of his men had been wounded, and one died.[18]

Early the next morning, the Seminoles watched their enemy break camp and move downstream. Gliding swiftly through the underbrush, the warriors easily outdistanced the heavily equipped soldiers. The army headed for a point two or three miles away where the guides now insisted the elusive ford was located. Presently, the troops emerged from dense thickets into a pine barren covering both sides of the river. Because this open area lessened the danger from ambush, Lieutenant James F. Izard was ordered to investigate the possibilities for crossing.

But the pine barren along the trail from Fort Brooke to Fort King had easily concealed Dade's attackers. Now there was similar cover on the Withlacoochee's southern bank. Hidden behind trees, the Indians and blacks watched a squad enter the water to plumb its depth. The lieutenant stood on the bank holding his horse and directing their efforts. The best Seminole marksmen aimed at him and fired. Izard collapsed, mortally wounded, and his men dove for cover.[19]

Bullets flew viciously, accompanied by shrill war cries from the southern bank and shouted orders from the northern one. But the ground was too open for the intense fire directed against the soldiers on the previous day. So when the Americans finally withdrew about noon, they lost only one man dead and two others wounded. In the two clashes, however, two officers had died or were mortally wounded. Once more, the Seminoles had shrewdly targeted them.

The Withlacoochee remained uncrossed, but the troops did not give up. They began felling trees to build a log barricade, rafts, and a pontoon bridge. General Gaines finally realized that his guides either did not know or would not tell the location of the ford. Provisions were running low, so the soldiers needed to defeat their foe quickly. Presently, Gaines sent a runner to General Clinch at Fort Drane. Gaines ordered Clinch to march at once and cross the river ten miles upstream to attack the enemy's rear.

Late that afternoon, the general heard much yelling from across the water. The guides said it meant reinforcements, probably Micanopy with "330 warriors."

A council was likely held that night. Head chief Micanopy, if not there himself, was well represented by his brother-in-law and chief counselor, Jumper; his kinsman and war leader, Alligator; and the black Alachua chief, Abraham. Osceola, recovered from the wound he had received at the first Battle of the Withlacoochee, brought his personal following of blacks and Mikasukis. They had borne the brunt of the fighting thus far. Additionally,

John Caesar (if present at the meeting) probably described the successes in the St. Johns valley, particularly the slave recruitment.

The warriors knew that the soldiers, one thousand strong, soon would be behind the walls they were building. Several hundred more troops were at Fort Drane, only thirty miles away. The warriors' own number, despite the exaggerated reports, was perhaps seven hundred, including "a great many" blacks.[20] Still, they decided to attack. The Seminoles did not expect another Dade massacre, which would be impossible to duplicate. Rather, they hoped to inflict enough losses so that the whites would be forced to withdraw before reinforcements could arrive.

Before daybreak on February 29 the warriors crossed the Withlacoochee River. Unlike General Gaines, the Seminoles knew where the fords were located. They used crude rafts, made of two or three logs lashed together with rawhide or vines, to ferry across their arms and ammunition. Undetected by the sentries, the men quickly climbed the northern bank. Then they silently slipped into the hammocks—islands of virgin soil supporting dense vegetation in the midst of a pine-barren sea—one east, and another west of the breastworks christened Camp Izard.

As dawn broke, dark figures crept out of the hammocks and quickly formed a long line behind their enemy's rear. Hidden in the grass and scrub palmetto, the attackers surrounded the post, leaving only the riverside free, which was monitored by their comrades across the water. The concealed warriors were not waiting for an opportunity to storm Camp Izard; their numbers and arms were inadequate. Rather, they waited for the soldiers to get up and expose themselves.

As the bugle blew reveille, the men rolled out of their blankets. Bleary with fatigue, they hastily snatched a scanty breakfast from their sparse provisions and proceeded to their stations. About one-third of the men remained on duty in the half-completed post. The remainder worked on the riverbank, hewing logs for pontoon rafts and splitting slabs for the bridge planks. Only a few sentries scanned the opposite shore for signs of the hostiles—unaware of danger on their flanks and rear. The ax strokes continued until mid-morning, uninterrupted by war cry or rifle shot; and the sentinels imperceptibly relaxed. Meanwhile, the tribesmen and blacks waited with the patience of deerstalkers.

Suddenly, the shrill Seminole battle cry screeched from one hammock and was answered from the other. Rifles cracked. Soldiers dropped their axes and reached for their muskets. Some men staggered and fell as others, supporting the wounded, rushed inside the camp's still unfinished walls.

Although the gunfire from the hammocks was continuous, the Americans coolly returned it. Then flames leaped toward them and surged down upon the breastworks. Soon the warriors were attacking through the smoke, firing as they came. Cries of pain told attackers that they were hitting their marks. One of the yelps came from General Gaines himself, directing the battle from a chair in the camp's midst. His lower lip was pierced by a bullet, and two teeth were knocked out. Showing grace under pressure, the general reportedly said: "It is mean of the redskins to knock out my teeth when I have so few!"[21]

His soldiers were frustrated and angry, especially those on the windward side, who fought an unseen enemy. Smoke and flames engulfing them, the men choked on acrid fumes. From both front and flank, bullets whizzed by. The harsh Seminole war cry was incessant and drawing nearer. The whites were also exasperated by the unorthodox tactics. It was unheard of for an opponent—even one with superior numbers—to charge a fortified position defended by regular troops.

Suddenly the wind shifted and carried the fire back to the attackers. They hesitated momentarily, then veered right and left for the sheltering hammocks. As the smoke cleared, the camp defenders could see bloody tracks on the blackened earth where the warriors had retreated. They had taken all but one of their fallen with them.

The battle lasted for two hours. The soldiers had one dead and thirty-three wounded, including the general. Gaines quickly put his men back to work on the barricade and sent off another runner to General Clinch at Fort Drane, urging him to send reinforcements and provisions immediately.[22]

In the warriors' camp Osceola spoke in council that night as never before. The other chiefs were gloomy. They wanted to retreat before fresh troops arrived and take their families to safety. But Osceola argued so passionately for continued hostilities that some American officers, who had slipped out of their camp to reconnoiter, could recognize his characteristic shrill tones.

"What does he say?" they asked their Indian scouts.

"He say . . . 'keep on . . . fighting,'" the tribesmen tersely muttered.

Eventually, the council agreed to maintain the siege. But they refused to attempt costly assaults like the one carried out that morning.

The first of March began peacefully with no sound of Seminole rifles or war cries, but General Gaines did not dare to hope that the enemy had left. At best, he felt that they, like his command, were merely resting. Therefore, the lull was more threatening than reassuring. His concern increased after he checked the provisions. Although three days' rations should have remained, the food supply was virtually exhausted except for the horses' corn. After it was divided among the men, it provided only one pint per person.

The following afternoon, the ominous silence ended when another attack began. The warriors, concealed in the hammocks, shot at every soldier who showed himself. The troops retaliated in kind. The Seminole firing and whooping were almost constant. Although the loss from the sniping was small (one white killed and three wounded in three days), the incessant hostile fire further demoralized the hungry Americans.

Soon the pint of corn distributed to each man was gone. On March 3 the horses were slaughtered and their flesh divided. Dogs were also eaten. Lieutenant Prince of the Fourth Infantry stated, "A quarter of dog meat sold for 5$."[23] By March 5 those refusing to consume horse or dog meat had eaten nothing for three days. It appeared that General Gaines's march was about to finish disastrously, either in an enemy-harried retreat or with his troops dying from starvation.

But if Gaines had been as well informed as his foe, he would have been optimistic. The Seminole scouts knew that Clinch's relief expedition was finally coming, so the tribal council likely discussed its next move. Some of the more cautious probably insisted again that the families should be withdrawn. During the siege, the women had prepared food and molded bullets for the warriors. Obviously, their services would no longer be needed if the Seminoles withdrew. The more militant warriors must have advocated pressing the attack. Osceola, however, opposed that plan; his courage was tempered by shrewd intelligence and unhampered by recklessness. A compromise must have been reached that took advantage of the Americans' plight and did not involve immediate action.

On the evening of March 5 a black man appeared out of the darkness and hailed Camp Izard. He said that the Seminoles were tired of fighting and wanted to talk. General Gaines agreed to parley the next day at 10 A.M. At the agreed time, several hundred warriors filed up from the riverbank and formed a line three hundred yards behind the camp. A group detached itself and warily approached the whites. Captain Ethan Allen Hitchcock went to meet the negotiators, who were led by Osceola. The delegation also included Jumper, Alligator, and Holata Mico. Abraham and John Caesar were the interpreters. John Caesar had been the previous night's envoy and perhaps the originator of the plan.

Jumper acted as spokesman and Abraham interpreted. He said that many of the Seminoles had died. Now they wanted a truce. Jumper asked that the soldiers retreat from the Withlacoochee and leave them alone. Gaines initially denied his request. But after more meetings, the general declared on March 8 that if the warriors withdrew out of the Withlacoochee area, abstained from hostile acts, and came to treaty talks when summoned, he would not attack them.

The Seminole leadership agreed that the Withlacoochee would mark the boundary between Indians and the Americans. But before the negotiations could be successfully completed, the vanguard of General Clinch's relief column arrived. Unaware of the peace parley, the men fired at the warriors who raced for the sheltering hammocks. After quickly crossing the river, they hastened to join their families who had relocated to more secure camps during the lengthy conferences.

Thus, the siege of Camp Izard was finally lifted. The Seminoles had lost three men—including a black—and five were wounded. In contrast, Gaines's losses were five dead and forty-six wounded.[24]

The troops remained at Camp Izard until March 10. They were in no condition to march and resembled, according to one observer, "living skeletons." The recuperating soldiers were unmolested. The Seminoles treated the armistice as binding, despite Clinch's rude interruption of the negotiations. When the Camp Izard garrison was finally ready, the troops returned with Clinch's command to Fort Drane.[25]

General Gaines soon left Florida, issuing a statement that the enemy had been "met, beaten, and, forced to sue for peace." But his men had not crossed the Withlacoochee River, and the allied tribespeople and blacks still held the region.[26]

CHAPTER FIVE

▨ General Scott, Governor Call, and the Great Wahoo

At the battle of the Wahoo, a negro, the property of a Florida planter, was one of the most distinguished leaders.

GENERAL THOMAS SIDNEY JESUP

The Indians and blacks of the Withlacoochee region did not rest long after General Clinch returned to Fort Drane with Gaines's exhausted troops. The warriors soon learned that three separate armies were either advancing or preparing to advance against them. They may even have known of the campaign plans before the soldiers marched. Slaves listening to officers discussing strategy could have alerted the Black Seminoles who often slipped into camps or settlements to spy.

On January 21, 1836, Brevet General Winfield Scott was appointed to lead the Florida offensive. One month later, he officially assumed command at Picolata on the St. Johns River, eighteen miles west of St. Augustine. Scott called for volunteers, but the battle plan he presented was designed for an opponent who waged "civilized" warfare. Unfortunately, the Seminoles were not inclined to fight that way, as both Clinch and Gaines had quickly learned.

Scott ordered three divisions (called wings) to drive and eventually surround the hostiles. The right wing, to be commanded by General Clinch, consisted of Florida, Georgia, and Louisiana volunteers plus regulars. They were to advance southwest from Fort Drane to Camp Izard on the Withlacoochee River. The left wing—South Carolina militia under Brevet Brigadier General Abraham Eustis and regular artillery troops led by Major Reynold

M. Kirby—would march south and then west from St. Augustine. They were to cross the St. Johns River at Volusia and move toward Micanopy's bases at Okihumpky and Peliklakaha. The center wing, mainly Alabama volunteers under U.S. Army Colonel William Lindsay, would move north from Tampa Bay to the Chocachatti settlements.

The divisions' movements would be coordinated by signal guns fired daily at different times. When the columns reached their destinations, they were to announce their arrival by discharging cannon. Then they would simultaneously move upon the Cove of the Withlacoochee (now Lake Tsala Apopka), where Scott believed the encircled enemy would be found and crushed.

That was the theory. But in the trackless Florida swamps, daunting logistics alone doomed the ambitious operation from the start. Furthermore, the Seminoles were a formidable foe. After annihilating Dade's command, they had repulsed Clinch's six hundred soldiers at the Withlacoochee River and then immobilized General Gaines's thousand troops at Camp Izard. Moreover, they had maintained their position south of the Withlacoochee even after Clinch's five hundred men had joined Gaines.

Now three armies were to march simultaneously and launch a coordinated attack against them from three different directions. The Americans had 4,800 soldiers, probably four times the number of resistance fighters—both tribesmen and black—that could be mustered in all of Florida. General Scott himself had estimated that the enemy force, including blacks, did not exceed 1,200.[1] Each army division included infantry (to clear hammocks) and artillery (to dislodge the Seminoles from strong positions). Additionally, the cavalry could ride the warriors down when they were flushed from cover. It remained to be seen how the Seminoles would cope with these new tactics.

The scouts watching Fort Brooke were the first Seminoles to observe a troop movement in General Scott's campaign. On March 10 they saw the center wing's Alabamians leave Tampa Bay. The soldiers headed north toward the Hillsborough River, where they erected pickets. The rudimentary post, called Fort Alabama, was initially garrisoned with seventy to eighty men.

After the center wing returned to Fort Brooke, Scott ordered the soldiers to go to the Chocachatti settlements. During the march, the Seminoles harassed the division by constantly picking off stragglers. When they reached their destination, the troops waited in vain for General Scott's signal gun. Then, after consuming all their provisions, they returned to Fort Brooke on

April 4. As before, small war parties "followed them . . . and killed and wounded several men." In the interim, on March 27 other warriors struck Fort Alabama. One white died and two others were wounded in the attack, but the Seminoles reportedly suffered heavy losses.[2]

Meanwhile, the left wing was operating below St. Augustine in the devastated plantation region. On March 17 the soldiers arrived at Volusia on the east bank of the St. Johns River but did not cross the river until five days later. The Seminoles were ready for them. As in the First Battle of the Withlacoochee (with Clinch), they waited until two companies had forded the river, stacked their arms, and engaged in camp duties. The ambushers then "crept . . . within 25 yards of the sentinel before being perceived" and opened fire at close range with murderous effect. When reinforcements were rushed across the St. Johns, the attackers withdrew before they could be intercepted. The Americans had three killed and several wounded, with two hit by friendly fire. Only one Seminole lay on the field, but "it was ascertained that four Indian bodies had been thrown into the river."[3]

The warriors allowed the troops to cross the Oklawaha River without much opposition on March 19. Yaha Hadjo, the Oklawaha chief who had been Abraham's associate in stirring up the plantation slaves, fired the only shot of resistance. Mortally wounded in a personal encounter with Brigadier General Joseph Shelton, he still managed to shoot the officer through the hip. Surrounded, Yaha Hadjo died while trying to reload.[4]

By now the left wing's objective was obvious. They were heading slowly but deliberately toward head chief Micanopy's principal towns of Okihumpky and Peliklakaha. The latter, the major Black Seminole village (sometimes known as Abraham's town), lay in the column's path and had neither river nor swamp to protect it. Thus, the tribesmen at Okihumpky and the blacks at Peliklakaha either had to retreat into the Wahoo Swamp or resist. They chose to fight.

On March 30 fifty warriors concealed in a dense hammock near Okihumpky ambushed a mounted troop, wounding three and killing one during the hour-long battle. Then the Seminoles skillfully executed a fighting withdrawal as the horsemen repeatedly charged them. Later that day the Indians and blacks saw the left wing enter abandoned Peliklakaha. On March 31 the troops torched the village. Dense smoke eventually obscured even the orange tree in full bloom that towered above the settlement's largest dwelling, supposedly

Micanopy's own residence. As Peliklakaha burned, the Seminoles moved west and plunged into the Wahoo Swamp. Their scouts soon brought word that, for now, they need not fear an attack. The left wing was proceeding south for Tampa, not west toward them.[5]

On March 26 yet another army (the right wing) departed from Fort Drane for Camp Izard on the Withlacoochee. General Scott, who had just arrived at the post, rode with the nearly two thousand soldiers. The column, which was stronger and better equipped than either Clinch's or Gaines's earlier commands, included infantry, artillery, and cavalry. It also was equipped with flatboats for crossing the river.

About this time Osceola decided to withdraw most of his force up the Withlacoochee toward the Cove, so the whites forded the river with little resistance on March 29. They were fired upon during the crossing, but the ambush caused no major damage. The next morning Seminole scouts reported that the troops were on the same trail that the tribespeople and blacks were using to retreat up the Withlacoochee. About five miles from the river, the soldiers came to a deserted camp and an abandoned town. They burned both.

Three miles away, the Seminoles lay hidden in a dense hammock facing a prairie and soon saw the advancing army. They called out to the Indian guide, Billy, and the black interpreter, Nero, who were moving cautiously ahead of the soldiers. (Nero was one of the few blacks who worked with the whites when the fighting started.) After talking with the warriors, the two men told General Scott that the Seminoles wanted a meeting.[6] The officer quickly agreed to their request. So the column withdrew to the still smoldering Seminole camp as preparations for the negotiations began. Meanwhile, a few tribesmen hurried the families into the Withlacoochee wilderness while the other men remained in the hammock.

The next morning, when no negotiators appeared, the troops again advanced across the prairie. The warriors began to fire heavily, particularly at the Louisiana volunteers. Cannons were deployed. As they blasted the hammock, the Seminoles gradually retreated. Fighting all the way, they withdrew through the pine woods into yet another hammock and finally reached the treacherous swamps of the Withlacoochee River.

Carrying their many casualties, the regulars and volunteers struggled back to the prairie. After establishing a special camp for the sick and wounded, garrisoned with Major Mark Anthony Cooper's Georgia battalion, the main body proceeded southwest for Tampa Bay. They torched a large village en route and arrived at their destination on April 6. During their march, "the men and horses suffered greatly for want of provisions and good water." The right wing's expedition had ended.[7]

"The campaign, so far," wrote a participant, "had been a complete failure. The enemy had not been found in sufficient numbers to induce any thing like a general engagement; and when met and defeated, he had always succeeded in effecting his escape." Logistical and communication problems had also prevented the three columns from linking up. Still, the failure of his plan did not dissuade Scott from further efforts to locate his enemy. He was convinced that, because no Seminole women or children had been seized, they were near Pease Creek. His opinion was confirmed by a "mixed Indian" captured near Charlotte Harbor. General Scott decided to find the families.

He ordered the Louisiana militia under Colonel Persifor F. Smith to sail to Charlotte Harbor and the mouth of Pease Creek. Colonel Goodwyn's mounted South Carolina volunteers were to ride overland from Tampa Bay for the upper part of the creek where the Seminole noncombatants were supposedly concealed.[8] But Smith's men discovered no traces of them except for a recently deserted camp. Goodwyn's column found no one but burned a large village that reportedly included three hundred huts. The soldiers returned, both men and horses having "suffered dreadfully in the expedition."

The failure of these two operations did not prove that there were neither tribespeople nor blacks on Pease Creek. In fact, it was later reported that the army on the Withlacoochee had unwittingly passed within two miles of a large Seminole town where the families were concentrated. One officer wrote, "This fact speaks volumes as to the character of the country, and the difficulty of finding the savage in his fastnesses, and of bringing him to battle."[9]

As Scott's campaign ended, he decided to abandon Fort Alabama. A detachment of regulars under Colonel William S. Foster was ordered to join Colonel William Chisholm's Alabama volunteers. The command, "in all about seven hundred and fifty men," left Fort Brooke on April 26. Their mission was to evacuate the sick and wounded and then destroy the post.

The men arrived at Fort Alabama near sunset. Before leaving the next morning, they armed a contraption that, if tampered with, would blow up the fort's magazine. Nicknamed the "infernal machine," the device exploded around 10:00 A.M. when the departing troops were a few miles away. It was never determined how many Seminoles, if any, died from the blast.

Later that afternoon, the soldiers found the remains of two men missing from Fort Alabama for the last two days. As they milled around the corpses, they were ambushed by "between one & two hundred Indians and negroes" who were concealed in a hammock on the opposite side of Thlonoto-sassa Creek. According to the official report on the action, "the first fire, as is usually the case with Indians lying in ambuscade . . . was stunning[,] killing and wounding a considerable number of troops and many horses."

But the Americans quickly rallied. Chisholm deployed the cannon being hauled back to Fort Brooke and ordered a bayonet charge. As usual, the counterattack scattered the hostiles, who then melted into the thick vegetation. Sixteen soldiers were wounded and four killed. An unspecified number of warriors lay dead on the field.[10]

Meanwhile, a frustrated Winfield Scott was recalled to lead the campaign against the Creeks in Alabama in May 1836. They were also resisting removal, although less effectively than their Seminole kin.

Before reporting to his new duty station, General Scott had once declared that "the season for operations in Florida is from the 25th of November to the end of April. I assert that an army cannot be safely put into the field earlier nor continued later." So as summer approached, the volunteers, their enlistments expired, went home and the regulars returned to their quarters. But the heat did not hamper the tribesmen and blacks, who did not stop fighting.[11]

The principal military posts in the Seminole country west of the St. Johns and north of Fort Brooke on Tampa Bay were, from south to north, Fort King, Fort Drane, and Fort Defiance (later named Micanopy). The Seminoles hit them all. The forts were also weakened from within by the effects of heat and disease.

Fort King was abandoned at the end of May because of sickness. On June 9, Osceola, leading 150–250 warriors, including 60 blacks, struck Fort Micanopy but was driven off. Fort Drane, located on General Clinch's plantation, was evacuated in early August because of illness. Osceola's followers then moved in and camped there. They were attacked by a company from Fort Micanopy on August 21, but the outnumbered soldiers were forced to retire after an hour's fighting. Early in September, Fort Micanopy was also abandoned because nearly half the garrison was sick.[12]

At this low ebb in the American fortunes, Florida's governor, Richard Keith Call, was selected to relieve General Scott. An old foe of the Seminoles, Call had been with Andrew Jackson when he destroyed the Suwannee settlements in 1818. The new commander quickly decided to mount a summer campaign, but due to the inevitable delays it did not begin until September. On September 19, Governor Call left Tallahassee for Suwannee Old Town with 1,200 mounted Tennessee volunteers and 140 conscripted Florida militia. They reached their destination six days later.[13]

On September 29, Call's army marched against Osceola's camp at Fort Drane. For more than a month, the chief's people and their cattle had feasted on General Clinch's corn and sugarcane. But their respite from fighting soon ended. On October 1 several warriors, some wounded, galloped into the Seminole encampment. They announced that horsemen—the vanguard of hundreds more—had surprised them ten miles back and killed several of their comrades. Although Osceola's forces had repelled one hundred soldiers a month before, they knew they could not defeat ten times that number. The only recourse was, once again, to seek refuge in the Cove of the Withlacoochee. The Seminoles quickly broke camp and left.[14]

Presently, Call's main command arrived at the now deserted Clinch plantation. The troops stayed for a week and rested their tired horses. On October 8, Major Benjamin K. Pierce and two hundred U.S. Army regulars joined them. Pierce soon marched after Osceola's band, taking Cudjo as his interpreter and guide. The Seminoles had reportedly destroyed Cudjo's considerable property, which possibly explains why he was aiding the whites. A friendly Indian named Billy also accompanied the column. His brother-in-law was the late chief Charley Emathla, whom Osceola had executed for complying with the emigration orders.[15]

Early on October 12 five weary men, some of them wounded, staggered into the new Seminole camp south of the Withlacoochee. Their band had been ambushed the previous evening, four miles north of the river. One woman and a child had died during the attack. More significantly, four women and seven children were captured. They represented a real prize; for during the nine months or so of warfare, almost no prisoners had been seized.

With the enemy almost upon them, scouts were dispatched to locate their base camp on the opposite bank of the Withlacoochee. Runners also alerted nearby Seminole villages. The more imaginative chiefs may have chuckled grimly when they thought how surprised the soldiers would be when they saw the swollen river.[16]

On October 13 daylight revealed a turbid flood at least two hundred yards across. Governor Call likely remembered the stream, perhaps one hundred feet wide, that he had crossed nearly a year before. At first he may have thought that his guides had led him astray and that he was on the shore of one of the region's many lakes. But as driftwood slowly floated by, he knew this body of water had to be the Withlacoochee.

A double column of mounted men rode forward, the leaders forcing their reluctant horses into the flooded river. As the first two animals began swimming, Seminole riflemen aimed at their riders and fired. With bullets flying around them, the horsemen unhesitatingly wheeled their mounts and regained the bank while their comrades returned fire.

Soon the Seminole fire became increasingly sporadic. Then it stopped. Obviously, the whites could not cross the river. Why waste more powder? On the opposite bank, the officers conferred with Governor Call. A Floridian, he knew that it would be easier to construct rafts from lead ingots than from the nearby pitch pines. Furthermore, the troops lacked tools except for a few axes.

The warriors spent the rest of the day observing various futile attempts to ford the river. But the troops succeeded only in occasionally drowning their horses or themselves. The Withlacoochee remained impassable.[17]

The day's real fighting occurred a few miles away. Under duress, one of the women taken prisoner the previous night had disclosed the location of a black settlement—on a fork where a stream joined the Withlacoochee. The town's inhabitants had been alerted and were ready to fight. As four hundred Tennessee volunteers advanced toward them, black warriors and some Seminole tribesmen hid either behind trees lining the creek bank or in their leafy branches. The Indian guide, Billy, and the female prisoner rode next to the troop commander, Lieutenant Colonel Josephus Guild.

The warriors targeted Billy and riddled him with bullets. Because they knew that the woman had been coerced, they spared her; but Billy was willfully betraying his people, so he had to die.[18] Although Guild's volunteers repeatedly approached the creek's edge, they were beaten back by the deadly fire. After an hour and a half, the Tennesseans regrouped. In addition to Billy, they now had two men dead and eight wounded. The soldiers had seen one black sharpshooter fall from a tree and believed they had inflicted other casualties. An elderly black, captured later, said that "there were twenty eight Indians and five negroes killed, besides many wounded."

Guild's command eventually withdrew. They subsequently reported that their enemy had been "driven from his position . . . with considerable loss." Governor Call tactfully did not inquire why the Tennesseans had failed to cross the fifty-yard-wide stream to take the town.[19]

With rations almost exhausted, Call's army soon returned to Fort Drane, arriving on October 17. For the third time in less than a year—and the second time for Governor Call personally—an expeditionary force from the post had been forced to retreat from the Withlacoochee.

The failure of Call's campaign did not dissuade him from attempting another, particularly after 750 Creek auxiliaries joined his troops. The tribesmen had landed at Tampa Bay at the end of September, proceeding overland to Fort Drane and reaching it on October 19. Wearing white turbans to distinguish them from the Seminoles, the Creeks were "to receive . . . such plunder as they may take from the Seminoles." "Plunder" primarily meant captured blacks.[20]

On November 10, Governor Call, with mounted Tennesseans, Creek volunteers, and some regulars (well over two thousand men), left Fort Drane for the Withlacoochee. Because the river had subsided from its crest, it was now fordable. Without their natural moat, the warriors could not risk a pitched battle with a force probably three times their own number. Moreover, half the force was mounted and accompanied by hostile Creeks. So the Seminoles abandoned their settlements and moved upstream with their families to the final refuge of the Wahoo Swamp.

Although the Seminoles did not fear the Creeks, they despised them. Those advancing upon them came from the group that had fought the Red Sticks twenty years earlier and had accompanied Andrew Jackson on his 1818 raid into Florida. This same faction had consented to selling Creek lands to the United States and had just participated in a war in Alabama against fellow tribespeople who were also resisting removal. The Black Seminoles had even more reason to hate the Creeks because they had helped to destroy the blacks' Suwannee settlements less than twenty years before. The blacks probably also knew that the Creeks had been promised all the plunder they could take;

namely, the blacks themselves. As one Seminole chief emphatically stated, he "understood the Creeks had come for negroes."[21]

Nevertheless, the warriors admired their kinsmen's combat skills, bravery, and courage. They knew the Creeks could live off the land and follow a trail for days without rest. In contrast, the whites seemed inept in the wilderness. They were always marching out with heavy carts and packhorses loaded with provisions that, when gone, forced them to return to their bases. Their big wagons could not cross a river without a bridge or a fleet of flatboats. Because the Seminoles felt that one Creek warrior was worth two or three soldiers, they decided for now to trust their feet rather than their rifles.

On November 13, Governor Call's army crossed the Withlacoochee without opposition, exactly one month after they had turned back from the river. His command soon found and torched "three large towns" with houses "built of hewn logs." The dwellings had been recently constructed, probably during the preceding spring or summer. Because of their superior workmanship, the burned villages most likely belonged to Black Seminoles, who were known to be better builders than the Indians. Trails led from these settlements to the east and northeast. An elderly black prisoner, the only person encountered during the whole operation, said that the inhabitants had fled to the Wahoo Swamp. He also said that the people had been subsisting on scrawny cattle. Indeed, there was little evidence of cultivation near the towns.[22]

Meanwhile, the Seminoles prepared to fight a delaying action like that used so effectively against General Scott. Their scouts reported that Call's forces were advancing in two columns. The mounted Tennesseans, the Floridians, and a few regulars were coming up the Withlacoochee along the right (north) bank. The main body of regulars and the Creeks were marching on the left (south) side. Call had ordered the two divisions to meet at Dade's battleground.

Understandably, the warriors preferred to engage the right wing, principally Tennessee volunteers, rather than the left one with the Creeks. They fought the right wing on November 17 and 18. The first clash lasted "about an hour, when the Indians were routed and disappeared in the hammock . . . one man [was] killed and ten wounded. Eighteen of the Indians were killed."[23]

The second encounter was a major affair that reportedly involved several hundred Seminoles near the Wahoo Swamp. The tribesmen lost heavily. The whites estimated that they had killed fifty warriors while themselves losing only four dead and a score wounded. The action gained the families no more than an hour to escape deeper into the swamp as the Tennesseans marched on. On November 20 they joined the regulars and the Creeks at Dade's battle-ground.[24]

Although his command had been on half rations for several days, Governor Call ordered yet another effort to find and crush the foe. The chiefs, however, probably knew about the military's precarious supply situation. Black Seminoles hidden just outside the circle of campfire light could have eaves-dropped on the soldiers' conversations. The uncanny tracking skills of the Seminoles—both black and Indian—also enabled them to inspect a deserted encampment and accurately determine the status of enemy provisions. Perhaps the dwindling rations would force the troops to withdraw.

But by the morning of November 21 it became evident that Call intended another expedition. His opponents were equally determined to defend every hammock and island. They had been pushed back nearly to the limits of their defenses. Thus, the day would probably be decisive. Either the Seminoles would be vanquished or they would continue the struggle.

The warriors waited in a hammock on the edge of the Wahoo Swamp near the November 18 battlefield. They watched the army advance in three columns. The Tennesseans were on the right, the regulars and Florida militia in the center, and the Creeks on the left. There was also a detachment of horsemen in reserve.

The Seminoles fired heavily as the regulars and militia charged. Then they retreated into a marsh. Their pursuers followed, sometimes "above their waists in mud and water; and . . . at least an hour advancing three-quarters of a mile."[25] The last Seminole stronghold was a mile and a half away through a bog beyond the main stream of the Withlacoochee. Although they seemed to flee in all directions, the warriors headed—as soon as they were out of the soldiers' sight—for a final stand. Gliding along a hidden trail through a dense hammock, they skirted the morass and soon outdistanced their enemy. After splashing across a shallow tributary, they took up positions in a cypress swamp facing a ford. Its water was so "black and sluggish" as to appear impassable to outsiders.

When he arrived, each man drew a stick from his pouch and gave it to his chief so that the captains could determine the number of casualties and survivors. They had lost only a few thus far, perhaps four or five killed. Eventually, as more warriors appeared, the force totaled 620 men, 200 of them black.

The resistance united tribesmen, Black Seminoles, and fugitive slaves. Yaholoochee (Cloud) and Osuchee (Cooper) were the principal Indian commanders; but "one of the most distinguished leaders" was a runaway, "the property of a Florida planter." Behind them, on higher, firmer ground, were horses packed with their scanty belongings. The families waited beside the animals, ready to flee if their men were defeated.

The warriors crouched behind whatever cover was available. They scanned the foliage across the Withlacoochee from which, at any moment, the final assault would come.[26] The bushes soon parted. Into the open, running like bloodhounds on a trail, came the Creeks. As they splashed through the mud and shallow puddles on the flooded riverbank, would they realize that this was a ford—and an easy one at that—with water just three feet deep? Or would they be deceived by the stream's sinister blackness, suggesting unfathomable depths?

Major David Moniac, a full-blooded Creek and an 1822 West Point graduate, boldly advanced to the river's edge and waded in. But before he could advise the others that the water was shallow, the officer was cut down when the cypress exploded in flame and smoke. As his body sank, the Creeks hastily returned to the bushes, threw themselves down, and returned the fire.[27]

The Seminoles howled gleefully. For about an hour, they traded shots with their kinsmen. Finally, after having struggled through the swamp, the regulars and volunteers arrived. The Seminole fire redoubled and then slackened. They were conserving their ammunition, which was running low. Also, with more troops present, they expected a bayonet charge.

Lieutenant Colonel Pierce, commanding the regulars, noted the diminished firing and guessed the reason. The Creeks had convinced him that the river was fordable, and a bayonet attack would carry the position and perhaps end the war. So the officer passed his orders to his second in command and informed the Tennessee commander, Robert Armstrong, of his decision. Armstrong, however, objected to the charge. Whatever his reasons, they were decisive. To the Seminoles' surprise, the soldiers began to withdraw as night fell.[28]

The relieved warriors also retreated, carrying their dead and wounded. Meanwhile, Governor Call's hungry and exhausted men struggled back to Volusia on the St. Johns River. The Battle of the Wahoo Swamp was officially proclaimed "a brilliant day, redounding to the honor of our arms, and calculated to bring the war to a speedy termination." A later report more accurately described the expedition as "a lesson to other commanders."[29] Governor Call had twice failed to get his armies across relatively narrow bodies of water and successfully engage large numbers of hostiles. He, like Generals Clinch, Gaines, and Scott, found the Seminoles—both Indian and black—to be formidable foes.

Where was John Cavallo during all these clashes with the American forces? He is not mentioned in the official records. Yet because of his later association with Alligator, John could have participated in the clashes at Peliklakaha or in the fighting at the Withlacoochee.

CHAPTER SIX

▨ There Is No Peace

This . . . is a negro, not an Indian war.
GENERAL THOMAS SIDNEY JESUP

Brevet Major General Thomas Sidney Jesup was appointed to replace Governor Call, who had been relieved of his duties in late November 1836. Jesup assumed command of the Florida campaign at Volusia on December 8, 1836. He was appointed because he had quickly crushed the Creek uprising in Alabama after replacing an ineffective General Scott in June 1836. As he had in Florida, Scott did not move quickly enough to satisfy Washington. Perhaps Jesup's experience with logistics during his stint as U.S. Army Quartermaster General also influenced his superiors' decision to reassign him.

Jesup faced a tough challenge. The first year of the war had been a complete failure for the military. Besides the lack of success on the battlefield, official estimates of enemy casualties from December 1835 to November 1836 were just 131 Seminoles killed (probably including blacks). The whites had lost nearly as many men in Dade's massacre alone. Furthermore, they had captured only fifteen warriors.[1]

Jesup intended to pursue the war more aggressively and effectively than previous commanders had. His predecessors had ordered large armies to march into the wilderness to locate and engage the enemy. But the Seminoles resisted savagely when their numbers and position were favorable and, if badly outnumbered, would melt into the swamps after waging minor evasive and holding actions.

Like those who preceded him, General Jesup was very willing to fight the warriors if given the opportunity. His primary aim, however, was to seize Seminoles and imprison them. Although the captives would be mostly women and children, he felt that such hostages would be a powerful incentive for the men to surrender.

To implement his goals, Jesup planned to deploy relatively small mobile units, principally horsemen and Indian scouts. An early test of his tactics took place on December 3, 1836. Even before assuming command, he had ordered Lieutenant Colonel Caulfield's Alabama mounted volunteers to raid a black village on the lake from which the Oklawaha River rose. They captured forty-one people, almost three times the number of those taken the previous year.[2]

General Jesup also enjoyed certain advantages over his predecessors. He had many troops, mostly accumulated through the efforts of previous commanders. Additionally, a year's experience in Florida warfare had produced useful information that made his task somewhat easier. The mistakes of those he succeeded became a source of inspiration. Finally, he had wisely concluded: "This . . . is a negro, not an Indian war; and if it be not speedily put down, the south will feel the effects of it on their slave population before the end of the next season."[3]

One of Jesup's first moves was to determine the location of the various enemy bands. He soon learned that Osceola was somewhere in the Wahoo Swamp with a group of tribespeople and blacks. Echo Emathla was also there, and Yaholoochee (Cloud) was nearby at the Cove of the Withlacoochee.

Additionally, Osuchee (Cooper) had a few Seminoles and a number of runaway slaves on the Apopka Lake. Cooper, Philip, and Micanopy reportedly each had about "one hundred and twenty to two hundred Indian and negro warriors; the latter, perhaps the more numerous." They were about a day's march from one another and not far from Jesup's base near Dade's battleground.

Micanopy, Jumper, and Abraham—the last two probably influenced by their leader's apathy—allegedly wanted to avoid fighting by hiding in the Everglades. But Osceola, characteristically, planned to remain on the Withlacoochee. He would move south into the Everglades only as a last resort.[4]

General Jesup decided to scout the Wahoo Swamp for Osceola's camp, but his soldiers found nothing. Their Indian guides believed that the Seminoles had gone south shortly after Call's forces had withdrawn to Volusia in late

November 1836. The next step, then, was to explore the greater Withlacoochee region. But the initial effort was unproductive. On December 23, 1836 reports declared that there were no signs of hostiles. All trails pointed south. A more careful search, however, revealed that Osceola was still in the area. He was ill and had retired to a black village in the Panosufkee Swamp.

On January 10, 1837, a mounted detachment, including some Creeks, surprised Osceola's camp and seized sixteen blacks. Two days later, thirty-six others (officially identified as Black Seminoles rather than recent runaways) and three tribesmen belonging to Osceola's band were also captured.

One of those taken was Primus, formerly a slave of Erastus Rogers, the sutler murdered on the same day as Agent Wiley Thompson. The military had used him at least twice as a messenger during the preceding winter. But Primus had a wife among the Seminoles; and the last time he had left the whites, he did not return. After his captors threatened to hang him, Primus disclosed that Osceola's warriors numbered a hundred if assembled but the chief was now fleeing through the swampy wilderness accompanied only by his family and three men. Primus also stated that Echo Emathla was still on the Withlacoochee.[5]

The army headed down the Withlacoochee from the Cove to find Osceola and Echo Emathla, marching in two columns, one on each side of the river. The expedition soon produced "positive knowledge" that there were not many Seminoles left in the area. The few still remaining were running through the swamps "with no other means of subsistence than roots, palmetto cabbage, and occasionally indifferent beef."

Lieutenant Colonel Foster was dispatched to find a camp of twenty to thirty warriors in a large swamp south of the Withlacoochee's mouth. The Seminoles supposedly wished to surrender. But when Foster's men encountered a "hostile" group of Indians and blacks, the Georgia volunteers killed two tribesmen "after (it is said) they had thrown down their arms." The others, six black men and twelve women and children, were taken prisoner.

Satisfied that the Withlacoochee region was now largely empty, General Jesup decided to move to the headwaters of the Oklawaha River where Micanopy, Jumper, and Alligator were reportedly concentrating their forces.[6] Early on January 22, 1837, the main body of the army marched for the Oklawaha. The advance guard, which included a Creek contingent, soon captured a black man. Possibly under duress, he agreed to lead a detachment to the camp of Chief Osuchee (Cooper), Micanopy's brother-in-law. Cooper had led blacks at the Battle of Wahoo Swamp, during which he had been shot. Osuchee and another wounded man, with their families and several companions, had returned to the southern border of Apopka Lake to recuperate. An Indian medicine man accompanied them.

On January 23 the Creeks located the camp and, without orders, charged it. They killed Cooper, his oldest son, and the medicine man. A fourth man, before dying, fatally shot one of the attackers. The Creeks captured Cooper's wife and three children, another tribeswoman and her two children, as well as two black men and their families.[7] The newly captured prisoners indicated that most of the Seminoles had withdrawn from the Oklawaha and were moving southeast toward the Caloosahatchee River. A brigade composed of Alabama volunteers, U.S. mounted marines, and Creek scouts was sent after them. Colonel Archibald Henderson, the U.S. Marine Corps commandant, led the unit. They followed the trail left by the Seminole cattle and on January 27 spotted herds of livestock grazing on the open ground. The animals clearly indicated the enemy's presence.

Colonel Henderson dispatched a detachment to find the hostiles. As his men proceeded south, they collected a large number of cattle, which were left behind under guard. The soldiers also seized a black man resting at a campfire. He said that many blacks were ahead of them and "from forty to fifty Indians, with Abraham" were in their rear. Meanwhile, Lieutenant James Chambers, who had also separated from the main command, located and charged the enemy baggage train. He captured five Seminoles, two women and three children, and about twenty blacks, also mostly women and children. The catch included one hundred ponies, fifty of which carried "a large quantity of plunder."

Henderson ordered Major Morris and his Creeks to follow the remaining Seminoles, who had fled into the Great Cypress Swamp (not the one with the same name located south of Lake Okeechobee). The mounted marines were in the vanguard.[8] Frightened fugitives from the pack train soon reached the main body of the Seminoles and warned of the enemy's approach. The warriors—probably led by Abraham—immediately prepared to fight. They felled two trees across the twenty-yard-wide Hatcheelustee Creek so the families could cross it. Then the men stationed themselves on the opposite side to cover their escape.

Shortly before noon, the marines cautiously approached the primitive bridge. After allowing them to get within easy range, the blacks and tribesmen opened fire, killing one and wounding three others. As Henderson's men counterattacked, the Seminoles retreated. They crossed a pine woods, plunged back into the swamp, and assumed another defensive position. The warriors were not dislodged until they killed another marine and wounded a corporal. But as they withdrew, their pursuers were right behind them.

A Black Seminole named Ben, about forty years old, fleeing with his wife, Jane, and their infant son, Robert, lagged behind the other fugitives. Suddenly they heard a menacing order to halt. Trapped and not wanting to endanger their child, the couple surrendered. Ben quickly informed his captors that he had never been owned by a white man and that he was one of Micanopy's people. After the unimpressed marines hustled the trio to the rear, Ben found the rest of his family, who were already prisoners.

The troops maintained the chase, without further success, until 4:00 P.M., although another detachment, under Lieutenant Colonel Caulfield, took another black into custody. When the men returned to their base about 10:00 P.M., they learned that the main command had discovered a recently vacated camp but had seen no action. Two blacks and an Indian were reported to have died during the day's skirmishing. Colonel Henderson later praised his forces, especially the marines, saying that their "killed and wounded show where they were, and render any further comment from me unnecessary."⁹

The captured cattle, baggage train, and women and children indicated that Jesup's army was very near the enemy's main body. If they marched rapidly, a decisive battle could occur. But Jesup was contemplating peace talks, not more fighting. He undoubtedly reasoned that his men could handle the outnumbered warriors but, at best, could only kill or catch a small percentage of the entire tribe. The survivors would then scatter and possibly take weeks or months to regroup. Jesup also felt that the Seminoles might now reconsider emigration negotiations.

The tribespeople had been roughly handled for more than a month. The soldiers had forced them from their favorite haunts in the Wahoo Swamp and the Cove of the Withlacoochee, and several villages had been destroyed. A principal chief (Cooper) and several warriors were dead; and more than 150 Seminoles, primarily women and children, had been captured—ten times the number taken the preceding year. Additionally, many of their cattle and most of their belongings had been seized. Planting season had begun; but because Jesup intended to harry them until it was too late to sow corn, they would only have koonti root to eat. Finally—and most important—Osceola, the principal war spirit, was ill. He was now a fugitive with his band entirely disrupted, and his martial influence was greatly diminished.

General Jesup was prepared to offer terms to the Seminoles as generous as his instructions permitted. He realized that his comparatively impressive accomplishments fell far short of what was still required. Although his troops had detained one hundred women and children in January alone, Jesup admitted that "not a single first-rate warrior has been captured, and only two Indian men have surrendered. The warriors have fought as long as they had life, and such seems to me to be the determination of those who influence their councils—I mean the leading negroes."[10]

As he considered his options, the officer must have thought about the black man named Ben whom the marines had just captured. Jesup learned that Ben was "one of the most important and influential characters among the Indian negroes." If this information was true, he was the ideal envoy. He could receive, in English, a conference request and then translate it for Jumper, Micanopy's chief counselor. As a prominent Black Seminole, Ben could also best express the communication's proper significance. Finally, only a prisoner whose family was held hostage could be trusted to leave and return.

The general sent Ben to find Jumper and tell him that he wanted to talk. The black man left the next morning, January 28; and shortly thereafter, the army marched to Tohopekaliga Lake, collecting several hundred more cattle en route. The troops camped on the lake, a few miles from the Great Cypress Swamp, where General Jesup anxiously waited for the answer to his message.[11]

Meanwhile, the blacks and tribesmen in the Hatcheelustee Creek fight had scattered ahead of their pursuers. Many a warrior, when the chase ended, found himself alone. One was Abraham. After backtracking and determining Jesup's new location, he searched for his people, especially his family. He must have been overjoyed when he found them safe, but his son cried about losing his pony with the captured baggage train.

More seriously, all of Abraham's personal property had been taken. His wife's cookware, the family's blankets, and one hundred dollars in silver were gone. Even worse, all his papers, including his priceless certificate of freedom, had been lost. If he were caught, the missing document could have prevented him from being sold into slavery.

Most distressing of all, the Seminole gunpowder supply had been seized. It had been obtained at a high cost—successfully smuggled into Florida through Charlotte Harbor via Spanish fishing boats from Havana, then shipped from St. Augustine down the St. Johns by sympathetic free blacks. But the warriors were left with no more than the powder that remained in their horns and flasks.

A troubled Abraham received Ben when he arrived at the Seminole camp. After a quick explanation of events, Ben gave him gifts from General Jesup as a gesture of good faith. It is unclear why Ben decided to go directly to Abraham. Perhaps he knew him better than Jumper or he could not locate the chief.

On January 31, Ben returned to Jesup's camp with Abraham. He went in first to advise the officer that Micanopy's leading black counselor and "the terror of the white people, for the last year" was ready for a parley. Abraham soon appeared, carrying a white flag of truce. He headed down the path leading to the largest tent, which he knew had to be Jesup's. As Abraham walked, he overheard some soldiers muttering about "the 'niger' who was going to hang."

When Abraham reached the commanding officer's quarters, he saw the general standing inside. He stopped and deliberately thrust his flagstaff into the earth beside the pole bearing Old Glory. He was a chief and would behave as such to the end. Then he crossed his arms as Jesup approached. The officer smiled and extended his hand, which Abraham took.

Although their conversation was unrecorded, its basic content can be surmised. Jesup surely emphasized the absolute necessity of Seminole emigration and must have stressed the government's resolve to enforce it at whatever cost of time, money, and lives. In turn, Abraham was undoubtedly an effective advocate for his people. He likely said that they required iron-clad assurance regarding their freedom and property before he could attempt to persuade the tribespeople to seek peace.

General Jesup did not need much convincing to understand that Black Seminole assistance was essential to end the war and remove the Seminole Indians from Florida, and thereafter he strongly asserted their position. Although there were some lapses in actual practice, his official communications stressed the importance of extending the utmost consideration to them.

Abraham rode back to the Seminoles with tobacco and messages for Jumper and Alligator. After much talking, he convinced them to visit Jesup the next day. He returned to inform the officer of their decision, but Jumper and Alligator failed to appear. When Abraham went searching for them, he discovered the two men just four miles from their camp. They had become apprehensive and had stopped. Only after much cajoling did he persuade them to continue the journey.

On February 3, Jesup finally met with the two tribesmen. The Seminoles eventually agreed to a truce while their other principal headmen were assembled. Messengers were sent to ask them to meet with General Jesup at Fort Dade on February 18. After the two negotiators departed, the army started for the fort, located on the Withlacoochee about fifty miles east of Tampa Bay. They marched on February 4.[12]

In the meantime, the St. Johns Seminoles, relatively quiet since destroying the plantations below St. Augustine at the war's onset, became active again. But the renewed hostilities apparently were now largely due to blacks, both Seminoles and recent runaways. While the elderly King Philip failed to act, the Black Seminole leader, John Caesar, decided to seize the initiative. He created a diversion in the St. Johns area, hoping to draw some troops from the Withlacoochee. John Caesar may have been the only principal St. Johns warrior who had visited that arena of conflict. He had participated in the siege of Camp Izard and was unwilling to let the St. Johns Seminoles do nothing while the bands formerly operating on the Withlacoochee were crushed.

During the spring and summer of 1836, St. Augustine had been harried by tribesmen and Black Seminoles, who often slipped into the town to spy. Although some were captured, many induced slaves to escape and smuggled out ammunition. Various free blacks and slaves were arrested on suspicion of conspiracy, but evidence sufficient for conviction was nearly impossible to obtain.[13]

About mid-January 1837, as General Jesup's forces were mopping up the Withlacoochee region and preparing to move against the Seminoles whom they believed were near the Oklawaha and St. Johns headwaters, John Caesar began his raids, targeting those plantations that, because of their proximity to St. Augustine, had escaped earlier devastation. He deployed small partisan bands of perhaps a dozen men each. Almost all were runaways who intimately knew the terrain.

But John Caesar was killed on January 17, 1837, one day after attempting to steal horses from the Hanson plantation, two miles west of St. Augustine. He apparently did not anticipate being followed and was surprised in his camp the following night. During the ambush, he and two others were killed. A fourth man was badly wounded and later captured. The attackers were dismayed that the group contained very few tribesmen and Black Seminoles. The rest were fugitive slaves belonging to prominent St. Augustine citizens. One belonged to the local Florida militia commander, General Joseph M. Hernandez. Another was a free black man from St. Augustine named Joe Merritt.

The local citizens realized that many of their runaways were now active Seminole allies. John Caesar's raids soon produced new city ordinances to control St. Augustine's blacks, both free and enslaved; and the town council demanded that the Florida militia remain nearby for protection, which deprived General Jesup of men that could have been used against the main force of the Seminoles. Thus, John Caesar accomplished his goal of tying up troops.[14]

Meanwhile, Wild Cat and about two hundred warriors attacked a fortified army camp on Lake Monroe (near present-day Sanford) early on February 8, 1837. "A sharp contest ensued" in which Wild Cat was the actual field commander. Although the garrison outnumbered them almost two to one and was supported by a steamboat equipped with a cannon, the Seminoles maintained a heavy fire for three hours before withdrawing. They killed Captain Charles Mellon and wounded fourteen others, some seriously. The assault on the post, which became known as Fort Mellon, marked the appearance of the war leader who eventually succeeded Osceola. After Osceola's captivity and death, Wild Cat surpassed him in militancy and continued the fighting for more than three years.

General Jesup was understandably dismayed by the attack at Lake Monroe. He feared that some of the Seminoles with whom he had negotiated had participated and might not honor the agreement of February 3. In fact, Wild Cat and his St. Johns warriors were unaware of the proposed armistice; but they were ready, when instructed, to suspend hostilities.[15]

The day after the Lake Monroe raid, troops operating "on the Gulf south of the Withlacoochee" destroyed eight Indian villages. They also encountered and routed a party of about fifty Seminoles. A sergeant was killed during the clash. General Jesup learned of this skirmish just before the peace conference was to begin. The action reinforced his impression of continued widespread Seminole resistance and stressed the need for an agreement to end the bloodshed.

Jesup anxiously awaited February 18, when the chiefs were to appear for treaty negotiations. But he knew that they might not come and understood their reasons. "I have required . . . immediate emigration," he wrote. "There would be no difficulty in making peace . . . were it not for that condition; . . . The negroes who rule the Indians are all averse to removing to so cold a climate."[16]

Abraham, however, was laboring to produce peace talks. He realized the Seminoles could not remain in Florida if the U.S. government wanted to expel them. Instead, his objective was to demonstrate clearly that they would mount a protracted and costly resistance unless the Black Seminoles were given satisfactory assurances. His point made, Abraham felt it was now time to negotiate.

The day of the conference came, but no Seminole leaders appeared. Finally, about mid-afternoon, Abraham arrived carrying a white flag. He said that Jumper, Holatoochee, Alligator, and others were on the way. The next day, about ten Black Seminoles showed up; and on Monday, February 20, about fifteen tribesmen came into camp. On Tuesday a few more arrived, but the leaders were absent. Abraham left that night to locate the missing chiefs and hurry them along. Shortly thereafter, Alligator and Cloud finally appeared, saying that Holatoochee would come the next day. Abraham returned on February 24 and said that Jumper was sick. Holatoochee, Micanopy's heir and representative, arrived immediately after Abraham.

The conference was finally held that day. Holatoochee, Cloud, and Alligator represented the Seminoles, with Abraham as translator. General Jesup spoke for the U.S. government, and Cudjo and a Black Creek named Cow Tom were his interpreters. Holatoochee said Micanopy wanted to remain in the "bad swamp" where he was living because he had been forced from his good land. But Jesup reasserted the absolute need to emigrate. The Seminole negotiators quickly declared that they had no instructions from Micanopy on the subject; he must approve such a serious matter. It was therefore agreed that they should meet again on March 4. In the interim, Holatoochee would talk to Micanopy, and Alligator to Jumper. When the delegates departed, they left twelve hostages, including a nephew of Micanopy.[17]

At one point during the negotiations, John Cavallo came into the camp. Twelve years later, he reminded General Jesup, "In January, 1837, Brevet Major Graham 4' Inf took ninety head of cattle belonging to me from Tokope keliga Florida—and used said cattle to subsist his troops on—telling me that I should be paid for them by the United States." He signed himself "John Cowaya, alias Gopher John" and asked for reimbursement. Lieutenant John T. Sprague supported his request.

The episode involving John's cattle was not such an orderly process of bargaining and sale, but there is no doubt that Graham's men seized John's livestock. The officer had commanded a company of the Fourth Infantry on January 27 when the Seminole baggage train was taken in the Great Cypress Swamp. His troops rounded up several hundred cattle grazing near Lake Tohopekaliga, probably John's herd among them. John could have identified his animals by their branding or ear cropping and then lodged his claim upon entering the camp a few days later.

Years later, an officer named S. F. Whitney testified that he had impounded seventy to eighty cattle during the 1837 expedition. Then he drove the livestock to the camp where John found them. Whitney also added that no one else had claimed those particular animals. But when Major Graham was questioned about the episode in 1849, he could not recall it. This is understandable; twelve years had elapsed, and John's herd had been only part of a large number of cattle taken that day. Graham could not remember having promised him payment because one of the major's subordinates had made the actual capture. Despite his best efforts, John was never paid for his livestock. But his claim established a link between the warrior of 1837 and the "lathy boy" of 1826 who had played the gopher trick on Lieutenant Colonel Brooke.[18]

On March 4 the Seminoles promptly appeared for the conference with Jesup, arriving at his base camp at Fort Dade on the Withlacoochee River. Jumper was with them. Micanopy, whether from indolence or timidity, was absent but had authorized Holatoochee to represent him. Cloud was also present. Alligator, for some reason, did not come but sent two surrogates: "his nephew, Philip's son," named Cotza Tustenuggee (Panther Warrior) and a Black Seminole called "Pease Creek John"—possibly John Cavallo.

John had progressed a long way in just over a year. He had proven himself as a warrior and risen from relative obscurity to become a subchief. Because the Seminoles had no medals, wound stripes, or written commendations, we can only speculate on the leadership qualities that impressed the chiefs. John's position as brother-in-law of the prominent headman Holatoochee possibly contributed to his success, but information about this relationship is too vague to allow an assessment of its significance on John's career.

On March 6, 1837, an agreement captioned "Capitulation of the Seminole nation of Indians and their allies, by Jumper, Holatoochee or Davy, and Yaholoochee, representing the principal, chief Micanopy" was endorsed by the Seminole negotiators. John Cavallo (Cowaya) and Cotza Tustenuggee also signed it, the latter clearly representing Alligator. The document stated that hostilities were to cease immediately and permanently and stipulated that the entire nation would emigrate to the West. To ensure their cooperation, the Seminoles would furnish hostages. Additionally, they were to withdraw south of the Hillsborough River and then assemble near Tampa Bay no later than April 10. The United States would pay their relocation expenses; and the Seminoles were to receive government rations before, during, and for a year after removal.

Significantly, the treaty was made with "the Seminole nation of Indians and their allies." Undoubtedly, *allies* referred to the blacks among them. Their rights were further guaranteed in article 5: "Major General Jesup, in behalf of the United States, agreed that the Seminole and their allies, who come in and emigrate West, shall be secure in their lives and property; that their negroes, their bona fide property, shall also accompany them West; and that the cattle and ponies shall be paid for by the United States at a fair valuation."

The agreement apparently protected three classes of blacks among the Seminoles. The term *allies* must have implied runaways who had participated in the fighting and free Black Seminoles such as Abraham. *Bona fide property* evidently meant those individuals categorized as slaves. Ben and his family, whom Micanopy claimed, were in that group. Abraham's influence as the principal negotiator is clear in this provision of the document. Therefore, it was particularly appropriate that John, a man of African ancestry, was one of the treaty signers.[19] About this time, Micanopy had arrived and camped near Fort Dade. He finally signed the capitulation agreement on March 18.

As the officers awaited the arrival of more tribespeople and blacks, they fraternized with those already present. Abraham used this time to collect his cattle, which were nearby. He also provided the whites with game. His young son recovered his pony, which had been captured at the Great Cypress Swamp and was being held by an officer. When informed that the animal belonged to the little boy, the officer good naturedly returned it.

By the end of March, matters seemed to be proceeding satisfactorily. Ya-holoochee was at Tampa Bay with two hundred followers. King Philip and Tuskinia, from the St. Johns band, had also agreed to leave. Moreover, Philip had ordered Arpeika to accept emigration. Osceola, however, "folded his arms and walked away" when removal was mentioned. Still, it was hoped that the other chiefs would eventually persuade him to comply. Abraham's slowness in reaching the Tampa Bay relocation camp might have caused concern, but he explained that his father-in-law's illness had delayed him. The man was apparently dying.[20]

During this time, General Jesup increasingly appreciated the need for conciliating the blacks among the Seminoles. On March 26 he declared: "The negroes rule the Indians, and it is important that they should feel themselves secure; if they should become alarmed and hold out, the war will be renewed." But by the end of the month, so many tribespeople and blacks had gathered in the emigration camp to await departure that Jesup became overconfident. On March 29 he wrote: "I have some hopes of inducing the Indians and the Indian negroes to unite in bringing in the negroes taken from the citizens during the war." The runaways who had joined the Seminoles during the fighting were no longer considered allies, a point of view that Jesup tried to persuade some of the more amenable chiefs to accept.

Jesup was also greatly pressured by planters whose slaves had fled during the fighting. Therefore, on April 8 he made a secret arrangement with certain Seminole leaders, notably Coa Hadjo (the second in command of the St. Johns River band), to bring in the "captured Negroes." It soon proved to be an unwise move.

The next day, Micanopy, Holatoochee, Yaholoochee, Wild Cat, and John Cavallo—who had been held as hostages to guarantee the capitulation agreement—were allowed to leave General Jesup's camp at Fort Dade. They proceeded to the Tampa Bay relocation center.[21] At the camp, John undoubtedly enjoyed seeing old friends and making new ones. Among them, the most important was Wild Cat, whom he had already met at Jesup's headquarters. John was then about twenty-five and Wild Cat just a little older. Probably at this time, the two young warriors forged a friendship that lasted some twenty years until Wild Cat's death.

Still, with all the arrivals and departures in the camp, the number of Seminoles who remained was fairly constant. Although many of the principal headmen were present, their followers were trickling in. On May 5, Jesup reported that several groups had scattered because of reports that they were to be punished. Then, surprisingly, Osceola and other chiefs suddenly appeared at Fort Mellon. They were coming to the emigration center.[22]

Meanwhile, unknown to him, General Jesup's secret April 8 agreement for the return of runaways had begun to unravel all his carefully constructed peace plans. Specifically, Coa Hadjo had instructed his associates in the scheme to not take the escaped slaves to Tampa Bay. To avoid a stampede, he ordered them to concentrate the runaways at different points away from the embarkation camp. The blacks could then be seized without causing undue alarm.[23]

By now, troops had gone into the Seminole country to watch the Indians, see that they were in the region assigned to them, guard against any revival of hostilities, and hurry them along to Tampa. They were also to receive the "captured Negroes." But often the soldiers did not have to search for the runaways or force their surrender. In fact, many just turned themselves in. They had suffered severely along with the Seminoles, perhaps even more, because the blacks were not used to surviving in the wilderness. They arrived in little groups, half starved and clad in rags, complaining of ill treatment from the tribesmen. They probably hoped their allegations, whether true or false, would lessen the punishment for leaving their masters' plantations.

Nevertheless, others, tougher and more combative, refused to surrender. A party of runaways located on Cedar Creek defied the Seminoles and were quoted as saying that "they [the Indians] had not taken them & that they [the Negroes] would not give up." Militants such as Osceola supported them. When Coa Hadjo announced in council that the fugitive slaves were to be returned, Osceola angrily arose and declared that, so long as he was in the nation, such an event would not happen.

General Jesup was still not fully aware of what was going on, but he glimpsed the future when he noted that "the arrival of several Floridians in camp for the purpose of looking after and apprehending negroes spreads general consternation among them. Those that were in camp fled, and carried the panic with them, and we cannot induce them to return."[24] Concerned about the blacks' flight from the relocation camp, Jesup decided to parley with the principal chiefs to induce the rest of the Seminoles to come in. But they failed to appear for the conference on June 2. That same night, a band led by Osceola and Arpeika forcibly abducted Micanopy, Jumper, and Cloud. Many warriors and their families left with them. John Cavallo was considered prominent in the raid. In fact, Jesup later identified him, along with Osceola and Wild Cat, as an organizer. The officer was particularly wary of John. On another occasion, he would write, "[W]herever John Cavallo was, foul play might be expected."[25]

Thwarted in his attempts both to end the war and to return the runaways, a dejected General Jesup announced yet another plan. Perhaps if the Indians surrendered the fugitive slaves among them, they could be allowed to stay in a small area to the south, "near Florida Point." His superiors, however, refused to make such a concession; and the proposal was never presented to the Seminoles.

The blacks and tribespeople tried to keep their distance from the army. They knew there would be no summer campaigning, and if necessary the warriors could defend themselves. During their months in the emigration camp, they had stockpiled supplies and ammunition. But at the Fort Dade capitulation, the Black Seminoles had lost almost two hundred people, including twenty-two adult men, three of them chiefs and six of them first-class warriors. General Jesup, still somewhat optimistic, was certain that he had captured "all the prominent Indian negro leaders." He declared that "the negro portion of the hostile force of the Seminole nation not taken is entirely without a head."

During July and August 1837, the Seminoles continued to play coy. They sometimes approached military posts but avoided clashes or friendly encounters. So matters remained until September brought renewed fighting.[26]

CHAPTER SEVEN

⊠ Okeechobee!

Wherever John Cavallo was, foul play might be expected.
GENERAL THOMAS SIDNEY JESUP

The solidarity of the Seminole resistance, which remained unbroken from December 1835 to early spring 1837, was badly weakened by the Fort Dade capitulation. Although the Alachua chiefs had signed the treaty and the St. Johns leadership had agreed to honor it, Osceola and the Mikasukis had rejected it. Furthermore, the secret deal of April 8 between General Jesup and Coa Hadjo, who had agreed to return the runaway blacks, had produced an even greater split between the conciliators and Osceola's militants. The appearance of slave hunters at the Tampa Bay emigration camp had divided the ranks even among those groups who had originally accepted the Fort Dade agreement. A younger group of leaders, represented by John Cavallo—quickly becoming the most important Black Seminole still at large—and Wild Cat, had recently aligned themselves with Osceola. Still, the disunity among the various factions did not become fully apparent until September.

During the summer of 1837, a beleaguered General Jesup despaired that the Seminoles would never surrender, despite their infighting. After the June 2 breakout from the Tampa Bay relocation center, the general inadvertently made matters worse for himself and the blacks. In a misguided effort to appease his Creek allies, who had been promised all the plunder they could take, Jesup offered them $8,000 for some ninety runaways that they had seized earlier that year. Thus, he was now making the U.S. government a slave owner. Then on September 6 Jesup further complicated the issue. He declared that *all* the blacks that his troops captured would be held at Fort Pike, Louisiana, (where the Creeks' "plunder" had already been shipped on the way to Indian Territory) until the secretary of war decided their fate.

Suddenly the situation changed. In early September, the first important warrior to surrender and ally himself with the whites came from the resistance's most hostile element: the Black Seminoles. Previously, only two blacks—Nero and Cudjo—had willingly aided the soldiers. A third man, a free mulatto named Ben Wiggins who once had lived among the tribespeople, had also assisted the military but was never considered a Black Seminole.[1]

On September 4, 1837, four fugitive slaves "belonging to Major Heriot, who were captured by the Indians at the commencement of the war," arrived at Fort Peyton, south of St. Augustine. Complaining of mistreatment by their captors, they disclosed the location of nearby tribespeople. The Florida militia's Brigadier General Hernandez marched with his command to the deserted Bulow plantation, thirty-three miles south, where the hostiles were said to be camped.

Early on September 8 four more of Heriot's runaways approached the Hernandez encampment and surrendered. Black Seminole John Philip, previously a member of John Caesar's band, accompanied them. John Philip was apparently in love with one of the Heriot slave women. She had been carried off or had deserted to the Seminoles at the war's onset. But by late summer 1837, weary of wilderness life, she apparently longed for the peace and comparative security that Major Heriot had provided. The woman was so insistent that John Philip decided to go with her. He probably hoped that, in exchange for returning voluntarily, they would be allowed to remain together.[2]

On the evening of the eighth, John Philip and two black translators, Abraham (probably not the famous interpreter of that name) and George, guided a detachment of 170 regulars and militia to the deserted plantation of Dunlawton, where King Philip's band was located. After surrounding the camp, Hernandez's men seized the chief and all his people. Only his eighteen-year-old son escaped. There was no bloodshed on either side. King Philip's favorite son, Wild Cat, was not present. Otherwise, matters might not have proceeded so smoothly.[3]

King Philip's capture delighted General Jesup. It was the best news he had received since three months earlier, when the Fort Dade agreement was still in effect. Optimistically, he claimed that John Philip had been the last prominent Black Seminole leader still at large. But on October 1 Abraham gave Jesup a roster of chiefs with the number of warriors under each. "John Cowaiya" was recorded as having fifteen men. Another seventy-six black warriors were listed with no designated commander.[4]

Meanwhile, Wild Cat learned of his father's capture from a prisoner specifically released to inform him about it. He immediately put on his finest clothes, placed a white crane's feather in his silver headband as a sign of peace, and rode with four other chiefs to St. Augustine. General Hernandez, however, seized the men and held them in the fortress. He then advised General Jesup of his actions.

Jesup initially considered hanging Wild Cat for his role in the recent kidnapping of the Tampa Bay detainees. But after the Seminole promised to return all the runaways and stolen cattle, the officer decided to use him to lure in others. So Wild Cat was allowed to leave, taking a message from his father that requested those who owed King Philip allegiance to meet with the soldiers.

About this time, in an apparent attempt to come to terms with General Jesup, Micanopy and his lieutenants sent John Cavallo to confer with the St. Johns Seminoles and Osceola. Their condition for negotiations remained the same: the Seminoles wanted to remain in Florida's southern extremity.[5]

When Wild Cat returned to St. Augustine bearing a white flag, he was accompanied by John Cavallo and the others who had helped kidnap the hostages in June. A wary Jesup secretly ordered Lieutenant Peyton, commanding the fort bearing his name, to seize them—despite their flag of truce—if they entered the post. But Wild Cat's group was also suspicious and could not be persuaded to come in. John Cavallo took a message to General Hernandez asking him to visit the Seminole camp, without an escort, for a parley. Informed of the invitation, General Jesup warned "that wherever John Cavallo was, foul play might be expected." He "had no doubt [that] the intention of the Indians was to seize a sufficient number of officers to exchange for Philip and the Euchee [Yuchi] chiefs."[6]

Hernandez was less apprehensive than Jesup. He met the delegation at Pellicer's Creek for a preliminary talk conducted by "the sub-chief, John Cavallo," representing Micanopy, as well as Jumper and Holatoochee. The parley demonstrated John's increasing importance. He was now speaking for the major Seminole leaders, including the headman.

At the October 18 conference with Hernandez, John Cavallo reported that Osceola and Coa Hadjo would be coming soon. Two days later, John told Hernandez that the two men had arrived and wished to see him at their camp. Advised of their presence, Jesup decided to spring a trap. He ordered Hernandez to increase his escort and negotiate with the Seminoles using only the written questions that Jesup would supply. If their replies proved unsatisfactory, Hernandez was to seize them.[7]

On the morning of October 21 General Hernandez's command reached the designated point near Fort Peyton. They found the chiefs, subchiefs, and principal warriors of the St. Johns band and Osceola's group in a grove under a white flag. John Cavallo was Micanopy's representative and probably served as interpreter. Few other Black Seminoles were present, possibly because they were aware that the tribespeople had just surrendered more than seventy runaway slaves belonging to whites.

The preliminary pleasantries were abruptly interrupted when General Hernandez began reading Jesup's list of questions. One of the first concerned the fugitive slaves. Why had all the blacks not been returned as promised by Coa Hadjo? More queries followed in rapid succession. As the chiefs tried to answer, Hernandez gave a prearranged signal. Suddenly, more than two hundred dragoons and Florida militiamen, commanded by Brevet Major John Ashby, surrounded the delegation with carbines poised. The flag of truce had been violated again.

It was not Seminole tradition to grab weapons and fight at close quarters against such overwhelming odds. The warriors offered no resistance as their arms were taken at gunpoint. Then the sullen captives marched for several miles under heavy guard to St. Augustine.[8]

Later that day, a jubilant Jesup wrote to Adjutant General Roger Jones about seizing notables such as Osceola, Wild Cat, Coa Hadjo, and John Cavallo. His claim that "nearly all the war spirits of the Nation" were in custody was—this time—justified. The treachery at Fort Peyton had deprived the Seminoles of Osceola, the principal war spirit; Wild Cat, "the Napoleon of the Seminoles"; and John Cavallo, the only Black Seminole leader not yet captured. Now only Micanopy and his circle were still at large. More than any other event, with the possible exception of the Fort Dade capitulation, the Fort Peyton affair dramatically weakened the Seminole resistance and eventually ended the fighting. Nevertheless, hostilities lasted almost five years more.[9]

After the prisoners reached St. Augustine, they were herded into the casemates (large rooms in the walls) of an old fortress, the Castillo de San Marcos. Renamed Fort Marion, it already held some forty people who had been taken the previous month. Osceola, Wild Cat, John Cavallo, and twenty others were detained in a cell measuring about eighteen by thirty-three feet. Located on the southwestern corner of the courtyard, it was feebly lighted by a thin shaft of light from a narrow opening fifteen feet up the wall. Beneath the loophole, nearly one-third of the room's area was occupied by a platform about three feet high. Otherwise, it was absolutely bare.

At this point, John Cavallo's role in the Second Seminole War seemed to have ended. That was not the case, however; he and Wild Cat probably began plotting an escape as soon as the jail doors slammed shut. Osceola, on the other hand, sank into a deepening apathy as they schemed.

The imprisonment was not harsh. Food was ample, and the Seminoles were given the freedom of the courtyard several hours a day. But despite such amenities, the news that reached the inmates was discouraging. On November 9 General Hernandez returned from a raid on Spring Gardens with fifty-three more prisoners, including twenty warriors. Among them were Wild Cat's oldest and youngest brothers and sixteen fugitive slaves.

Moreover, a Cherokee delegation led by Chief John Ross was coming from Georgia, officially sanctioned to urge the Seminole leadership to make peace and leave Florida. On November 10 the five Cherokee delegates arrived.[10] The next day, a full council between the Cherokees and the Seminoles was held in the fort's courtyard. John Ross's address was read and interpreted for the prisoners by the Black Seminole Pompey. Coa Hadjo replied, probably speaking for the elderly King Philip. He expressed the conventional desire for peace, and Osceola stated that "he was tired of fighting." About a week later, the Cherokee delegation left St. Augustine for Fort Mellon, located to the south on Lake Monroe. Accompanied by Coa Hadjo, they intended to contact personally the hostile chiefs still at large in the area.[11]

In the prison, escape plans were moving rapidly. The captives in John's cell apparently secured a file, probably passed to them by a friendly black on the fort's staff or bought from an impoverished soldier for a silver bracelet or gorget. General Jesup later stated that they had received "aid from without. There are too many," he declared, "who would be ready to aid them[,] particularly among the blacks." Indeed, numerous free blacks—suspected Seminole allies—lived in the St. Augustine area.[12]

Late on November 29, 1837, the carefully designed plan jelled. Either with a file or through strenuous and repetitive manipulation, one of the two rusted bars was removed from the loophole fifteen feet up the cell's wall. Canvas bags, which the captives slept on, had been torn into strips and braided into a strong rope. One of the tallest and strongest of the warriors vaulted onto the wide platform some twelve feet beneath the porthole and lifted a slighter fellow prisoner to his shoulders. That man, using toeholds carved in the hard wall (or perhaps stepping on a knife handle, its blade wedged firmly in a crevice), grabbed the ledge immediately beneath the loophole. As the Seminole pulled himself up, he kept one end of the makeshift rope gripped between his teeth. After tying the line to the remaining bar, he tossed the other end—possibly weighted by a stone or a piece of iron—through the five-foot-long narrow passage in the wall down to the muddy moat surrounding it. When the captives gathered below the porthole, mortally ill Osceola and feeble King Philip did not join them.

The most difficult part of the escape lay ahead. Even without a bar, the exit was exceedingly small—only about eight inches wide. But one by one the Seminoles wiggled through and tore their bare skin on the rough rock lining the cramped passage to the outer wall. Although they faced a steep descent some twenty feet down the fort's rampart, the cushioning mud at the bottom of the ditch softened their fall once they released the rope and dropped. Eventually, twenty people stood next to the moat, among them Wild Cat, his two brothers, John Cavallo, and two women. They were nearly naked, virtually unarmed, and hurt from being cut by the hard rock. But they were free. After moving south, the fugitives reached the remnants of King Philip's band encamped on the headwaters of the Tomoka River near the Atlantic coast.[13]

By now, the Cherokee delegates had entered the hostiles' country. Coa Hadjo, who had confidently assured General Jesup on October 27 that "Micanopy . . . was anxious to surrender," was their guide. After easily locating the Seminole chief, who was unaware of the breakout from Fort Marion, they escorted him and his lieutenants to General Jesup's headquarters. The group arrived, under a white flag, on December 3. The Seminoles were immediately ordered to collect their wives and children. Osceola's family, along with many blacks, had already surrendered at Fort Mellon on November 30.

On December 6 the Cherokee delegation contacted the Mikasuki chief, Sam Jones, who refused to join them. When they returned empty handed on December 14, Jesup angrily told Micanopy that he and his companions were now prisoners. He sent them off to join King Philip and the other captives in St. Augustine, an act that greatly offended the Cherokee delegates, who were unwittingly involved in yet another of Jesup's violations of a truce flag. Nevertheless, Micanopy ordered Jumper and Holatoochee, who remained at large, to gather their families and come in. Thus, his inner circle was either in detention or about to surrender.[14]

Colonel Zachary Taylor, the future U.S. president, had just arrived in Florida and was now ordered to proceed southeast from Tampa Bay to search for hostiles. He soon encountered both Indians and blacks who wanted to surrender in compliance with Micanopy's orders. Taylor reported that "Charles, John & August[,] three negroes of Micanopy's people," were among those who came into his camp. This John was not John Cavallo; but August may have been the man who, with July and Abraham, had led the blacks at Peliklakaha.[15]

Taylor dispatched messengers to urge more Seminoles to surrender. Two of them were Tony Barnett, a Black Seminole, and Captain Parks, the mixed-blood leader of the Delaware and Shawnee detachment, who were sent to find Alligator. But Barnett and Parks located Jumper instead, who agreed to go with them. Accompanying him were "his family and a part of his band, consisting of fifteen men, a part of them with families, and a few negroes, in all sixty-three souls." They reached Colonel Taylor's command on December 20. Holatoochee and sixteen warriors were reportedly coming as well.

Tony Barnett was also successful with some of the Black Seminoles. He later stated that he had received "strict orders when I first went out, that if I met with any of the colored people, to tell them to get away from the Indians . . . and no doubt something would be done for them, GOOD, and so I did." Among those who listened to the appeals was John's sister, Juana, who was with her Seminole owner in Alligator's band. Barnett reported that "Warner [Juana] . . . and children followed Jumper and Captn Parks, and myself, saying she wouldnt go any further with her mistress after hearing what the general had said. For he said that every colored person that came in should be well treated, and not harmed."[16]

Meanwhile, Wild Cat, John Cavallo, Sam Jones, and Alligator were moving toward the lower Kissimmee River and Lake Okeechobee, gathering their men to fight. Wild Cat eventually collected eighty warriors. Sam Jones probably commanded the largest force because his group had not fought much so far. Alligator most likely retained some of his personal following and may have led the remnants of Micanopy's and Cloud's bands. John Cavallo surely mustered a group of leaderless Black Seminoles because he was now a principal chief.

On the morning of December 20 Colonel Zachary Taylor left Fort Gardner, near the Kissimmee River, with more than a thousand men, including Missouri volunteers, Delaware and Shawnee auxiliaries, and a company of "Morgan's spies." The rest of the command comprised regular soldiers. The Seminoles withdrew before this overwhelming force. They wanted to find an advantageous battleground like the Withlacoochee crossing two years before. As the warriors retreated, they passed apathetic groups of Seminoles camped along the way. Tired of the fighting, they would not join the hostiles. On December 22 twenty-two such war-weary people, mostly women and children, surrendered to Colonel Taylor.

The next day, the army was right behind Alligator's band; and Taylor's advance guard soon captured a few stragglers who said that the Mikasukis were ten to twelve miles ahead, ready—at last—to fight.[17] But the warriors continued withdrawing through a cypress swamp. After entering another, they stopped for the night, built fires, and slaughtered cattle. The next morning, alerted that Taylor's forces were closing in, the Seminoles hastily abandoned their camp. The blacks and tribesmen pushed on to a large prairie bordering a great swamp. Beyond it was a dense hammock. On its farthest edge, Sam Jones and the Mikasukis were staying on the shore of Lake Okeechobee. This was the position that the warriors were looking for. They decided to stand and fight.

On December 24 Taylor's scouts captured an Indian who reported that "a large body of Seminoles, headed by John Co-hia [John Cavallo], Co-a-coochee [Wild Cat], and no doubt Alligator . . . were encamped five or six miles from us, near the Mikasukies." The captive said that he was John Cavallo's brother-in-law. On Christmas morning, the troops reached the recently vacated camp. They found the cooking fires still smoldering and breakfast food scattered about. On the prairie beyond, a large herd of cattle and about one hundred horses were grazing. The animals had been abandoned, perhaps that very day, by their fleeing owners. The soldiers soon seized another warrior. He pointed to the right, where the Seminole force was located in a hammock.

It was about noon. The army scouts cautiously advanced across the prairie and encountered a swamp "three-fourths of a mile in breadth . . . totally impassable for horses, and nearly so for foot, covered with a thick growth of saw-grass, five feet high, and about knee-deep in mud and water, which extended to the left as far as the eye could reach, and to the right to a part of the swamp and hammock we had just crossed, through which ran a deep creek." Beyond this formidable barrier, in a dense hammock, the enemy was waiting.[18]

Some four hundred hostiles—blacks and tribesmen—were concealed in the trees on the hammock's swamp side. The center was commanded by Alligator, who led 120 men. The right was under Sam Jones, who had nearly two hundred Mikasukis. Wild Cat and his eighty warriors anchored the left flank, while John Cavallo and an unknown number of blacks probably supported him. Lookouts were perched in tall trees. Hidden by the thick moss on the leafy branches, they would also serve as sharpshooters when the fighting began. The Seminole front and flanks were protected by the deep, wide swamp. At their rear was the vast Lake Okeechobee. Along its shore, the Mikasuki camp extended for a mile.[19]

As the men up in the trees watched, Taylor's forces began forming a line of battle on the prairie. But the Delawares refused to lead the way, so Colonel Taylor ordered them to take the right flank. They were replaced by the Missouri volunteers and Morgan's spies, who were also mainly from Missouri. After dismounting, they left their horses and baggage under guard. The regulars of the Fourth and Sixth infantries fell in behind the militiamen. The First was held in reserve, and Taylor remained with them.

The army, now numbering slightly under a thousand men, marched forward across the prairie for a quarter of a mile. When they reached the swamp, the men began floundering through the mud, water, and razor-edged sawgrass. They had to cover almost a mile before closing with the warriors.[20]

The Seminoles on the ground could see nothing except the sawgrass swaying in the distance, but the lookouts in the trees undoubtedly informed them that the enemy was advancing in large numbers. As the troops slowly came nearer, the chiefs ordered their men into defensive positions. Every tree on the hammock's swamp side soon concealed two warriors—one standing and the other prone, each covering the other. Every rifle and musket had been carefully prepared for that first fire, which was so important in deciding a battle. The powder was scrupulously measured, and the rifle bullets had been meticulously shaved to fit the bore before the Seminoles thrust them home. Carefully molded musket balls were tightly wadded into position, flints adjusted and pans primed with powder of special quality. Everything had been done to ensure a quick and accurate discharge.

As the soldiers drew closer, the blacks and Indians on the ground could now see them. Because the advancing troops wore civilian clothes, they had to be volunteers, who usually were riflemen. Their weapons were more accurate and had a longer range than U.S. Army muskets. Still, as the Withlacoochee had proved, militia were more easily rebuffed than the regulars, who could now be seen in the second line.[21]

The whites approached the hammock's border. They sank less deeply into the mud and water with each forward step. As the ground became firmer, their pace quickened. Suddenly a withering blast of firepower, at point-blank range, swept their line. The Seminoles, as usual, targeted the officers. Colonel Richard Gentry of the Missouri volunteers fell, dying. His young son, Sergeant Major Harrison Gentry, also was seriously wounded. A captain and two lieutenants of the Missouri regiment, three officers from the spies, and twenty-four soldiers were hit almost immediately.[22]

Gentry's men, their bodies screened by the tall grass, briefly held their ground and returned fire. They plied ramrods frantically in an attempt to reload, but the volunteers could not withstand such murderous fire. They had come to Florida in a festive spirit. But now, after struggling through a miry swamp, the Missourians faced a savage and desperate foe. They had been ordered to withdraw and re-form behind the regulars if heavy fire prevented them from advancing. The men did not doubt that those directives now applied, at least as far as retreating was concerned. So except for a few stalwarts (mainly officers), they broke ranks and fled, floundering back across the swamp until they reached the prairie. Collapsing on the ground among the baggage train, the volunteers refused to return to action.[23]

Not all the waverers were in the Missourians' ranks. The venerable Mikasuki chief, Sam Jones, had thus far succeeded in avoiding major encounters with the troops. Frightened, he began retreating with some of his warriors. But Alligator, stationed next to the Mikasukis, stood in their way. Prodding them with his loaded rifle, he successfully returned most of them to their posts.[24]

Meanwhile, the regulars, with five companies of the Sixth Infantry in the center, continued to advance. The Seminoles fired heavily, especially at the officers. Lieutenant Colonel Alexander Thompson and his adjutant, Lieutenant John P. Center, were mortally wounded. Every commissioned officer of the Sixth and most of its noncommissioned ones were also either killed or wounded. So many enlisted men suffered the same fate that in one company only four soldiers remained unhurt. Finally, the few survivors of the Sixth's five units were ordered to retreat.

By now, six companies of the Fourth Infantry were advancing on the Seminole right flank. They eventually reached the hammock with 160 men. With firm ground beneath their feet and trees to protect them, they consolidated their position and began returning enemy fire, rebuffing several counterattacks. Soon the First Infantry, previously held in reserve, also moved on the Seminole right flank, which had been weakened by the defection of some Mikasukis and the Fourth Infantry's work. While another unit attacked the left side of the hammock, fresh soldiers from the First charged with fixed bayonets from the right. At the same time, the Sixth, having rallied and re-formed, advanced again on the center. By now it was three o'clock in the afternoon, and the firing had been continuous for two and a half hours.

With their enemy converging from three different directions, the outflanked warriors retreated through the hammock in small groups. They fought from tree to tree, in their usual fashion, until reaching Lake Okeechobee. Some leaped into canoes drawn up on the shore, pushed off, and paddled swiftly away. They headed for islands hidden in the vast watery expanse and were soon lost to view. Others fled right and left into the swamp. The Seminoles easily avoided their heavy-footed pursuers, who soon abandoned the chase.

The soldiers found only ten tribesmen and one or two blacks dead on the field, but signs indicated that at least nine had escaped wounded. They also found marks scrawled on the sand. Abraham, who later visited the scene, said that Alligator had made them to indicate his intent "to war to the death."[25]

After the Seminoles had vanished, Zachary Taylor soberly considered his heavy casualties. The many dead and wounded were slowly removed from the swamp on improvised litters over a hastily constructed causeway. Twenty-six corpses were placed on the prairie and covered with blankets. The entire next day was spent burying the dead and constructing additional litters for those of the 112 wounded who required them.

Colonel Taylor's battered force struggled back to Fort Gardner on December 31. On January 4, 1838, he hailed the costly action as a decisive victory. But Taylor had taken no prisoners except those who had voluntarily surrendered on the march to Okeechobee. Furthermore, for every casualty inflicted on the Seminoles in battle, he had lost nearly seven of his own men, killed or wounded. He did, however, seize six hundred cattle and about a hundred horses.[26]

When Jesup's subordinates next encountered the warriors, they found them still full of fight. Navy Lieutenant Levi M. Powell had been ordered to explore "the coast and rivers of south Florida, and to cooperate with the Army." He commanded fifty-five sailors, including many blacks, and twenty-five regular soldiers and volunteers. On January 15, 1838, Powell and his landing party of eighty men captured an old Indian woman, near Jupiter Inlet on the Atlantic coast, who offered to guide them to the enemy's hideout. After they had marched about five miles, the Seminoles ambushed them.

During the furious three-hour fight, the sailors were routed. Only the regulars' staunchness prevented a massacre. Nevertheless, five whites were killed and twenty-two wounded, some mortally. At least one of the fallen, Navy surgeon Frederick Leitner, was left behind alive. The Seminoles reportedly killed him later. The bodies of three tribesmen and a black were seen on the ground and as many more were reported to have died.[27]

Five days later, General Jesup, with five hundred horsemen and an artillery unit, left Fort Pierce on the St. Johns River headwaters. They rode southward on the eastern side of Lake Okeechobee. Shortly before noon on January 24 the column arrived at the Indian Crossing of the Lockahatchee River. On the opposite bank, two to three hundred warriors—nearly equally divided between tribesmen and blacks—held a strong position. They were in a dense hammock "so thick a man could not see two feet ahead of him." A Seminole named Tuskegee led them. He was a former companion of Micanopy and had left Jesup's camp before the head chief's seizure.

Accounts of the Lockahatchee clash are not numerous, probably because it reflected little credit on the military. Although General Jesup's men eventually dislodged and dispersed the enemy, they themselves had "seven killed and thirty wounded; many of whom afterwards died from the severity of their wounds." Jesup himself was shot in the face, shattering his glasses and injuring his left cheek. Reportedly, only one warrior was killed, but many of their livestock were taken. This costly encounter was General Jesup's last battle in the Florida war.[28]

Meanwhile, reports filtered in that Alligator's band, and probably also Wild Cat's, had separated from Sam Jones's Mikasukis because of his alleged cowardice at Okeechobee. But the Seminoles still remained in the wild and trackless region bordering the great lake. Although the warriors never again gathered in numbers like those that opposed Taylor's forces on December 25, 1837, the clashes at Jupiter Inlet and Lockahatchee proved that they were still prepared to launch punishing hit-and-run operations.

After building a small stockade at Jupiter Inlet, christened Fort Jupiter, Jesup soberly considered his next move.

CHAPTER EIGHT

⊠ From Suspicion to Responsibility

I believe . . . [John Cavallo] to be one of the most artful and faithless of his tribe.
BRIGADIER GENERAL ZACHARY TAYLOR

By early 1838, the whites were war-weary. Unlike a year earlier, it now seemed that the fighting would never end. As February began, Brigadier General Abraham Eustis and a committee reportedly representing all of Jesup's other senior officers urged Jesup to end the conflict by declaring a truce that would allow the Seminoles to stay in the southern part of Florida.[1]

General Jesup needed little persuading. He had always believed that such a plan might work. He dispatched a Black Seminole to invite the chiefs to yet another conference and on February 7 talked with the young subchief Halleck Hadjo. The next day, he met with Hadjo's superior, Tuskegee. The tribal leaders agreed to assemble within ten days near Fort Jupiter while the general contacted the president. Jesup wrote, with real conviction: "In regard to the Seminoles, we have committed the error of attempting to remove them when their lands were not required for agricultural purposes; when they were not in the way of the white inhabitants; . . . My decided opinion is, that, unless *immediate, emigration* be abandoned, the war will continue for years to come, and at constantly accumulating expense." Time would demonstrate the accuracy of his predictions.

Jesup proposed that the tribespeople still in Florida be permitted to remain, but only south of the Kissimmee River and Lake Okeechobee. Those already shipped to Charleston and New Orleans would not return but would continue their journey to Indian Territory.

Tuskegee's band began gathering near Fort Jupiter. By March 7 "more than three hundred Indians, and one hundred and fifty Seminole negroes, had come in." A military surgeon from South Carolina described the blacks as "the most diabolical looking wretches I ever saw; their style of dress contributing much to render them ferocious and oriental in aspect." He said that they were constantly offering to shake hands, "with as much hauteur, and nonchalance, as if they were conferring a vast deal of honour, of which we should have been proud." Forced cordiality with confident black warriors particularly galled the officers from the South.[2]

Despite their arrogance, General Jesup was delighted that so many of the Black Seminoles had assembled. He knew that the blacks would cause problems while they remained in Florida and realized that the tribespeople would not capitulate until the Black Seminoles did. Furthermore, he was certain that the blacks would not surrender until their freedom was assured. Therefore, he issued an order, saying "that all the negroes [who were] the property of the Seminole . . . Indians in Florida . . . who separated themselves from the Indians and delivered themselves up to the Commanding officer of the Troops, should be free."[3]

Jesup justified his offer of emancipation by explaining that splitting the blacks from the tribespeople would "weaken them more than the loss of the same number of their own people." But they were not to stay in Florida, where their presence would constantly encourage runaways. Rather, "they should be sent to the west as a part of the Seminole nation, and be settled in a separate village, under the protection of the United States."

The appeal of Jesup's proclamation did not lie so much in freedom from the Indians, who had been more protectors than masters until now. But with that relationship disrupted by war, Jesup's proposal and the security provided by federal troops seemed attractive. Emigrating might be worthwhile after all.[4]

On March 7 Abraham, probably hoping for the success of the new policy that he had helped negotiate and also wanting to obtain his family's freedom, claimed that there were "not more than ten or fifteen negroes left in the nation." His statement seems to have been exaggerated. A few black leaders and their followers were still at large, notably "the negro chiefs August and John Cavallo, to whom, and their people . . . [Jesup had] promised freedom and protection on their separating from the Indians and surrendering." July, another prominent Black Seminole who later became John's father-in-law, received similar blandishments. Significantly, Jesup asserted that his proposal "was distinctly understood and assented to by the chiefs Holatochee, Toskegee and Halleck Hadjo."[5]

On March 6 John Cavallo and Alligator were reportedly seen together. The commander of Fort Lauderdale said that Wild Cat and Alligator were nearby, apparently not disposed to fight. General Jesup may have considered these reports a hopeful sign because the freedom offer might influence John to persuade Alligator to give up.[6] But on March 17 the secretary of war rejected Jesup's plan to keep the Seminoles in Florida without the blacks. He was ordered to continue with the removal, regardless of difficulties.

The general now faced a dilemma. How should he handle the hundreds of tribespeople assembled near Fort Jupiter who believed that they would be permitted to remain permanently in Florida? To inform them that his proposal had been denied could precipitate renewed hostilities. Therefore, it was probably better just to seize them. Although it would be another betrayal of trust, Jesup may have felt that he would save countless lives and avoid much human suffering by doing so.

On March 19 he summoned the Seminoles to a council to be held the next day. Possibly aware of his change in plans, they failed to appear and began breaking camp. General Jesup quickly ordered his troops to surround them starting at midnight on March 21. During the next two days, 513 Indians, including 150 warriors armed with rifles, and 161 blacks, "forty four of whom capable of bearing arms," were captured.[7]

The episode was a triumph equal to the treachery that enabled it. At a single stroke, almost as many tribespeople and blacks were seized as had surrendered or been captured during the preceding fifteen months. Still, the bands of Sam Jones, Wild Cat, and Alligator were unaccounted for. General Jesup decided to use persuasion to bring them in.

On March 24 he sent Abraham and Holatoochee to help Zachary Taylor negotiate with Alligator. Their arguments were effective: "Alligator . . . surrendered at Fort Bassinger on the 4th of April . . . with 88 of his people . . . [including] John Cowaya [Cavallo] and 27 blacks." Taylor also said that "Alligator will send for Coacoochee [Wild Cat]." A delighted Jesup declared: "If these three chiefs can be detached from the hostiles the war may yet be closed this summer."[8]

John Cavallo apparently remained behind to gather stragglers and bring them in. On April 14 Col. Persifor F. Smith reported that John and his family had arrived. He also said that John's owner "Charley Coh-wy-yah will be here tomorrow with his people." But Wild Cat remained at large.

On April 25 a relieved Abraham wrote to General Jesup: "All the black people are contented[.] I hope . . . John Cavallo is in and contented. Glad to hear of the peace." Thus, by early 1838, John had achieved full status as a Black Seminole leader. Like Abraham, he now realized that the war in Florida was impossible to win; so he pragmatically cast his lot with the whites.[9]

During the rest of the conflict, blacks no longer played an important part in the fighting. But throughout the war's first two years, when the major battles were fought, they had been prominent. Their influence had certainly been the primary factor in the fierce Seminole resistance to removal.

Alligator, John, and their followers were soon marched to Tampa Bay to await relocation West. For the next month, they remained in the detention center. But as departure approached, their fears must have returned. On June 4—a year after the kidnapping of Micanopy, Jumper, and the other hostages from the emigration camp—another breakout was attempted. Guards recaptured all except thirty of the fugitives, who escaped by "plunging into a hammock" with mounted troops in hot pursuit.

Although Alligator was detained to leave with a later group (he would arrive out West on August 15), John and his family were among the 305 Indians and 30 Black Seminoles who reached New Orleans on June 14, 1838, where they boarded the steamboat *Livingston*. Passing Little Rock on June 23, the Seminoles arrived at Fort Gibson five days later. Their journey was unusually short and successful, with only one death.[10] A large number of John's old associates had preceded him to Indian Territory. A party of 1,069 Seminoles— including Micanopy, Cloud, and Coa Hadjo—had reached Fort Gibson on June 12; but both King Philip and Jumper had died en route.

The Seminoles soon discovered that the land promised to them was not available. The Fort Gibson treaty had set aside the region between the Canadian River and its north fork, extending west to the branches of the Little River, for their settlement. But the Creeks already occupied that location. So the Seminoles remained camped around Fort Gibson, drawing rations and waiting for a separate tract of land to be assigned to them.

Meanwhile, in May 1838, Brigadier General Zachary Taylor (promoted by brevet for his performance at Okeechobee) had replaced a weary General Jesup. Taylor persuaded Holatoochee and other chiefs to return to Florida to induce the remaining Seminoles to emigrate.[11] John apparently wished to accompany them. On September 12 General Mathew Arbuckle, commander of Fort Gibson, wrote to Adjutant General Roger Jones: "John Ko-wa-e, the Speaker of the Seminoles in this country has requested . . . to [go to] Florida this fall . . . [to urge] all the Seminoles to remove to this country (among whom he has two married sisters and two children). . . . [A]s his Mother, one of his children . . . and other relations are now in this country there is much reason to believe that he could have no . . . [other] motive for returning to Florida." John's first wife was never mentioned among his relatives in either Indian Territory or Florida. It is unclear what happened to her.[12]

On October 17 General Arbuckle was authorized to allow John Cavallo to return to Florida "to persuade the Seminoles . . . to emigrate to their new homes in the West." He could either accompany the Seventh Infantry, which was being transferred to Florida, or the U.S. Army Quartermaster General could provide separate passage.

When Adjutant General Jones informed Zachary Taylor of his decision, Taylor was outraged. On 17 November he wrote to Jones: "I regret that permission should have been given for the return to Florida of the Seminole Indian 'John Co-wia' as I believe him to be one of the most artful and faithless of his tribe." Taylor continued: "I cannot therefore give my consent to this man's landing in the Territory, and if time allows will take the responsibility to order him to be halted at New Orleans." His hostility possibly stemmed from the fact that John had been one of the leaders at Okeechobee.

Nevertheless, Taylor did not prevent John from reaching Florida. In fact, by May 1, 1839, he was employed there as a military interpreter. Meanwhile, Taylor had been temporarily superseded by Major General Alexander Macomb. Although he could have conducted the entire war, the senior officer chose to negotiate with the Seminoles and leave operations to Taylor. John's services would be particularly useful during Macomb's peace talks, especially since Abraham had been shipped West early in February.[13]

Macomb had been authorized to implement the terms that Jesup had suggested the previous year: the tribespeople would be allowed to remain in Florida's southern extremity. After parleying with the chiefs at Fort King, he announced the end of hostilities in May 1839. Then Macomb returned to Washington, and General Taylor reassumed his command.[14]

Peace prevailed for about two months. But the Seminoles left in Florida were leaderless, and Macomb's agreement was considered binding only by those who had directly negotiated with him. At least four bands did not participate in the process.

Early on July 23 a detachment of thirty men under Lieutenant Colonel William S. Harney, en route to establish a trading post, was ambushed in their camp on the Caloosahatchee River. The attackers were the so-called "Spanish Indians," who had not attended the Fort King meeting with Macomb. Chekika, Hospetarke, and Billy Bowlegs (Holata Mico) led the war party. They killed about sixteen soldiers and captured Harney's two Black Seminole guides, Sandy Perryman and Sampson. The warriors burned Sandy at the stake but spared Sampson at Billy Bowlegs's orders, probably because the black had "lived with Osceola, who was his . . . friend."[15]

The Caloosahatchee attack shattered the fragile armistice, and war erupted again. By now, guides were scarce. Abraham was in Indian Territory, Sandy Perryman was dead, and Sampson was a prisoner. Murray, "the best and most useful" translator and guide in Florida, had been recently murdered by a sergeant with whom he had quarreled. Because Fort King had no interpreters, John's services became more important and were in great demand.[16]

But why would John, who for more than two years had fiercely resisted compulsory removal, willingly assist the military? One explanation (besides his stated desire to locate missing family members) was that he owed no allegiance to the bands that remained in Florida. The Alachuas and those chiefs with whom he was closest, Alligator and Holatoochee, had given up. Even Holatoochee was openly cooperating with the whites. Furthermore, his friend Wild Cat was operating in the St. Johns area, far from where John was located.

In any case, John Cavallo shed his Black Seminole warrior identity to become a popular guide and interpreter with the officers for whom he worked. A generation later, he still figured in the traditions of one of the regiments in which he had served. In 1873, the Eighth Infantry historian described him as "six-feet-two in his bare feet, broad shouldered and straight as a gun-wiper." He "could smell an Indian a mile off . . . follow a trail by moonlight, at a gallop over a burnt prairie; talk English . . . and . . . supply any quantity of gophers for the Commanding General's table at an hour's notice." His proficiency at providing fish and game for the officers was probably as prized as his uncanny tracking ability. A talented impromptu cook, he could prepare savory items such as catfish chowders and yellow perch baked in campfire ashes.[17]

When John had surrendered in 1838, he was described as wearing ragged, mismatched clothes. But now the well-paid guide dressed like a Seminole dandy. His brilliant turban was graced with plumes. His hunting shirt was studded at the lapels with silver clips and gathered at the waist with a broad sash supporting a handsome dirk. His leggings were elaborately decorated with gaudy ribbons. The whole outfit was set off by an ever-increasing number of silver gorgets and bracelets. Dressed in such regalia, John must have attended the frequent dances held at the Black Seminole camp. He was likely among those who, according to an observer, "cut up all imaginable capers before their dusky sweethearts to music play'd on a crack'd fiddle & tin pan." Their long legs, bare beneath their hunting shirts as they spun about, formed "quite a contrast" to the carefully laundered "white frocks" of their partners, who "were deck'd out . . . with considerable taste."[18]

It was probably on one of these occasions that John met a young woman who captured his heart. Nineteen-year-old Susan was a good match. Her father July had stayed in Florida as an interpreter and formerly was one of the head chiefs of Peliklakaha. By the spring of 1840, at the latest, John and Susan were wed. They remained married for more than forty years, until he died.

Years after his Florida duty, John reported on his U.S. Army service. Although some dates are wrong, many of the activities he listed are corroborated by other sources.[19] Initially, he apparently acted only as guide and interpreter. But in May 1840, according to his own account, he "was sent from Cedar Key to join *Major Loomis* who was exploring . . . the wicthlokkoochee & destroyed Corn fields," an assignment that probably actually happened in April, when the hostiles were enraged by "the destruction by major Loomis' command, of some of the crops."

Inevitably, John began participating in actual combat. In the summer of 1840, he "joined *Major Beall* & went with him to *Chokkotratee*[.] Had a fight with Coosa Tustenukkee & the party went to Tampa & were reinforced by Major Staniford—returned & fought again on which occasion one old woman was killed and Coosa was wounded."

Major Beall also reported this event. The officer said that he had crossed the Withlacoochee River at Fort Clinch on September 21, 1840. Two days later, he engaged some warriors. "My interpreter [presumably John] called to one of them, who had reached an island, to come back, but his reply was, that he could or would not as he was badly wounded." On September 25 the major wrote: "I came to the Chocohattee savannah" and found an Indian village that was surrounded. "I directed my interpreter to talk with them. A negro in their camp called to my interpreter and said that they 'did not want to talk, they were ready for a fight,' and immediately eight or ten rifles were fired on me, but without effect."[20]

On May 5, 1840, Brevet Brigadier General Walker K. Armistead replaced Zachary Taylor as Florida commander. John quickly impressed Taylor's successor. On June 15, 1840, Armistead wrote: "Gopher John . . . who appears honest and intelligent, declares that the return of two or three Chiefs from Arkansas [Indian Territory] . . . will . . . [induce] those now here to emigrate. He states that . . . the Indians [believe] that those shipped for the West were afterwards thrown overboard and if they can be shown that their brethren have not only been spared but well treated, they will be inclined to join them."[21]

General Armistead was eventually authorized to implement John's proposal. One of those selected for the Florida mission—perhaps at John's suggestion—was Holatoochee. On October 1, 1840, the chief, thirteen other Seminoles, and two interpreters left Fort Gibson and arrived at Tampa on 2 November. The delegates soon managed to contact the two most prominent hostile leaders still at large: Halleck Tustenuggee, a Mikasuki, and Tiger Tail, a Tallahassee. A meeting was arranged with General Armistead for November 7, 1840.

During the meeting, the two chiefs asked to remain in Florida. If that was unacceptable, however, they would reluctantly emigrate. Armistead promised to write to his superiors about their request and told the two to collect their followers in the interim. But after two weeks the assembled tribesmen disappeared. Again, hopes were dashed for quickly ending the war.

Nevertheless, during early 1841, Holatoochee and his companions continued gathering as many Seminoles as possible. On March 21, after much delay, 220 members of the Tallahassee band had come in. They were later shipped to the Indian Territory.[22]

John's most important activity in 1841 was facilitating the surrender of his old friend Wild Cat, now the most influential chief still at large. Wild Cat's most recent exploit was attacking a company of actors near St. Augustine in the summer of 1840. The warriors had killed two people and plundered their wardrobe, but the ambush had been promptly avenged by Lieutenant Colonel Harney's capture of Wild Cat's mother and daughter.[23]

As Wild Cat's former comrade, John was particularly suited to help bring him in. In his record of service, John stated that he and the chief's daughter accompanied Colonel William J. Worth to Fort Gardner on the Kissimmee in February. Mico, an old associate of King Philip (Wild Cat's father), was sent to find the young Seminole leader. After two attempts, he located him.

Wild Cat came into camp on March 5, 1841 attired as Hamlet. Some of his warriors also wore Shakespearean garb, their costumes part of the plunder from the ambushed actors. Hearing his voice, Wild Cat's little daughter ran from her prison tent and proudly slipped him some musket balls and packets of powder that she had pilfered. Her father broke down and wept. He then consented to remain in the camp but refused to commit to emigration.[24]

During his stay, Wild Cat probably spent some of his time with John. One day the two men watched some officers drinking. The tribesman hoped to be invited to join them. He was curious about their behavior because each man raised his glass before drinking and declared, "Here's luck!" or "The old grudge!"

Wild Cat asked John what the expressions meant. His friend "was puzzled but finally explained by saying 'It means, How d'ye do!'" The Seminole chief tried repeating the interpreter's phrase several times. When he felt he had mastered it, he boldly approached the group of whites, halted, and glared at them. One of the officers quickly gave him a full cup. The men stared as Wild Cat lifted the goblet and grunted "in a deep, guttural and triumphant voice" the single word, "Hough!" A burst of appreciative laughter arose, flagons were refilled, and the men toasted him with a chorus of "Here's—how!" John Cavallo and Wild Cat may have added an imperishable phrase to the vocabulary of conviviality.[25]

After four days of hospitality and conversations with John and the Indian Territory delegation, Wild Cat finally agreed to emigrate. But the Seminole doubted that he could assemble his band and persuade them to leave before the green-corn dance in June. He promised to try and would return in ten days.

On March 9, Wild Cat departed with his companions and his daughter. He duly returned on the nineteenth, lamenting his failure to collect his people. Nevertheless, he still wanted to meet the commanding general at Tampa. This time he probably left his daughter with Colonel Worth, either as a hostage or so that she might enjoy better food and care.

Wild Cat's interview with General Armistead at Fort Brooke on March 22, 1841, largely duplicated his earlier conversation with Colonel Worth. They agreed that Fort Pierce on the Atlantic, commanded by Major Thomas Childs, should be the assembly point for Wild Cat's followers before they left Florida. Active military operations in his band's area were suspended, which would allow them to gather undisturbed.

During April and May, Wild Cat frequently visited Fort Pierce, collecting food and whiskey but producing no one who wanted to emigrate. Reports state that his behavior was obnoxious, partly because of his drinking. Nevertheless, because the whites wanted his support for relocation, he evidently knew that, at least temporarily, he had the upper hand.

Finally, Wild Cat reported that a council was to be held near Lake Okeechobee. Holata Mico (Billy Bowlegs), Arpeika (Sam Jones), and Hospetarke planned to participate. Wild Cat said that he would urge them to accept removal but demanded a large quantity of rations and whiskey for the meeting. To Major Childs, this demand was the last straw. Childs wrote to his commanding officer, saying that he believed the Seminole leader was accumulating supplies before vanishing into the Everglades for the summer. Childs received permission to capture Wild Cat and his band at the next opportunity.

A young second lieutenant named William Tecumseh Sherman was given the mission of capturing Wild Cat. Along with the chief, Sherman seized his brother, an uncle, thirteen warriors, and three blacks. Wild Cat was handcuffed, loaded on a transport, and shipped to New Orleans on his way West.[26]

About this time, John Cavallo, according to his own claims, played a part in bringing in Coosa Tustenuggee, second in command of Halleck Tustenuggee's war party. On December 28, 1840, exactly five years after the Dade massacre, the band reportedly killed an officer's wife and four of her escorts. The ambushers scalped and mutilated the bodies.

On March 21, 1841, on Orange Creek near Fort Brooke, Halleck Tustenuggee's men clashed with Lieutenant William Alburtis and nineteen soldiers. The band lost four of its thirty-five warriors. Coosa Tustenuggee apparently became discouraged and worried about his fate if captured; so when the Indian Territory delegation located him, they convinced the subchief to consider giving up.[27] Meanwhile, Colonel Worth had talked with Coosa Tustenuggee and reportedly bribed him into surrendering all his people. John briefly summarized the affair: "[I] accompanied Genl. [Colonel] Worth . . . to *Towachotka* where they got in *Coosa Tustenukkee*." His skills as an interpreter were no doubt helpful during these negotiations. On May 7, 1841, two hundred tribespeople, including Coosa Tustenuggee, sailed from Tampa for the West.

On May 31, 1841, at his own request, General Armistead was relieved by Colonel Worth. The retiring commander had made good use of John's services. Years later, he declared that John had "aided him in getting . . . five hundred and thirty five Indians." Worth, who already knew John's ability, used and appreciated him perhaps even more in his relentless pursuit of the war-weary Seminoles.[28]

After learning that Wild Cat and his band were en route to New Orleans, Colonel Worth immediately ordered that they should be intercepted and returned to Florida. On July 4 the officer met their ship at Fort Brooke. When he boarded their transport to interview the Seminole chief, John accompanied him as interpreter.

The tribespeople were heavily manacled. Wild Cat remained "calm, quiet and subdued" as Worth spoke about the absolute need for Seminole removal. The officer concluded by solemnly warning Wild Cat that the fighting must end. He told the chief to send out a few men, who would have up to fifty days to induce the rest of his people to emigrate. Unless the envoys were successful, Worth would hang the chief and his remaining warriors at sunset on the fiftieth day. Wild Cat grimly noted: "I feel the irons in my heart."

By mid-July, Wild Cat's followers began to surrender. "From day to day they arrived in small parties . . . [and] on the last day of the month, the entire band . . . was encamped at Fort Brooke." Wild Cat's shackles were removed, and he was permitted to dress in gala attire and greet his people.[29]

John was next involved in capturing Hospetarke, one of the most prominent Seminole leaders still at large. Wild Cat had received permission to send men into the Big Cypress Swamp to ask his brother, Otulke, to surrender. After about ten days, a messenger returned with Otulke and an unexpected request from Hospetarke. He wanted to see Wild Cat. Colonel Worth offered Wild Cat and his followers freedom for their help in bringing in Hospetarke.

Wild Cat went to Hospetarke's camp and soon returned with the chief and eighteen warriors. But the Indians did not have their families with them and showed other signs of not wanting to emigrate. By now, Wild Cat agreed with Worth that only force would cause Hospetarke's band to surrender.

On the afternoon of August 26, 1841, Hospetarke and his men were ushered into the cabin of a boat. They were seated, according to rank, around a long table. Colonel Worth sat at its head. "The black interpreter . . . Gopher John, stood in the vicinity." A company of troops remained on shore in their tents. When needed, they would assemble on the bank as sharpshooters to prevent escape by swimming. Several officers, pistols in their pockets, unobtrusively prepared for action.

After the negotiations became increasingly heated, Worth signaled his men to draw their weapons. He told the Seminoles that they were now his prisoners. During the ensuing melee, Wild Cat reeled into the cabin, "a rifle in one hand, a bottle of whiskey in the other." In feigned outrage, he harangued the soldiers for their treachery, thus preserving his influence with the captives.

After the confusion subsided, five messengers were selected to gather the remainder of Hospetarke's followers and bring them to Punta Rossa at the mouth of the Caloosahatchee River. A steamboat would wait there to convey them to Fort Brooke. According to John's record of service, he "accompanied Genl. [Colonel] Worth to Caloosa Hatchee where they got in the people of *Hospotakee & Sowannukkee* & returned to Tampa."[30] Meanwhile, Wild Cat continued to collect other Seminoles. Finally, on October 11, 1841, he and 211 members of his and Hospetarke's bands were shipped West. Eighteen blacks traveled with them. The emigrants finally arrived in Indian Territory as the year ended.

By now, the military authorities thought that Alligator could possibly convince the Tallahassees under Nethlockemathla and Tiger Tail to surrender. He and two other chiefs left Fort Smith on September 20, 1841, and reached Florida on October 14. Shortly after his arrival, Alligator did persuade Nethlockemathla to come in; and Tiger Tail soon followed him. But the hostiles killed two of Alligator's men who were attempting to bring in Halleck Tustenuggee. The deaths ended the mission, during which John served as interpreter and guide.[31]

The next year, John was involved in a major clash with Halleck Tustenuggee on April 19, 1842, at Peliklakaha. Colonel Worth personally led the troops. During the fight, the "fire of the enemy was concentrated principally upon the Indian guides and negro interpreters. . . . The tall figure of . . . Gopher John, his loud voice, and negro accent, the repeated discharge of his unerring rifle, well known to the Indians as he was, made him a conspicuous object of assault." The casualties included one soldier dead and four seriously wounded. One warrior was killed, two wounded, and one captured. Halleck Tustenuggee was seized a few days later. He and his men had fought the last real battle of the war. Worth's policy of keeping the Seminoles constantly on the run had finally worn them out.[32]

John's last mission in Florida apparently was to accompany Captain Kerr of the Second Dragoons on an expedition sometime around May 14, 1842. But by then, with the fighting almost over, his services were needed less often.

On April 30, 1840, Brevet General Zachary Taylor had certified that "John Cohai and his wife indian negroes gave themselves up to me under the orders given by Bvt General Jesup . . . which set forth that all Negroes the property of the Seminole . . . who . . . delivered themselves up to the Commanding Office of the Troops should be free." On February 22, 1842, Colonel Worth reaffirmed this statement and explicitly added: "Gofer John, his wife and increase" are free.

On July 14, 1842, Worth reported that a party of 120 Seminoles, mostly from Halleck Tustenuggee's band, was going West. John Cavallo, with his wife, Susan, and their child, and the delegation that had come from Indian Territory at John's suggestion were included in the group. As they departed, Halleck Tustenuggee declared: "I have been hunted like a wolf . . . and now I am to be sent away like a dog."[33]

The war continued until August 14, 1842, when Colonel Worth was authorized to end it, even though there were several hundred Seminoles still in Florida. Of all U.S. conflicts with Native Americans, the Second Seminole War was the longest—at seven years—and the most expensive. It cost well over 20 million dollars, four times what Spain had received for Florida. It was also the deadliest, with more than 1,500 regular soldiers and sailors lost. (It is impossible to determine how many militia died.) In contrast, from 1866 to 1891, when the many tribes in the West were conquered, total U.S. Army losses were less than two thousand. Until the Vietnam conflict, the Second Seminole War was the longest war ever fought by the United States—and like the Indochina fiasco, it did not end with an American victory. Moreover, as General Jesup accurately observed, this was "a negro, not an Indian war"; for blacks were prominently involved in nearly all its major battles.[34]

Hostilities ignited again in 1855 during a new round of fighting later called the Third Seminole War. The main Seminole leader was Billy Bowlegs. The conflict was primarily one of attrition and lasted three years. There were several blacks in Billy Bowlegs's group, including one of his wives; and his principal interpreter and counselor was a Black Seminole named Ben Bruner.[35]

PART TWO

The Lean Years, Indian Territory, 1842–1850

CHAPTER NINE

⊠ Seven Lean Years

Some say there is no law against stealing negroes.
JOHN CAVALLO

John's party left Tampa Bay on July 14, 1842. After reaching New Orleans, they boarded a steamboat on July 22 heading upriver; but low water in the Arkansas River forced them to disembark and go overland. Unfortunately, they had problems obtaining wagons, it rained incessantly, and many fell ill. In addition, a road had to be cleared for part of the way. Finally, on September 6, they reached their destination. Their relieved escort, Lieutenant E. R. S. Canby, delivered them to Indian agent John McKee.

During the journey, young Canby had been embarrassed by his inability to "negotiate drafts" to pay travel expenses, unexpectedly large because of the trip's difficulties. But John Cavallo had intervened and given the officer $1,500 in cash to cover the deficit, money he had earned during his Florida service. When they arrived at their destination, Canby left a draft for the loan "in the hands of Capt. E.B. Alexander[,] Asst. Q.M. at Fort Smith." Alexander presumably repaid the Black Seminole.[1]

Shortly after his arrival, John Cavallo found the bands of Wild Cat, Alligator, and Holatoochee camped near Fort Gibson. Numbering more than 1,100 and unwilling to settle among the Creeks, they had remained near the post on the land of friendly Cherokees. Although allowed by their hosts to till the soil, the Seminoles were discouraged by their uncertain position and also lacked tools.

Only the more tractable chiefs—Micanopy and Black Dirt, an early supporter of emigration—were in the Creek country. On September 10, 1842, William Armstrong, acting superintendent of the Western Territory, wrote about the black contribution to Micanopy's prosperity. He also described the dangers the blacks faced:

> Micanopy and the other leading Seminoles have settled on the Deep Fork [of the North Canadian River]. . . . They have many negroes that have participated in the Florida war. . . . In many cases the Creeks claim negroes which are the property of the Seminoles. These negroes the Creeks allege ran away from them before and during the Florida war, and were either captured with the Seminoles or came in under a proclamation from some of the commanders in Florida. These negroes are now with the Seminoles. . . . The labor . . . is principally performed by the Seminole negroes, who have thus far conducted themselves with great propriety.

Another observer noted that "the Seminoles who had settled in the Canadian Fork raise corn and rice; [they] have 1000 blacks among them . . . who pay a small tribute to their [Indian] master, say two of three bushels of corn." Apparently, the Florida system of democratic feudalism had been partly transferred to the Territory.[2]

Unlike other blacks, John Cavallo did not have to immediately find work but could live off his savings from his Florida service. It is unclear what he actually did during his first year back in the Territory; however, after about eighteen months passed, he replaced Abraham as Micanopy's chief interpreter. Abraham had been hired as the Seminole subagent's official interpreter for $300 a year.

John, who by now was probably homesteading at Deep Fork, also had his freedom reaffirmed. In July 1843—at Micanopy's direction—the Seminole council had validated Charles Cavallo's will. Thus, John was officially recognized as free.[3] Still, despite his prominence and comparative prosperity, he was unhappy. It was cold, and drought had halved the 1843 corn crop. Furthermore, he recognized the tenuousness of his position: a free black man among a people who practiced slavery.

John sympathized with his friends Alligator and Wild Cat, who were impoverished and living miserably. To help them, he apparently persuaded Micanopy to visit Fort Gibson in April 1844 to meet with the Seminoles camped nearby. John interpreted at the council that took place on April 8. The next day, Micanopy met with Judge Richard Fields, a merchant and member of the Cherokee bench. They decided that the Seminoles should send a delegation to Washington to plead their case. Alligator and Wild Cat led the group. Thomas L. Judge, the Seminole subagent; Judge Fields; and John accompanied them. They embarked on the steamboat *Trident* on April 16, 1844.

Soon thereafter a number of Seminole chiefs and subchiefs headed by Micanopy were induced to disavow the mission and its leaders. They claimed that Wild Cat and Alligator were renegades living in the Cherokee country.[4] This event marked the first serious factionalism among the Seminoles in the Territory. As in Florida, the schism lay roughly between the militants—Wild Cat's and Alligator's followers—and the appeasers, who were more willing to conciliate the mixed-blood Creek leadership. Moreover, Micanopy possibly feared that his able nephew Wild Cat might usurp him. But the young chief later responded that he was only going to Washington to help his starving people. He would not meddle in tribal politics.

The delegates arrived in Washington within a month. On May 16 they applied for land separate from the Creeks, who constantly threatened their slaves. John signed the petition as a witness. General Jesup, who received them in his home and whose children entertained the group with songs, supported their request. On May 30 Jesup wrote to the secretary of war urging that the Black Seminoles, to whom he had promised freedom, be protected from kidnappers.

After leaving Washington, the delegation went to Philadelphia, where they were hosted by Reverend O. Douglas of the Mariner's Church. Their next stop was Pittsburgh, where they visited their old Florida foe, Major General Edmund P. Gaines.[5]

When the party returned to the Territory, they found their people devastated by flooding from the Arkansas and Grand rivers. Those settled near Deep Fork and the Little River were better off because they had adequate food. Although John's family was among the more fortunate, it soon became entangled in the difficulties that almost immediately beset him.

John's problems began with an attempt on his life, but motives for the attack are unclear.[6] John claimed that the would-be assassin came from the "Seminole Indians,—Alligators people. . . . The fact of my having acted as guide & interpreter during the Seminole War is the cause of the enmity & murderous designs of the Indians." On another occasion, he identified the assailant as a "Seminole named Philip (Pascofa's brother)." The Cherokee agent, Pierce Butler, gave yet another reason: "After his return, he became . . . obnoxious to many of the Seminoles[,] particularly his former owner."

Undoubtedly, the tribespeople who had most recently surrendered or been captured hated those who had served in the military. General Jesup commented that, because the Black Seminoles had translated at treaty negotiations, the Indians—after finding such agreements unfulfilled—blamed the blacks for deceiving them. As John said, "they murdered some of the guides & I am confident such will be my fate if I remain."

Still, there is no rationale for his assertion that the assassination attempt was made by "Alligators people." John had cooperated with Alligator in Florida and had just been his interpreter in Washington. Because it was unlikely that the chief's followers would have turned against him so suddenly, Agent Butler's explanation seems more logical.

According to Butler, shortly after returning from the Washington mission, John borrowed a horse from Captain Nathan Boone so that he could visit his family at Deep Fork. About a mile from Fort Gibson, John encountered a Seminole tribesman named Philip, who apparently had some shadowy claim to the black man. A confrontation developed, and "obnoxious language" was exchanged.

Suddenly John's opponent leveled a loaded rifle. With no time to bring up a weapon or flee, John dug his heels into his horse's flanks and jerked the bridle rein. The maneuver made the animal rear, disrupting Philip's aim as he fired. Nevertheless, the ball grazed John and killed his mount. The horse fell backward, pinning the rider beneath it. Philip quickly threw down his firearm, pulled out a knife, and stalked his virtually defenseless victim.

Help arrived unexpectedly. John must have accumulated much goodwill since arriving in Indian Territory because he would interpret free of charge, day or night, for anybody who asked. Now his kindness was rewarded when some Seminole women observing the struggle joined the fray. They tackled Philip and seized his knife, and John wriggled free from the dead horse.

A shaken John hurried back to Fort Gibson and sought sanctuary. Convinced that it was no longer safe to stay in Seminole country, he went to Deep Fork and brought his family, "three in number, besides himself," to the post, leaving behind fifty head of livestock, a wagon, and other items. The fort's commanding officer warned the Seminole chiefs that they would be held responsible for the abandoned property.[7] Presently, John also brought "his mother in law 'Teena'" and her ten children to Fort Gibson. Her husband, July, had been killed in Florida while serving as an interpreter.

After settling into his new quarters, John wrote to General Jesup, asking for help in obtaining land in the Choctaw country or, better yet, in Florida to "live in peace and security." John also requested freedom papers for his sister Juana and her children, who had come in when informed that "all negroes who surrendered themselves to the United States should be free." Unable to cultivate his land on Deep Fork because of the death threats, John applied for an additional payment of $2 per day for his Florida service, which he claimed had been promised to him.

On August 31, 1844, the Seminole chiefs disavowed the attack on John and pledged to reimburse him for the $30 he had to pay for the dead horse. But three years later, John was still trying to collect the money.[8]

By now, however, John had become more concerned about his people's plight. He claimed that the Seminole subagent Thomas Judge "urged the Indians . . . in open council, either to sell or make slaves of them again." Two other interpreters, James and Tony (probably Jim Bowlegs and Tony Barnett), joined him in asking to leave the Territory. They, too, feared being killed by the vengeful Seminoles or seized by the Creeks and then sold.

About this time, two slaves belonging to Nelly Factor, Hardy and Dembo—both to be long and closely associated with John Cavallo—also appeared at Fort Gibson requesting emancipation papers under Jesup's freedom proclamation. Lieutenant Colonel Richard B. Mason, the post commander, wrote: "Gopher John, Hardy and Dembo tell me that the Seminole keep . . . the negroes that were sent to this country, under General Jesup's promise of freedom . . . and sell them whenever they choose." Although Mason supported John Cavallo's request, he noted that "John is here with his family, lounging about the garrison in idleness, and if he can be sent where he can gain a living by his own labor, and be safe from the Seminoles . . . I . . . recommend that it be speedily done."

General Jesup quickly authorized Mason to allow John and his family to stay at the fort and continue drawing rations. But he said that his freedom offer had applied only to those Black Seminoles who had voluntarily surrendered, not to those whom their masters had brought in. Still, Jesup confirmed that John, Juana, and their families should be free.[9]

Then John was presented with another opportunity to be useful. The delegation to Washington had produced a treaty among the Creeks, the Seminoles, and the U.S. government. Enacted on January 4, 1845, it allotted the Seminoles land in the Little River area and granted them local autonomy, although the tribespeople were placed under the general control of the Creek council, in which they were to be represented. Additionally, a small sum was paid for their Florida holdings.

Most important, the agreement stated that "all contested cases between the two tribes, concerning the right of property, growing out of sale or transactions . . . previous to the ratification of this treaty, shall be subject to the decision of the President of the United States." The Seminoles believed that *property* referred to their slaves claimed by the Creeks. Naïvely confident that the government would protect their rights, they accepted the treaty. Now the two tribes were bound by federal law, with the Creeks having the upper hand.[10]

The Seminoles soon began moving from the Cherokee country near Fort Gibson to Little River. For sixty days in the early spring of 1845, John used his ox-driven wagon to transport tribespeople and their baggage to the new location. But in 1848 he was still trying to collect pay from the government at $3 per day—rather below the usual rate—for his services.[11]

After the Seminoles were settled, John began planning what had probably been on his mind ever since his attempted assassination: he would go to Washington and personally lobby to return to Florida. He also wanted the money that the government still owed him. But John was also concerned for his people and planned to bring their plight to the attention of Washington authorities.

Before leaving, he obtained a letter from Subagent Judge introducing "Jno Goffer (alias Cowaniou)" to the commissioner of Indian affairs. The agent wrote that John's unpopularity among the Seminoles was allegedly related to his Florida service. Still, the problem remained of getting to Washington. It was one thing to accompany an Indian delegation, quite another to do it alone. The best solution was to travel with a white man.

Fortunately, in the late spring of 1845, a "General" John T. Mason (not to be confused with Lieutenant Colonel Richard B. Mason) prepared to make the journey and agreed to let John Cavallo accompany him as his servant.

This was probably the only way that Mason would have taken the Black Seminole with him, although nothing in his background qualified John for his new role.[12]

The two men left Fort Gibson early in May and reached Washington by the eighteenth of the month. During his first month in Washington, John lodged at Galibrun's European Hotel on the north side of Pennsylvania Avenue between Fourteenth and Fifteenth streets, near the White House and various government offices. Shortly after his arrival, John contacted General Jesup. With Jesup's assistance, he filed a petition to return to Florida and requested additional reimbursement for his military service and the cattle seized during the Second Seminole War.[13]

By now, however, John had tired of his arrangement with Mason. Perhaps he did not understand that his obligation extended beyond the journey, or possibly he disliked working as a servant. At any rate, after a month he arbitrarily left Mason and was on his own. But his employer did not graciously accept John's breach of contract as Colonel Brooke had done after the gopher hoax some twenty years earlier. On August 5 he obtained a lien on the property of "Gofer John (a free Seminole Negro)" for $68 plus $30 for expenses. The $68 debt included the passage price, travel costs, and various loans amounting to $83 against which was credited $15 for a month's wages. Secretary of War William L. Marcy wrote to District Attorney James Hoban asking him to defend the Black Seminole. It is unclear what motivated Marcy to make the request, but no record has been found showing that John ever repaid Mason.[14]

Meanwhile, John did make some progress in preparing his own financial claims. He established his right to an additional sum of approximately $1,075 for his services as guide and interpreter in Florida. In addition, his Washington expenses for board and lodging—which eventually amounted to $130.92— were approved for reimbursement. Whether this amount was ever paid is uncertain. As late as 1848 "the settlement of Gopher John's account" was still being called to the appropriate authorities' attention. But John failed to obtain payment for his cattle, which he alleged that Brevet Major Graham had seized at Tohopekaliga, Florida, in 1837. As late as the spring of 1849, he was still requesting reimbursement for them.[15]

John had also brought to Washington a list of infringements on his people by Creeks, Cherokees, and Seminoles. Although an officer at Fort Gibson actually wrote the document, its poignantly simple language is apparently John's own. The "Statement of John Cow-a-ya" contains the names of eighteen Black Seminoles who had been returned to slavery. One of the saddest cases was a family unit in which a grandmother, mother, and grandchild had been sold for "5 barrels of Whiskey."[16]

Nearly thirty years later, John stated that he had talked with President Polk while in Washington, affirming that General Jesup had recorded what was said during the meeting. He also said that Polk had assured him that the Black Seminoles would be treated like the other tribespeople. Unfortunately, no records have been found of the conversation, and Polk's published diary does not mention it.[17]

Early in April 1846, having done all that he could for himself and his people, John decided to return to the Territory, apparently abandoning his plans to return to Florida. Reports from General Jesup, who had visited Fort Gibson during the previous summer, probably made him uneasy about the welfare of his family and friends. On April 8, 1846, Jesup wrote to the Fort Gibson commandant: "John Cowayee . . . [needs] to return to his family, leaving the business of himself and his people in my hands." Jesup also said that "the case of the Seminole Negroes is now before the President."

The general gave John a pass to facilitate his trip through the South. It stated, in part, that John had "been in Washington City prosecuting the claims of himself and his people against the Government of the United States, and is now about to return to his family at Fort Gibson. . . . It is to be hoped that he may be allowed to pass on his journey without interruption."[18]

During John's absence, the Black Seminole situation had deteriorated. Removal to Little River had helped the tribespeople by giving them land to cultivate; but it exposed the blacks, now surrounded by the Creeks and distant from the protective garrison at Fort Gibson, to increased kidnapping danger. Moreover, their legal position was very confused. When he was in Florida, Jesup had assured them "that if they surrendered and agreed to emigrate they would be settled in a separate village . . . under the protection of the United States, as a part of the Seminole Nation, and were never to be separated or sold." But General Zachary Taylor had "told the Seminole Indians that those who surrendered and agreed to emigrate would be secure in their property, including their slaves." Thus, the exact circumstances of each individual black's "coming in" determined his or her status as "free or slave." Because the Seminoles saw no real difference between the two categories, this issue would have been comparatively trivial if they had been allowed to settle it by themselves. Unfortunately, members of other tribes—particularly mixed bloods—and unscrupulous whites constantly intervened.

The Creeks claimed almost all the Black Seminoles, alleging that either they or their ancestors had fled from the Creeks before the Florida conflict. The Indians also said that they owned those blacks whose parents had escaped from Georgia and South Carolina plantations to Florida when the Seminoles were still considered part of the Creek Confederation because the Creeks had been required to pay for those runaways. Furthermore, the Creeks who had fought the Seminoles in Florida had never received the payment promised for the blacks they had captured. Thus, it was possible for a black supposedly freed by Jesup's proclamation or possessing emancipation papers from a former Indian master to be enslaved by a Creek or a Seminole.[19]

Because few Seminole tribespeople had papers for their slaves and their inheritance customs were changing, the ensuing confusion aided the unscrupulous. Lieutenant Colonel Gustavus Loomis, the new commander of Fort Gibson, starkly described one of the methods people employed to snare free Black Seminoles: "A *half-breed* Creek goes to a Seminole & buys a title to a negro . . . no matter whether the Seminole has a shadow of a title himself. . . . The *half-breed* sells *his title* to a white man; & they . . . [run] the negro . . . to the States." There, it was impossible to trace the individual, and he or she was lost forever.[20]

Not surprisingly, when General Jesup had arrived at Fort Gibson on July 17, 1845, to plan for the construction of new buildings, the Black Seminoles reminded him of his freedom promise. After Jesup told them that his pledge was "in full force and effect," several hundred blacks left their alleged owners and sought sanctuary at the military post. While staying there, sixty or seventy of them helped build the new stone structures.

This relocation to the fort irritated the Creek claimants and those Seminoles who believed that the blacks among them were merely chattel that could be bought and sold like the whites' slaves. The Seminoles evoked the section of the 1845 treaty stating that the president of the United States should decide questions about disputed property. The matter was referred to the U.S. attorney general, but the case dragged on for years before an opinion was finally rendered.[21]

The plight of John's older half-sister Juana and her children typified the situation. Details about her difficulties are unusually well documented because of her brother's prominence and his untiring efforts on her behalf. Juana (her name appears as Warner or Wannah in the official correspondence regarding her case) and her children were claimed, via a complicated series of events, by a Seminole mixed blood named Jim. But Juana declared that she was free because she had "come in and surrendered voluntarily" before the Battle of Okeechobee under Jesup's proclamation. Tony Barnett, General Taylor's interpreter, supported her assertion.

Juana, like most other Black Seminoles, had understood Jesup's promise not as freeing her from her Seminole owner but providing protection from avaricious third parties like Jim. But Jim said that he owned Juana, her surviving child by an earlier marriage, and the "three or four children" she had given birth to "by another slave of his, *Sam Mills* to whom she was married." Jim had already "sold his claim to two of her children 'Sarah and Linus' for $400, of which he received $235 on account, to a Creek named Cyrus Hardridge [also mentioned as Siah or Sias Hardage]; who treated them somewhat roughly."

Juana, Sam Mills, and their remaining children took refuge at Fort Gibson. On March 11, 1845, the post commandant issued a proclamation "forbidding any person [from] Molesting Wannah or her children" until their case was adjudicated. General Jesup accepted her claim of freedom and noted that Jim's mother had freed Sam Mills. Nevertheless, Hardridge still had Linus and Sarah.[22]

Fortunately, the officers at Fort Gibson were generally sympathetic to the Black Seminole plight. Lieutenant R. W. Kirkham, the Sixth Infantry adjutant, had requested General Roly McIntosh, the Creek head chief, to return Juana's "children to their Mother & also tell this Hardinge that I wished to know for what sum he would relinquish his claim [to Sarah and Linus]—but have yet received no answer." McIntosh, however, was a mixed-blood slave owner who strongly supported reducing the Black Seminoles to conventional bondage.

Jim, meanwhile, proposed to "give up his claim" to Juana and her children for the "rather exorbitant" sum of $1,300. Lieutenant Kirkham wrote that the mixed-blood Seminole was "aware of the very slight claim he has upon the family, and I think an order from the Department setting them free would cause him to give them no more trouble." But no such directive was forthcoming.[23]

Fortunately, John had left the "business of himself and his people" in General Jesup's capable hands when he had departed from Washington. Determined to protect the Black Seminoles in every way possible because the matter concerned his honor as a soldier, the general kept up a constant correspondence on the subject. But Jesup lived in a proslavery era and answered to a proslavery president. Furthermore, the sympathetic Seminole subagent, Thomas L. Judge, had been replaced by Marcellus Duval, an Alabamian, in late 1845. Duval advocated strict bondage and quickly became the nemesis of John and his people.[24]

Those Seminoles who were not affected by the Creek mixed-blood influence viewed owing blacks in the Territory much as they had in Florida. One observer commented: "It is well known that the slaves are only slaves in name. . . . [They] are really of no value . . . beyond the imaginary distinction that attaches to the name of the master." This viewpoint obviously galled Duval and others like him.[25]

John's unofficial and unpaid interpreter duties occasionally allowed him to induce the military authorities to thwart, at least passively, Duval's mischief. But the subagent, recognizing John's shrewdness and his influence with some of the Seminole chiefs, harassed him constantly. While Thomas Judge had tried to help John collect the money for the horse killed in the assassination attempt, Duval stated simply that he "must look to the Indian who killed his horse [for payment]."

At this time John Cavallo was only in his early thirties, but he already displayed far more leadership ability and civic concern than he had as a reckless young warrior or a compliant guide. And the Black Seminoles badly needed a leader. Abraham, their principal chief in Florida, was now about sixty years old and reportedly drank heavily. He had retreated from public life, leaving only John to take command.[26]

As time passed, the Black Seminoles' predicament worsened. Early in June 1846, the kidnappers became bolder, targeting a black settlement on the Deep Fork of the Canadian River. Armed Seminole tribesmen descended on the community and "attempted to take by force some of the Children." But the blacks were not easily intimidated. Seventy-two men were "compelled to take their arms" and rebuffed the slavers.

Soon after this incident, John and two companions arrived at Fort Smith in Arkansas. They reported the Deep Fork raid to Brigadier General Mathew Arbuckle, who commanded the Second Military Department. The trio complained about the overall situation and requested land in Arkansas for the free Black Seminoles. Although removing from Indian Territory to Arkansas might appear imprudent, they probably felt that enough law and order existed in Arkansas to protect those legally recognized as free. In the Territory, only brute force seemed to prevail.

Juana was not the only grieving parent whose children had been kidnapped. "Tony Barnett," wrote Lieutenant Kirkham, "has lost two of his boys, one was sold by his master when they landed on the banks of the Arkansas, he has not seen or heard of him since. The other named Tony was bought of Dick Stinson by Mrs Coody and is living with her near the Garrison. Tony is very anxious, as he is free himself, to have his children so also."

August was another grief-stricken father. He was a Black Seminole who had been useful to General Jesup in Florida. John Drew, a Cherokee, owned two of August's sons but was "selling off his negroes and these two boys will go with the rest, although they have as much right to protection as the others."

At least the military sheltered the blacks within Fort Gibson. On August 1 Lieutenant Kirkham stated that "a few days ago three men came & carried off a boy living in and under the protection of the Post, he was recovered by a party of Dragoons sent after them, but it keeps up a constant state of excitement & annoyance among the poor people."[27]

The summer of 1847 was a sad one for Juana. Cyrus Hardridge took her two children to Fort Smith and sold them. They were never heard of again. Ironically, about this time Subagent Duval, who displayed no interest in the youngsters' fate, complained to Washington about U.S. Army protection of blacks at Fort Gibson. He was further irritated when the post commander, Lieutenant Colonel Gustavus Loomis, a devout Christian, opened a small Sunday school and taught the blacks "to read and possibly write." But not even Loomis, despite his best efforts, could shelter everyone. Late in 1847 John Cavallo and Tony Barnett appeared again at Fort Gibson. Despondent, the two men requested that their people be sent anywhere—even to Africa as Loomis suggested—where they could be free.[28]

Shortly thereafter, Major B. L. Bonneville replaced Loomis as commandant of Fort Gibson. In the spring of 1848, his efforts for John's people were even more vigorous than his predecessor's. On April 14, 1848, he requested permission to issue rations to eighty-seven blacks, including forty-three children, at the post. He also asked how to handle lawless Seminole tribesmen who stole horses and free blacks. Additionally, he exposed a kidnapping ring headed by a Cherokee woman named Mrs. Wilson. Although the gang members were later brought to court, the judge freed them.

After the disposition of this case, John Cavallo appealed once more to General Jesup. His words demonstrate his despair: "but the other day three of our people were stolen and more than a month has passed & have not yet been recovered. One of the principals in this theft has been placed before the law, and from some Cause or other she has been let go—Some say there is no law against stealing Negroes."[29]

Finally, John reluctantly realized that neither General Jesup, the Washington authorities, nor the commandants at Forts Gibson and Smith could protect his people. He knew they would have to fend for themselves.

CHAPTER TEN

⌧ The Exodus to Mexico

[In] Mexico . . . a negro [is] as big as any body.
GENERAL MATHEW ARBUCKLE

Before long, John Cavallo and his people faced an even greater threat to their liberty. On June 28, 1848, U.S. Attorney General John Y. Mason "decided that the Negroes should be restored to the condition in which they were prior to the intervention by General Jesup." Mason, a Virginian, felt that the general lacked the authority to grant them freedom. President Polk quickly approved his opinion. Thus, the Black Seminoles, who had regarded themselves as free for a decade, were now restored to their condition as Seminole slaves.[1]

John's people would probably have reluctantly returned to their former position, if that was actually what Mason's decision meant. But the Seminoles were now surrounded by the Creeks and subject to Subagent Duval's bullying. They could no longer protect their black comrades from kidnappings and fraudulent claims. Clearly, reestablishment of the blacks' status as the Indians' vassals and allies was impossible. Instead, they would become chattel slaves without rights.

Mason's ruling embarrassed General Jesup, who reacted somewhat uncharacteristically. On July 28, 1848, he wrote to Major Bonneville at Fort Gibson, saying that the blacks had "weakened their own cause" by allowing those not eligible for his freedom offer to join them. But his attempt to transfer responsibility for Mason's decision to the Black Seminoles was entirely unwarranted. In fact, nearly a week before, Jesup had rebuffed Secretary of War Marcy, who had asked him how to deliver the blacks expeditiously to their legal owners. In a curt, formal note that was far more creditable than his letter to Bonneville, he declared: "Genl Jesup considering that his personal honor is involved . . . declines any opinion as to the manner of returning negroes, whom he considers entitled to their freedom, to slavery."[2]

Mason's ruling did not impact John because the Seminole council had already freed him. But his family members were once again Nelly Factor's property, so he petitioned General Arbuckle for help. Arbuckle's adjutant wrote to the Fort Gibson commander: "Gopher John . . . is extremely anxious to purchase his wife and children, and the General would be grateful if you could be of any service to him." Although there is no record that John actually bought his immediate family's freedom, he did buy the freedom of his nephew Andrew, Juana's son.[3]

On August 5, 1848, General Arbuckle, stationed at Fort Smith, was ordered to deliver the Black Seminoles at Fort Gibson to their masters. Several months elapsed before the move took place. Finally, however, Arbuckle designated December 22, 1848, as the date and Fort Gibson the place for returning the blacks to their owners. But cold weather prevented the Seminoles from arriving on time, and the schedule was further disrupted by Micanopy's sudden death on December 22.

The original roster of blacks who said they were free included 286 names. Some were at Fort Gibson while others resided at Deep Fork and elsewhere. By now, however, many had died or had been sold. Micanopy had claimed the largest number on the list, seventy-eight. Nelly Factor (who owned John's wife Susan and her family) said she had forty-seven. Billy Bowlegs, still fighting the U.S. government in Florida, laid claim to forty-six. Harriet Bowlegs, Echo Hadjo, Holatoochee, Charley Emathla, and Miccopotokee claimed the rest.

By January 2, 1849, the Seminole owners appeared, either personally or by proxy, at Fort Gibson. Creek mixed bloods and whites, whose claims to many of the same blacks were still unrecognized, were also present. All the interested parties and the Black Seminoles in question, led by John Cavallo, gathered in the post chapel to hear the senior military official speak. He was Brigadier General William G. Belknap, who had temporarily replaced Mathew Arbuckle. Belknap allowed the blacks to remain at Fort Gibson until the spring, when they would join their masters. The officer admonished the Indians to treat their slaves well and not to sell them.[4]

Belknap's humane action gave John and the other black leaders more time to plan. Unfortunately, Jim Jumper—unscrupulous son of the old counselor and war leader, Jumper—had succeeded Micanopy. The new headman had been involved in the kidnapping of Black Seminoles and had negotiated with the Seminole subagent's brother, William J. Duval, to mediate the blacks' return even though he had no claims to any of them. In addition, Jim Jumper had ordered the blacks at Fort Gibson to settle near the Seminole agency when they returned to live among the tribespeople, a move that would allow Marcellus Duval to control them better.

But in April 1849, when John Cavallo led his followers from Fort Gibson, they headed southwest to the Canadian River away from the agency. Keeping to the hills and off the low land, the Black Seminoles came to Wewoka Creek, stopping near the falls that gave the stream its name, Barking Water. There, thirty miles from the Seminole subagency and Marcellus Duval (near present-day Wewoka, Seminole County, Oklahoma), they cleared land, built houses, and planted corn. The blacks had deliberately disobeyed Jumper's orders and established a separate town. They had finally quit relying upon Washington for protection and were ready to defend themselves.[5]

On May 15, 1849, "by a decree of the general [Seminole] council," "all the slaves and their increases, having formerly belonged to King Payne, were decided to belong to and be under the control of . . . Jem [Jim] Jumper, the principal chief." This declaration was obviously intended to increase Jim Jumper's domination of as many blacks as possible. At the same time, the Creeks began complaining that the armed black villages at Deep Fork and Wewoka violated their laws. They ordered all free Black Seminoles to leave the Creek Nation, warning the Seminole tribespeople to enforce these laws or the Creeks would be forced to intervene.

But John Cavallo and his people refused to capitulate. They preferred "to die where they were" rather than become property to be distributed among various claimants. He and his followers soon demonstrated how determined they were to protect themselves.[6]

In early June 1849, a Cherokee Indian alleged that a black man known as Walking Joe had stolen his pony. With the blessings of the Seminole chiefs, the Cherokee went to Wewoka with two Seminole tribesmen to recover his property. The three men found the stolen animal in the town's horse herd and located Walking Joe. When they attempted to seize him, Joe drew a knife but was overpowered, disarmed, and bound. Suddenly a group of heavily armed blacks led by John Cavallo advanced toward them. The rescue party released Joe and gave the Cherokee his pony. Then they ordered the posse to leave and tell the chiefs not to attempt to take a prisoner from their town again "*without consulting the head men* (meaning Gopher John & some others)." If not, "*some person might get hurt.*"

The Seminole leadership summoned John to explain the incident, which he dismissed with diplomatic references to "young unmanageable negroes." But an outraged Marcellus Duval did not buy his explanation. He declared that John and his followers should have been whipped. Duval also asked General Arbuckle for soldiers to disarm the blacks. Weary of the matter, the officer declined. He said that sickness among the troops and other duties left him with no available men.[7]

Meanwhile, Wild Cat, who had been unable to become the Seminole chief, decided to change his tactics by broadening his constituency. He and John Cavallo, who now recognized the need for even stronger action to protect his people, became much closer. An officer wrote from Fort Smith: "[Wild Cat] was strongly influenced by Gopher John and others of the chief negroes, to resist any interference in reference to the condition of the negroes. . . . They retained their arms, and lived under no restraint whatever from their owners." Indeed, early in September 1849, Wild Cat, George Cloud, Pasoca Yahola, and fifteen other warriors told the Fort Smith commander that, despite the Creeks' objections, they wished "the negroes to retain their arms." The Indians said that the blacks needed them for hunting game to feed their families.[8]

By now, Wild Cat and John were prepared to leave the Territory. The Seminole chief apparently planned to unite his disgruntled followers—including blacks—with other allies, such as tribespeople from Texas, and then move to Mexico where slavery no longer existed. John Cavallo knew that a land of liberty lay just across the Rio Grande. Reportedly, during one of his visits to Fort Smith, General Arbuckle had advised him to go to Mexico with all those who claimed to be free. The officer was quoted as saying that south of the border "a negro was as big as any body." But John apparently did not rely upon hearsay. According to his people's oral tradition, he went there before the final emigration occurred.[9]

During the summer and fall of 1849, the Black Seminoles prepared for the exodus. They needed to store enough arms, ammunition, and food for the long journey. It was also necessary to delay the departure for another reason: yet another group was headed to Florida to try to persuade Billy Bowlegs and Sam Jones to relocate to Indian Territory. Because the delegates, including Marcellus Duval, would not leave until after the sickly summer season, it seemed better to wait until the Seminole subagent had departed before they went to Mexico.

Although Wild Cat and John Cavallo were asked to join the Florida party, they "generally . . . refused to come." The delegation, led by Halleck Tustenuggee, finally left on October 16, 1849. Tony Barnett, Jim Bowlegs, and a black man identified only as Tom were the interpreters.[10]

With Duval gone, the emigrants hastened to depart in early November. It was reported on the fifteenth that, a few days before, "a considerable band of Seminole and Seminole Negroes . . . [had] left their houses with arms and provisions." The exodus to Mexico had begun.

The blacks and Indians traveled separately because Wild Cat did not want it to appear that he had lured John's followers away. Still, at least two blacks rode with the tribespeople: John Wood, Wild Cat's orderly, and Kitty Johnson, John Kibbitts's step-daughter, the nurse for Wild Cat's son Billy. The party also included twenty to forty-five warriors and their families.

The other group was primarily made up of John's kin. They included his immediate family, his sister Juana and her children, and his wife's relatives. Among them were her younger brother Sampson and her uncles Dembo and Thomas. In all, John Cavallo had about thirty men and their loved ones with him. John Kibbitts was his second in command.

There was sadness in John's band. Juana grieved for her son Linus and her daughter Sarah, sold away into slavery. Sampson July reluctantly left without his wife and some children who were at the Creek Nation. The group believed that any attempt to rescue them might have alerted the Creeks.[11]

Although the two parties traveled separately, all acknowledged Wild Cat's authority and leadership. The two groups moved south for about a month and then, when reunited, went into winter quarters in Texas. They stayed on the Cow Bayou, a branch of the Brazos River. A large number of Kickapoos camped close by. The plan was to remain near the Creek country to receive news about the Florida delegation. They would also plant corn while Wild Cat tried to recruit more tribespeople. The Seminole chief seemed unconcerned about pursuit, perhaps because, before leaving, he had curtly warned that "any whites or Creeks who undertook to follow him would be killed." But the nearby presence of a Texas Ranger company under S. P. Ross apparently shortened their stay at Cow Bayou. They departed without waiting for the Florida delegates to return or the corn crop to grow.[12]

The emigrants next rested near the Llano River. Early in April, it was reported that "Wild Cat . . . with about twenty Seminole warriors, twenty or twenty five negroes, and the usual number of women and children" were close to Fredericksburg, Texas. About one hundred Kickapoo warriors camped nearby. They claimed Wild Cat as their leader, who evidently was "determined to entice away as many Indians as possible and settle in Mexico where he . . . [would] not have to contend with rival chiefs."

The Seminoles again planted corn. They apparently intended to wait at the Llano until Wild Cat could visit Mexico and return with news that their services had been accepted to fight the U.S.-based hostiles, especially Apaches and Comanches, who regularly terrorized the Mexicans. While still in Texas, Wild Cat also attempted to confer with General George M. Brooke, the victim of John Cavallo's gopher hoax in 1826. Now at San Antonio, Brooke was commanding the Eighth Military Department. Wild Cat probably wanted both a safe-conduct pass through Texas and rations; the provisions his band had brought from Indian Territory were exhausted, and his followers were forced to scavenge for food. But the chief's two attempts to see the general were thwarted, and he gave up.

On May 15, 1850, Wild Cat and what seemed like "2,000 men, women and children" visited William Banta, a settler near Burnett, Texas. The Seminole chief demanded and received several bushels of corn from the startled farmer. A few days later, Wild Cat went to Fort Croghan. After listening to his claims that his people were starving, the military authorities gave him twenty cattle and fifteen pounds of bread.[13]

The "two nations," as elderly Black Seminoles referred to the two bands many years later, remained near Fredericksburg waiting for their crop. Then an event propelled them headlong toward Mexico.

The situation began because of Wild Cat's fondness for liquor. On a drinking spree in Fredericksburg, he brought along his aide, John Wood; his son's nurse, Kitty Johnson; and John Cavallo. At the saloon the chief's funds apparently ran out before he had finished drinking. Perhaps at the suggestion of the saloon owner, Wild Cat decided to sell John Wood and Kitty to obtain more money. But John Cavallo boldly intervened. He hustled the two blacks out of the bar, and the trio galloped back to their encampment.

Fearing pursuit, John's followers quickly broke camp and rode for the Rio Grande, abandoning most of their possessions and forfeiting the precious corn crop. "They never stopped till they got to Las Moras Springs," said Molly Perryman, one of Kitty's daughters. Molly also said that Wild Cat "was so drunk, he didn't know what he was doing. . . . John Horse liked his liquor . . . but he was the chief—he know when there was danger and he mustn't touch it. That was John Horse—always watching over his people!"[14]

Wild Cat and his group soon joined John's band, evidently without recriminations. This wasn't the first time the chief had peddled Black Seminoles when he needed cash or liquor. As Penny Factor, Molly Perryman's sister, explained, he once "sold Rosa Fay's mother, Clara [Dixon,] in Eagle Pass [Texas] for a barrel of whiskey—[then] stole her back."[15]

On July 6, 1850, at Las Moras Spring, the emigrants encountered a company of troopers, under Major John T. Sprague, escorting a government wagon train. They were camped near present-day Brackettville, Texas. The group was not frightened because soldiers had been their friends and protectors in the Territory. Moreover, they had known Major Sprague from their Florida days. Indeed, their initial reception was cordial; there was no reason to believe there would be any trouble.

According to Black Seminole oral tradition, Sprague's party fed the hungry people and offered whiskey to their headmen. Wild Cat evidently had not learned his lesson at Fredericksburg, and John Cavallo must have felt secure enough to drink heavily. Both men were soon drunk. But somewhere in the camp, a man watched over the unwary Seminoles. He was a Mexican *cautivo* (captive), formerly a prisoner of hostiles whom the troops had rescued. Nevertheless, he was little more than a slave again and sympathetic to anybody seeking freedom.

The Mexican had seen a man slip out of the camp on horseback. Understanding a little English, he also overheard the soldiers joke about the big force that was coming to capture the Indians and seize the blacks. The next morning, after Wild Cat and John awakened, the cautivo approached them. Using gestures and broken English, he told them that trouble was afoot.

The headmen went immediately into council. "Wild Cat talked for a long time in his own language, and John Horse too—everyone could understand

Seminole in those days." John wanted to fight because "he was not afraid of anything and half-drunk into the bargain." He defiantly declared, "I'm not going to run away!"

But Wild Cat realized that the odds were against them. So they hastily gathered their belongings and rode toward Mexico. Out of sight of the military camp, the emigrants split into two groups—the families, escorted by a few guards, in one and the warriors in the other. As they headed for the Rio Grande, the first party spread out to make a broad, confused trail while the men kept together to produce clear tracks. With luck, their pursuers would follow the warriors.

The fugitives apparently traveled two days before arriving at the Rio Grande. The men crossed it, according to one account, near the "Lehman's ranch, across from Moral [Mexico], above Eagle Pass." The women and children reached the river at a ford "between Eagle Pass and Del Rio, that they called San Felipe then." It was dark, and the Rio Grande was high; so the escorts lashed together logs to build crude rafts and spent all night ferrying the families across the swollen waters.

"Just at daybreak as the last raft was crossing—the water wasn't dry on the feet of their horses—they saw the troop . . . on the opposite bank of the river; . . . [the soldiers] waved red handkerchiefs and called to them to come back. 'Yes we'll come back all right,' the warriors shouted in reply, 'but we'll come back to fight!'"[16]

According to official Mexican documents, the actual crossing took place about July 12, 1850. On that date about three hundred persons belonging to the three tribes (the Kickapoos had joined them earlier) presented themselves to the Mexican commandant at Piedras Negras, across from Eagle Pass, asking permission to settle in Mexico. They evidently were well received. According to oral tradition, they were taken to a "big office and give[n] . . . [a] lot to eat." Negotiations started almost immediately concerning the land concession where the immigrants could settle.

On July 24, 1850 the captains of the three tribes, "Gato del Monte" (Wild Cat); "Papicuan" (Papicua), leader of the Kickapoos; and "el moreno John Hourse," chief of the free blacks or "Mascogos" (a term possibly derived from the word *Muscogee*), met Colonel Juan Manuel Maldonado, subinspector general of the military colonies, at San Fernando de Rosas (now Zaragoza). The headmen described their woes and asked for help.[17]

Wild Cat spoke in the Seminole language, which John Cavallo translated into English. Then Don José Antonio Menchaca, ensign of the colony of San Vicente, converted his words into Spanish. The Seminole chief requested arms, land, tools, mules, and other livestock so that the immigrants could establish themselves. He recounted the troubles they had experienced during their nine months of travel and asked for permission to return to Indian Territory with documentation of their agreement to obtain more recruits. In addition, he wanted to recover the belongings left behind near the Llano River in Texas.

The Mexican officials tentatively granted their petition. Temporary living arrangements were made until confirmation came from the central government. John Horse and the Mascogos stayed at El Moral, just north of Piedras Negras, while the Seminoles remained in San Fernando de Rosas. The Kickapoos were nearby. Delighted by the successful negotiations, Wild Cat soon rode for the Indian Territory to enlist more followers.[18]

During his absence, the plight of the blacks remaining in the Territory had worsened. Cyrus Hardridge (the Creek slaver who had bought Sarah and Linus) received permission to seize John Cavallo's land at Wewoka. He could do so because John had taken Hardridge's property to Mexico—undoubtedly a reference to Juana and her other children. A caretaker at John's place tried to resist Hardridge and was wounded.

The Creeks had also arrested Jim Bowlegs, who had interpreted for the latest delegation to Florida, for possessing arms and horses. But after either escaping or being freed, he reportedly led 180 blacks "en route for Texas, armed and bidding defiance to any person or persons who should attempt to take them." The group may have included some of the fifty-six Black Seminoles whom Billy Bowlegs, the last major Seminole chief still at large in Florida, had placed under his guardianship.

Meanwhile, on June 24, 1850, a party of Creeks under Cyrus Hardridge rode to Wewoka accompanied by three Cherokees and four white men, including Gabriel Duval, another of the subagent's brothers. The posse intended "to take forcible possession of a number of Negroes . . . residing in the Seminole nation . . . claimed by some of the leaders of the aforesaid party."[19] But when the neighboring Seminole Indians learned of the Wewoka raid, "many of them painted themselves for war and asserted their firm determination to assist the negroes in defending themselves." At this point, the military authorities at Fort Smith intervened to prevent a bloody civil war among the tribespeople. The Hardridge party withdrew, and a council was held. Its members decided to confine 180 blacks in the Seminole subagency to prevent them from following Wild Cat, John Cavallo, and Jim Bowlegs to Mexico.[20]

After arriving in the Territory in September 1850, Wild Cat tried to convince the Seminole chiefs to emigrate to Mexico. But only "a few Seminole and about 100 Negroes" wanted to go with him.[21]

In October 1850 Marcellus Duval wrote that, during "these past two months," two hundred blacks had fled, including those who went with Wild Cat. The fugitives belonged to whites, Seminoles, Creeks, and Cherokees. Duval also declared that they "would constitute a 'formidable band' in Texas where they would secrete, protect, and guide all runaway slaves who made their way to the Texas plains."

Disaster soon struck the group of blacks who left after Wild Cat's October recruiting visit. As in the first exodus, they traveled separately from the Indians and would join them later. Unfortunately, the Creeks "despatched a company after the negroes." A running fight ensued that continued for two or three days. The women and children were sent ahead while the men tried to hold the attackers back. But the Creeks overwhelmed them. On October 23, 1850, about sixty survivors, mostly women and children, some of them injured, passed Camp Arbuckle on their way back to the Territory.[22]

Well into the next century, the Black Seminoles of Brackettville described flights from Indian Territory to Mexico that went terribly wrong. Once, about twenty slaves escaped from Arkansas and reached the Territory. The fugitives subsequently joined some Black Seminoles, making a total of seventy-two. Then they tried to reach Mexico. Although seven were killed in clashes with white slavers, none of the group was recaptured. But while battling hostile tribesmen during their trip across Texas, they lost about half their number. This account might refer to a party mentioned by Duval in the spring of 1851. He wrote that "only a few women and children (some 10 or 15 out of about 60 Seminole Negroes) were spared, from a massacre by the wild Indians."

According to Black Seminole Curly Jefferson, another group had apparently journeyed for several days and nights. At one resting point, the men decided not to tie down their horses for the night. Instead, they hobbled them and turned the mounts loose. The animals were driven away by hostile Indians during the night; and the next day, while the Black Seminole men tried to recapture their horses, the camp was attacked. Reportedly, all the women and children were killed except for a little boy who escaped to the brush.[23]

In 1852 a member of a U.S. exploring party also wrote about the blacks' misfortunes: "Within the last few years the Comanches have (for what reason I could not learn) taken an inveterate dislike to the negroes, and have massacred several small parties of those who attempted to escape and cross the plains for the purpose of joining Wild Cat." When asked why they attacked the blacks, the Comanches sardonically replied: "because they were slaves to the whites" and "they were sorry for them." But apparently their true intent was to prevent Wild Cat's band from being reinforced, which would leave the Seminoles less able to challenge Comanche border incursions.

The Comanches once tortured two little black girls, the only survivors of a group they had annihilated. Their captors flayed the girls' skin to see if the flesh underneath was black and then "burned them with live coals to ascertain whether fire produced the same sensations of pain as with their own people." The pair were finally rescued by a Delaware Indian trader. He brought them to Little River where Captain Randolph B. Marcy reported on their pitiful condition: the "poor girls were shockingly scarred and mutilated when I saw them."[24]

Yet despite the slavers—both Creek and white—and the Comanches, other parties of blacks fought their way to the Rio Grande. According to one descendant of the original Black Seminole emigrants, "they . . . [came] in several little bunches."[25]

While returning to Mexico in 1850, Wild Cat picked up two hundred or so Kickapoos. He must have avoided settlements and military posts, for there are no known reports of his trip. He was wise to do so because the countryside was aroused against him. Marcellus Duval had run a reward offer in Texas newspapers for the recovery of the Black Seminoles supposedly with Wild Cat; and Judge Rollins, the Indian agent in Texas, notified his Comanche charges to bring in blacks for $50 a head. Duval also persuaded Governor Bell of Texas to ask General Brooke for troops to capture the fugitives. The commander of Fort Duncan (at Eagle Pass) was instructed "to arrest any runaway negroes crossing the Rio Grande near his post." Nevertheless, the Black Seminoles continued to battle their way into Mexico.[26]

Left: John Horse. (Courtesy of the Institute of Texan Cultures.)

Below left: Abraham. (Courtesy of the National Archives.)

Below right: Wild Cat. (Courtesy of the Institute of Texan Cultures.)

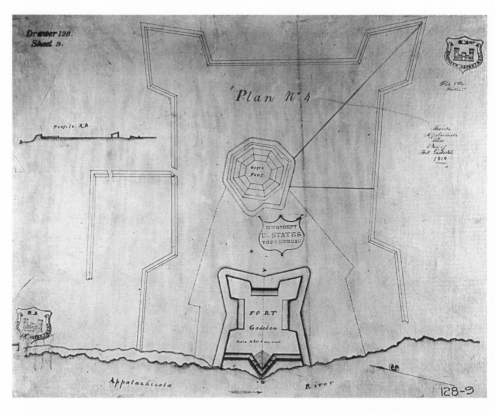

Plan Nº 4

Profile A.B.

Negro
Fort

ENGᵗ DEPT
U. STATES
TOPˢ BUREAU

FORT
Gadsden

Appalachicola   River

128-9

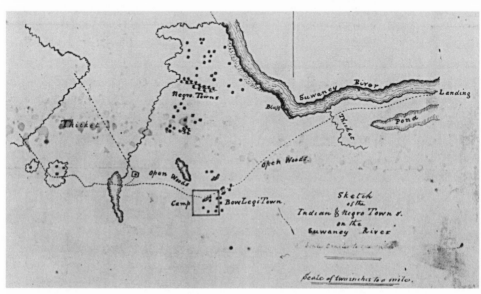

Negro Towns

Thicket

Suwaney   River

Bluff

Thicket

Landing

Pond

open Woods

open Woods

Camp   BowLegi Town

Sketch
of the
Indian & Negro Towns
on the
Suwaney   River

Scale of two inches to a mile.

Facing page, top: Plan of the Negro Fort on the Apalachicola River. The fort was destroyed by General Edmund P. Gaines's forces in 1816. (Courtesy of the National Archives.)

Facing page, bottom: Map of Black Seminole villages on the Suwannee River. They were attacked and destroyed by General Andrew Jackson in 1818. (Courtesy of the National Archives.)

Right: General Edmund P. Gaines. (Courtesy of the National Archives.)

Below: General Thomas S. Jesup. (Courtesy of the National Archives.)

Left: Marker at Ft. Duncan, Eagle Pass, Tex., celebrating the Seminole scouts' role in the pacification of West Texas. (Photograph by Alcione M. Amos.)

Below: A group of Black Seminole scouts on January 15, 1889. From left to right: Plenty Payne, Billy July, Ben July, Dembo Factor, Ben Wilson, John July, and William Shields. Dembo Factor participated in the "Dade Massacre" and the Battle of Okeechobee during the Second Seminole War. (Courtesy of the National Archives.)

The unit dismounted, early 1890s. Sandy Fay, who was John Bullis' striker (or orderly) is in the front row, second from the right. (Courtesy of Museum of the Big Bend, Sul Ross State University.)

The Black Seminole scouts mounted, early 1890s. The man on the left in the front row is Medal of Honor recipient John Ward. (Courtesy of Ben E. Pingenot.)

Joe Coon, son of John Horse and
Susan July and father of John Jefferson.
(Courtesy of Whitehead Memorial
Museum, Del Rio, Texas.)

John Jefferson, John Horse's grandson, late
1800s. Jefferson served in both the Tenth
Cavalry and in the scouts. Apparently he
closely resembled his grandfather. One of the
Black Seminoles said, "If you've seen John
Jefferson, you've seen John Horse!" (Courtesy
of William "Dub" Warrior.)

John July and wife Molly (later Mrs. Perryman), late 1800s. July served in the scouts from the mid 1870s until his death in 1900. Mrs. July was Kitty Johnson's daughter. (Courtesy of the Black Seminole Indian Scout Association.)

John Jefferson, 1919. Then aged forty, he was serving in the Tenth Cavalry when this photo was taken. (Courtesy of William "Dub" Warrior.)

Left: Scouts Fay July and William Shields, late 1880s. (Courtesy of the Black Seminole Indian Scout Association.)

Below: Scouts in dress uniform, ca. 1910. Left to right, back row: Fay July, John Shields, Joe Remo, John Daniels, Willy Wilson, and Ignacio Perryman. Front row: Thomas Daniels, George Kibbitts, John Jefferson, Sam Washington, Curly Jefferson, and Isaac (Ike) Wilson. (Courtesy of the Black Seminole Indian Scout Association.)

Above: Scout Billy July, date unknown. July participated in what was probably the unit's last armed conflict, in 1893. His granddaughter, Ethel (July) Warrior, is currently one of the leading Black Seminoles in the Brackettville–Del Rio area. (Courtesy of William "Dub" Warrior.)

Right: Scout Prymus Thompson, in civilian clothing, date unknown. He first joined the unit in January 1877 and served until August 1885. He reenlisted in 1889. (Courtesy of the Black Seminole Indian Scout Association.)

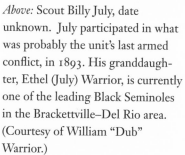

Left: Black Seminole Tobe Factor in civilian garb, date unknown. Factor served in the Scouts in the 1890s. (Courtesy of the Black Seminole Indian Scout Association.)

Above: Former scout Pompey Factor, probably in the 1920s. Factor received the Medal of Honor in 1875 when he, John Ward, and Isaac Payne rescued Lt. Bullis along the Pecos River. Denied a veteran's pension, he died penniless in 1927. (Courtesy of William Loren Katz.)

Left: Fay July and his mother-in-law, Phyllis Kibbitts. This photo was taken in the early 1900s. They are standing in front of one of the houses on the Fort Clark settlement. (Courtesy of the Black Seminole Indian Scout Association.)

Below: Sergeant Ben July (standing) with his parents, Sampson and Mary July (seated), on the Fort Clark settlement, date unknown. (Courtesy of the Museum of the Big Bend, Sul Ross State University.)

Sampson July, date unknown. He was John Horse's brother-in-law and first joined the scouts in March 1875 at age forty-nine. July served until May 1883. Miss Charles Emily Wilson is his granddaughter. (Courtesy of the Black Seminole Indian Scout Association.)

Rebecca and Jim July (brother and sister), date unknown. Their father was Sampson July. Miss Charles Emily Wilson is Rebecca's daughter. (Courtesy of the Black Seminole Indian Scout Association.)

Above: A Mexican and a Mascogo, date unknown. The architectural style of the building behind them suggests that the picture was taken in Mexico. The man on the right possibly is George "Dink" Gordon. (Courtesy of William "Dub" Warrior.)

Right: The man on the left is Charles James July, who served in the Seminole scouts before the unit's disbandment in 1914. His two companions are unidentified. Note the racial mix of the Black Seminoles clearly shown by the three men. Photo date unknown. (Courtesy of the Black Seminole Indian Scout Association.)

Top left: Scout Charles Daniels and family, early 1900s. Daniels first joined the unit in October 1871 and participated in such operations as the Zaragoza strike in 1876. He retired as a sergeant in 1909 and died in 1931. (Courtesy of the Black Seminole Indian Scout Association.)

Left: Penny Factor and Joe Remo, about 1930. He was a former slave and former Union soldier who joined the scouts in October 1875. Penny Factor was one of the informants Porter interviewed in the 1940s. (Courtesy of William "Dub" Warrior.)

Last mount of the Seminole scouts at Fort Clark, 1914.
From left to right: Kelly (Carolina) Warrior, Antonio
Sanchez, Billy July, Isaac (Ike) Wilson, Billy Wilson, Ignacio
Perryman, Caesar Daniels, Sgt. John Shields, John Daniels,
Fay July, John Jefferson, Charles James July, and an
unidentified scout. (Courtesy of William "Dub" Warrior.)

Above: Fort Clark, about 1890. The top photo is looking at the officer's row to the west; the bottom one is to the north toward Brackettville in the distance. Except for paved streets and sidewalks, the views today are remarkably similar. (Courtesy of the National Archives.)

Right: Post hospital at Fort Clark, about 1890. John Horse and Titus Payne were ambushed a few hundred yards behind the building, to its right, in 1876. The facility is now a recreation center for seniors. Its exterior has changed little since this photograph was taken. (Courtesy of the National Archives.)

107726

Above: Lieutenant John L. Bullis, as he looked while leading the scouts in the 1870s. (Courtesy of Doyle Crane.)

Top right: Major Bullis, 1899. President Theodore Roosevelt promoted him to brigadier general in 1905, on merit alone. It was apparently the first time in U.S. Army history that such a three grade advancement happened. (Courtesy of the White-head Memorial Museum, Del Rio, Texas.)

Right: Deputy Claron Windus, date unknown. Awarded the Medal of Honor like Black Seminole Adam Payne (Paine) was, he mortally wounded the former scout on New Year's Eve 1876. This is the only known episode where one medal recipient killed another. (Courtesy of Charles M. Neal, Jr.)

Left: William "Dub" Warrior, nephew of John Jefferson. He is also a descendant of both Elijah Daniels and Medal of Honor recipient John Ward. Mr. Warrior has been a leader among the Black Seminoles of Brackettville for years. His hat bears the crossed arrows insignia of the scouts. (Courtesy of William "Dub" Warrior.)

Below: William "Dub" Warrior and his wife, Ethel, next to Las Moras Creek in the pecan grove where many of their ancestors lived until evicted in 1914. This photo was taken in 1994. (Courtesy of Mr. and Mrs. William "Dub" Warrior.)

Left: Miss Charles Emily Wilson, standing by Las Moras Creek, 1994. She is the last Black Seminole still living who was born on the Fort Clark Reservation. John Horse was her great uncle. Miss Wilson has also been a leader among her people for many years. (Courtesy of Miss Charles Emily Wilson.)

Below: The Las Moras Creek, looking upstream to the west, 1994. It has changed little since the scouts and their families lived along it. (Photo by Thomas P. Senter.)

PART THREE

The Sanctuary, Mexico, 1850–1870

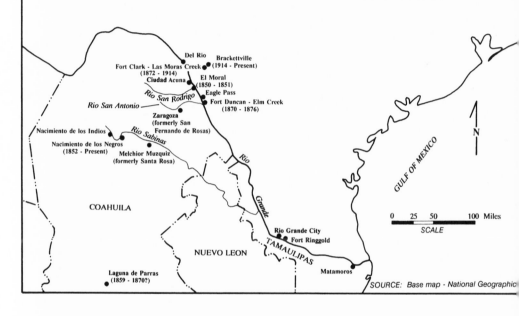

THE BLACK SEMINOLES ON THE TEXAS-MEXICAN BORDER

Del Rio
Brackettville
(1914 - Present)
Fort Clark - Las Moras Creek
(1872 - 1914)
Ciudad Acuna
El Moral
(1850 - 1851)
Rio San Rodrigo
Eagle Pass
Rio San Antonio
Fort Duncan - Elm Creek
(1870 - 1876)
Zaragoza
(formerly San
Fernando de Rosas)
Nacimiento de los Indios
Rio Sabinas
Nacimiento de los Negros
(1852 - Present)
Melchior Muzquiz
(formerly Santa Rosa)

COAHUILA

Rio

Grande

Rio Grande City
Fort Ringgold
NUEVO LEON
TAMAULIPAS
Matamoros

GULF OF MEXICO

N

0   25   50   100 Miles
SCALE

Laguna de Parras
(1859 - 1870?)

SOURCE: Base map - National Geographic

CHAPTER ELEVEN

⊠ This Land Was Bought with Blood

*When we came fleeing slavery, Mexico was a land of freedom,
and the Mexicans spread out their arms to us.*
JOHN HORSE

When the Seminoles, both Indian and black, arrived at Piedras Negras (across from Eagle Pass, Texas), they were greeted warmly. Their hosts' hospitality profoundly impressed John Horse. Reports state that he "would never let even the little children fight with the Mexican children" because their parents had "spread out their arms to us." John's policy also included nonintervention in Mexico's incessant civil wars. Although this neutrality exasperated those in power, it ultimately was the Mascogos' salvation.

The immigrants awaited presidential approval of their petition to be formally admitted as settlers. In the interim, they camped at various points on or close to the Rio Grande, near Piedras Negras and at San Fernando de Rosas.[1] Most of the blacks remained at El Moral, about thirteen miles above Piedras Negras, "for a year or more." But they soon discovered that, even on Mexican soil, slavers threatened them.

In fact, a nest of professional slave hunters—particularly the Town, Wood, and Morris families—operated from nearby Eagle Pass. They tried to intercept runaways at the border and reclaim those who were already in Mexico. The Rio Grande did not stop them from pursuing fugitive blacks.

"Old Man Townes and his family . . . [although] colored, but mostly white," were the worst of the lot. They were descended from David Town, a Georgian, who had moved to Nacogdoches, Texas, with a black woman in 1827.

He eventually emancipated her and their children; and in 1834 they were described as industrious and respectable. In 1850 his son David, now living in Eagle Pass, went into the slave-catching business.

Although the Town family was "mostly white," they appeared black enough to fool unwary runaways. Constantly looking for an opportunity to steal Black Seminole children, they once kidnapped a little girl playing on the riverbank. Fortunately, her people quickly dispatched a rescue party that recovered her before she could be sold.[2]

In addition to the threat from slavers, the immigrants also lacked food. They had arrived too late to plant corn and were forced to improvise. Initially, the Indians and Mascogos largely depended on government aid and neighbors' hospitality. They probably hunted as well, and some blacks likely worked for wages. Soon after their arrival, the Mascogos, Seminoles, and Kickapoos strengthened their petition for land and other assistance by demonstrating skills far beyond those of good hunters and industrious laborers. Although hostiles had regularly raided Coahuila for some time, the attacks were especially ferocious in 1850. That year, "Comanches, Mescaleros, and Lipans . . . marauded over the whole vast area . . . even attacking the town of Santa Rosa." The Seminoles and Mascogos were to be located near Santa Rosa the next year. But before the relocation could take place, and while Wild Cat was in Indian Territory, his band supported Mexican troops on two campaigns, battling U.S.-based hostiles "who were defeated with loss."[3]

On 16 October 1850 the president of Mexico approved the immigrants' request for land and tools. The area assigned to them lay at the headwaters of the San Rodrigo and San Antonio rivers in the Rio Grande district, state of Coahuila, about thirty miles above Piedras Negras. In exchange for the land grant, the colonists were supposed to obey the laws of Mexico. They also had to preserve the peace with friendly nations, especially the United States—a condition that obviously reflected the Mexican authorities' desire to avoid another war with their northern neighbor. Finally, they had to avoid contact with hostiles except to fight them.

On November 18 the captains of the Seminoles, Mascogos, and Kickapoos were summoned to the colony of Monclova Viejo (now Ciudad Acuña) across from Del Rio, Texas. Presently, the subinspector, Colonel Juan Manuel Maldonado, explained the terms of the grant to them. The three leaders swore an oath of fidelity the next day.

By February 4, 1851, Wild Cat had returned to Mexico. On that date, he appeared at Monclova Viejo and also pledged to honor the agreement. He was then appointed judge of the municipality and commissioned an army colonel. His cousin, Nokosimala, was made sheriff.[4]

U.S. authorities were understandably concerned about a large, independent band of tribespeople and blacks so close to their border and, moreover, led by the notorious Wild Cat. In the autumn of 1850, General Brooke reported: "Seminole and Kickapoo Indians, who have located themselves with Wild Cat in Mexico . . . are in the habit of passing and repassing the Rio Grande, and hunting on this side of the river." He considered this situation worrisome, especially because the tribespeople were frequently accompanied by blacks. The Mascogos might either provoke Texan hostility or encourage their slaves to flee.

The commander at Fort Duncan soon declared that the newly arrived colonists could not cross the border except for trade, and then only at Eagle Pass. The Mexicans duly informed "the chiefs of the nations which have emigrated to the Republic of Mexico from the United States" of this prohibition. The American military also decided to send a commission to ascertain Wild Cat's intentions. The Seminole chief told them that his goal was to remain only temporarily in Mexico until securing a permanent home for his people in Texas. While describing his plans to the commissioners, he was "respectful and kind."[5]

The Seminoles and Mascogos did not stay long at the headwaters of the San Rodrigo and San Antonio rivers after objections were raised to locating them there. On March 3, 1851, in El Paso de la Navaja, Captain Nokosimala, representing Wild Cat and accompanied by the interpreter August Factor, was given land near the colonia of Monclova Viejo. It was across from Del Rio and close to Guerrero below Piedras Negras. The Seminole grant was called La Navaja.[6]

The immigrants soon began paying in earnest for their land allotment. Hardly was their first corn crop planted before they rode against the Comanches. The colonists were then "engaged for two months in traversing the desert, and twice gave battle to the savages." Their families were left alone for forty-five days, during which their corn crop failed. Fortunately, the government of Coahuila gave them 470 pesos for their good conduct and need.

During the expedition, however, the Kickapoos defected with the livestock recaptured from the hostiles and returned to Indian Territory near the end of 1851. Only their chief, Papicua, with a few followers, remained loyal and stayed behind. Thus, "Wild Cat was . . . left with only about forty Seminoles and from fifty to eighty negroes in his band." This statement probably referred only to the warriors.[7]

The year 1851 was memorable for John Horse. Shortly after the Comanche campaign, he underwent a humiliating experience. In late August 1851 a U.S. Army scouting party picked up a stray horse that belonged to John and brought it back to Fort Duncan. Apparently without attempting to locate its owner, they sold the animal. After John heard of the affair, he laid claim to his property. But his request, although supported by Wild Cat, was ignored.

John went to Fort Duncan with some other Mascogos and loudly demanded the horse. Disregarding his protests, the soldiers expelled John from the post and hustled him across the Rio Grande. "The next day, having an order for goods on this side, he attempted to cross with great pomp, but was notified to keep himself out of sight until the commander of Fort Duncan could be seen." Until then, John was not permitted to set foot on American soil. He had to stand in the river, under a sudden rainfall, until negotiations were completed. John was eventually allowed to enter the United States and "did his business in a humble manner and vanished." Still, such demeaning treatment apparently did not discourage him. The next month he was again in serious trouble at Eagle Pass.[8]

Meanwhile, the Seminoles had barely returned from their recent expedition against the hostiles when they were asked to repel a group of Texas slavers. The filibusters knew that the Black Seminoles were not, by far, the only runaways south of the border. Indeed, "several thousand Negro slaves fled from the United States in the decades prior to the Civil War and gained freedom by setting foot on Mexican soil." Thus, Texas slaveowners were understandably receptive when insurrectionists from northeastern Mexico, such as José María Jesús Carvajal, offered to return fugitive blacks in exchange for help in setting up an independent Rio Grande republic. Their offer was especially timely because of the lack of cheap slave labor in Texas, where "a prime field Negro cost $1200 to $1500."

Carvajal invaded Mexico on September 18, 1851. His force consisted of three or four hundred men, including discharged Texas Rangers under the colorful John S. "Rip" Ford. The Seminoles were called out, with others, to resist them. Wild Cat led sixty warriors, including some twenty blacks. They rendered "efficient aid in the fight at Cerralvo," northeast of Monterey, and helped decisively defeat Carvajal. The following year, he attempted two more unsuccessful raids; and in April 1853 U.S. authorities arrested him as he was preparing for a fourth.[9]

In 1851 not all slave-hunting filibusters were as eager as Carvajal to enter Mexico and fight. Instead, some just gathered at Eagle Pass. Calling themselves volunteers, they hoped to use the border confusion to sneak across the Rio Grande for plunder. Chief among these volunteers was Warren Adams, a professional slave hunter. Marcellus Duval had commissioned him to recapture the Black Seminoles.[10]

John Horse, with a companion known as Hongo de Agosto, chose this unpropitious time to return to Eagle Pass for "some commercial affair." On September 19, 1851, just one day after Carvajal's first invasion of Mexico, Adams ordered the two men seized and confined in the local judge's house. John Horse was reportedly drinking just before his capture.

When the Mexicans learned of their detainment, they approached both the military and civil authorities in Eagle Pass, to no avail. Finally, on September 22 José Antonio Arredondo, chief justice of the eastern military colonies, submitted the matter's correspondence to Texas Governor Peter H. Bell. Arredondo formally requested freedom for the "two citizens of a friendly nation." But the Mexicans were unaware that only two days before Adams had seized John and his friend, Governor Bell had issued a proclamation urging all Texans to assist Warren Adams in recapturing the runaways from the Indian Territory and Texas. At this point, prospects for the release of the two prisoners seemed slim.[11]

Then Wild Cat intervened. A few days after the kidnapping, he went to Eagle Pass and talked to Adams. John Horse interpreted. The tribesman agreed to pay $500 in gold to free John and, possibly, the other captive as well. He also pledged to deliver other Black Seminoles that Adams had claimed for Marcellus Duval.

Wild Cat rode back to Mexico and soon returned with twenty-five $20 gold pieces. John Horse was freed. The fate of the other captive is unknown. Wild Cat then went to La Navaja, ostensibly to collect the other blacks in question. While he was gone, Adams examined the curiously stained coins and then submitted them to Dr. George E. Cooper, the surgeon at Fort

Duncan, for further study. The medical officer declared that they were covered with blood, most likely human. A shaken Adams decided not to wait for the additional Black Seminoles. Not only did he realize it was probably fruitless, but he may also have wanted to distance himself from Wild Cat, John Horse, and their warriors.[12]

Still, the slave hunter did not entirely give up. On the evening of November 2, 1851, the colonel commanding Fort Duncan advised Colonel Maldonado, the subinspector of the western colonies, that some filibusters were approaching the border. Numbering more than a hundred, they were proceeding from San Antonio and planned to seize the free blacks at Monclova Viejo. Warren Adams and seventeen men were already camped near Leona, twenty leagues from the fort. The American officer said that he would prevent the filibusters from crossing into Mexico at any point held by his troops, but he apparently felt that it was not within his province or power to disarm and disperse them.

Subinspector Maldonado ordered twenty men from the colony of San Vicente to reinforce Colonel Francisco de Castañeda, the commandant at Monclova Viejo. He also recommended arming the blacks and removing their families from harm's way.

Soon 150 mounted defenders rode to Sauceda in the jurisdiction of Villa de Nava, believed to be the intended point of attack. There they succeeded in repulsing the invaders, probably with little or no actual fighting. According to Black Seminole oral tradition, this was the first of three occasions in which their men repelled Texas slavers while in Mexico.[13]

But Adams did not leave empty-handed. Retreating from Nava, he swooped down on a black family living near Santa Rosa (now Melchor Múzquiz) and captured them. Pursued by a posse of thirty-five men, he nevertheless escaped with his victims.

His career was finally put to a halt by U.S. Army Second Lieutenant Daniel Huston, Jr. On February 5, 1852, the officer and his soldiers destroyed Adams's camp, scattering his force and confiscating whatever weapons they could find.[14]

Mexican authorities praised the work of the blacks and tribespeople, stating that "the immigrant Indians from the United States . . . the Mascogos and the Seminole have justified the Republic's hospitality, contributing faithful and useful assistance to such military operations as an expedition against the barbarians and the defence of Cerralvo."[15] Soon, however, the colonists were removed from the place where they had made such a favorable impression. The presence of Adams and his filibusters clearly showed that the Mascogos, living so close to the border, were a continual temptation to slave hunters from Texas. In addition, the owners of the lands where the immigrants lived had asked that they be relocated.

The government announced that La Navaja displeased the Seminoles. As an alternative, it would give them four *sitios de ganado mayor* and other irrigable property in the Hacienda El Nacimiento. (A sitio is a unit of pasture land amounting to 1,711 hectares, one hectare being equivalent to 2.47 acres.) The grant was in the Santa Rosa Mountains on the headwaters of the Sabinas River. It lay about twenty miles northwest of the town of Santa Rosa, which itself is eighty-four miles southwest of Piedras Negras.

The Mexican authorities were not entirely altruistic when they suggested that the Seminoles transfer to a safer point. Hostiles had ravaged the relocation area for some time and had nearly sacked Santa Rosa in 1851. Moreover, the Sabinas River sprang from the mountains through a gap that the raiders customarily used. A military colony could be strategically located there.

The immigrants began to head toward Nacimiento at the end of 1851 so that the women and children could be relatively safe while the men left to campaign in the Laguna de Jaco in Chihuahua. The families stayed for a time at Alto, just northwest of Santa Rosa, on the road to Nacimiento. This spot later became a favorite camping place for the Seminole tribesmen who were visiting the town.[16]

In December 1851 Colonel Emilio Langberg, the military commander in the region, was at Monclova Viejo enlisting Mascogos and Seminoles for an expedition against hostiles. But Wild Cat had felt that it was more important to visit Mexico City and obtain official confirmation of the Nacimiento grant. While he went to talk with the Mexican president, John Horse and a Seminole named Pasaqui assumed command of all the Seminoles. The black subchiefs were John Kibbitts and Hardy Factor. In early 1852 they rode with Langberg into Chihuahua to fight *los indios bárbaros*, returning to their new homes in Nacimiento by mid-June 1852.[17]

Shortly after their arrival in the Muzquiz area, hostiles struck the immigrants. Late on June 28, 1852, an unnamed Mascogo went to check on his horse. As the man stepped outside, several Indians ambushed him. Mortally wounded with an arrow, he died the next day.

A posse soon rode after the attackers. But because the raiders were so few and had collected little loot, they moved rapidly and left too faint a trail to be overtaken. Their victim was the first—but not the last—of the Black Seminoles to "buy with blood" their lands in Mexico.[18]

Meanwhile, Wild Cat and his companions, including the Kickapoo chief, Papicua, had reached Mexico City. Arriving there by May 18, they stayed for several months. During their visit the Seminoles called on various government officials, and a priest catechized them "with great care." On July 26 they were formally granted the promised sitios de ganado mayor at Nacimiento. Additionally, they were given four other plots in Durango under the same conditions as the agreement of 16 October 1850.

By September 1, 1852, word of the confirmation of the Nacimiento grant reached the Muzquiz authorities. Wild Cat and his delegation probably had returned from Mexico City by then. Interestingly, Papicua and his few Kickapoo followers never took advantage of the Nacimiento allotment. Instead, they settled near Morelos. In addition, the Seminoles and Mascogos apparently did not investigate the Durango grant and stayed only in Nacimiento.[19]

Their respective missions completed, Wild Cat and John Horse now helped their people settle. As in Florida and the Territory, they established two separate villages. The tribespeople lived at the head of the Sabinas River, where the present-day Kickapoo settlement is located. It was the more attractive but also the more exposed location. The blacks moved near the hill of Buena Vista, a few miles downriver. Wild Cat, John Horse, and some of their men scouted the nearby desert for water holes and favorable campsites so they would be prepared to pursue hostiles or mount expeditions against their strongholds.[20]

In the meantime, charges of misconduct plagued the colonists after their return from the Laguna de Jaco campaign. It is unclear if these charges had any foundation. Perhaps the Mexicans viewed the newcomers suspiciously and assigned every crime to them. In any case, the authorities summoned John Horse to be interrogated. Through an interpreter, they asked him about the damage that the Seminoles and Mascogos had supposedly caused. John categorically denied the accusations, but the controversy soon reignited. In November 1852 some Seminoles reportedly possessed a dead cow belonging to one of the prominent local gentry, Don Indalecio Elizondo.[21]

About this time, Wild Cat and the Black Seminoles confronted the U.S. Army once again. The troops were escorting some surveyors marking the boundary between Texas and Mexico. Their commanding officer, a junior lieutenant named Duff C. Green from South Carolina, reported being stopped on November 1, 1852, between the Rio Alamo and Santa Rosa "by some Negroes whom I found belonged to Wild Cat's band." He later encountered the chief himself, who "came out in his well Known manner demand[ing] why I had come into the Country."

After an exchange of boasts and threats, Green and his men proceeded to Santa Rosa. "It seems," he declared, "that the government of Mexico had given this Indian land on condition that he will defend the frontier from other Indians. He would, I have not the Slightest doubt, have given me Battle had he supposed for one instant that he Could gain the day. This settlement . . . is very injurious to the slave interests of Texas, as runaways will always find a safe home."[22]

John Horse was not among those who intercepted Green. In September 1852 he had gone to Piedras Negras in search of work, accompanied by several Mascogos and four tribesmen. While there, his life was again threatened. Early in November 1852 a fiesta, culminating in the evening with a boisterous fandango (dance), was held in the little Mexican border town. During the party John Horse fought with one of the boundary survey party. The cause of the altercation is unclear.

Fortunately for John's opponent, one of the celebrants was a man named Ed Stevens, the mail carrier between San Antonio and Eagle Pass. As John Horse, knife in hand, lunged at the surveyor, Stevens whipped out a revolver and shot him in mid-rush.

John's life hung in the balance, as it had in the assassination attempt near Fort Gibson seven years earlier. But before the man could fire again, angry Mexicans seized him. After he was disarmed, Stevens was "arrested, ironed, and cast into prison." He escaped during the night, swimming the river to Eagle Pass and safety, but had to leave his clothes and six-shooter behind.

John Horse eventually recovered from his wound, a fact that dismayed the journalist who reported the event. According to him, "Capt. Horse, as Gopher John terms himself . . . [was] an impudent and troublesome negro, and from his own accounts . . . [had] made many white men bite the dust."[23]

Wild Cat, meanwhile, had actively worked to establish the Nacimiento settlement. He had also led his warriors against the Comanches on his own volition. Soon the Seminole leader received "the thanks of the government, which, however, ordered that in future expeditions they should be accompanied by some Mexicans." This condition was intended to prevent the colonists from being accused of causing depredations.[24]

As they became more settled, the Mascogos were forced to learn some Spanish. But they did not abandon either the Creole of their ancestors or the Seminole language. John, however, reportedly never mastered "Mexican."[25] In addition, most of the blacks and some Indians were given or assumed Mexican names, either during baptism or for reasons of convenience. Some of the new names were straight translations. For example, Wild Cat became known as Gato del Monte. John Horse was called Juan Caballo. In some cases the modifications were slight. For instance, Bowlegs became Bully; Bruner, Bruno; and July, Julio. More frequently, the blacks adopted the names of the prominent families in the vicinity of Nacimiento. For example, the Factors were called Aldape; the Fays, Alvarez; the Perrymans, Flores; the Washingtons, Garza; and the Paynes, Morillo.

Less comprehensible are those names that could have easily been changed into Spanish but were not. For example, instead of becoming Juan Madero, John Wood was known as Juan Miguel. John Kibbitts, on the other hand, was called Juan Quivi, a close "translation." Similarly, the Wilson family became the Wills.

Yet in nearly every case, the Black Seminoles also retained their American names. Moreover, they kept their own dialect for use among themselves. They still do so to this day, in both Mexico and Texas.[26]

In addition to learning Spanish and acquiring new names, other adaptations were necessary. For example, the Mascogos had to learn irrigation methods—unnecessary in Florida and unknown in Indian Territory. Although corn continued to be a staple, they soon began using the Mexican *metate* to grind it. The local royal palms replaced koonti in the preparation of sofkee, and the palmetto-plank houses of Florida and the log cabins of the Indian Territory were replaced by the chink house and later by adobe dwellings.

The church was also an important institution within the community. Despite the requirement that newborn infants (and perhaps adults as well) should be baptized into Catholicism, the blacks mostly followed their ancestors' Baptist beliefs. Ignoring the Catholic ritual, they baptized by immersion in the Sabinas River—and later, in Texas, in Las Moras Creek.[27]

Marriage among the Mascogos took various forms. To wed "Indian fashion," the man chased and captured the woman in front of witnesses. Another ceremony was a legacy from slavery days in the antebellum South: the couple held hands and jumped over a broomstick held at either end by two friends. A more formal method was marriage with a Bible. The bride and groom clasped hands before witnesses and a master of ceremonies. He was not required to be literate; the mere presence of the Scriptures was evidently the only requisite. Joe Bruner, who could not read, had a Bible and used it to perform marriages.[28]

Thus, the Black Seminoles gradually adapted to their life in Mexico. Without discarding all their old traditions, they acquired new ones that they deemed necessary in their adopted land.

CHAPTER TWELVE

◼ Perils on the Border

Among the Seminoles [in Mexico] there are two hundred and fifty odd negroes. . . .
Fifty or more of these negroes are well armed and are good fighters.
TEXAS STATE TIMES

In 1853 the Seminoles and Mascogos began following a predictable pattern. Right after corn planting, they scouted for hostiles, usually in the Laguna de Jaco west of Nacimiento. Four or five Mexicans would ride with them. Generally, the authorities praised the blacks and Indians for their perseverance and zeal during these campaigns.

The Mexicans ordered frequent expeditions; and the Seminoles willingly complied, particularly because of the horses they might seize. If the captured animals' brands could be recognized, their legitimate owners could recover them for a small fee, usually two pesos per head. The colonists generally received the unclaimed ones for use on later campaigns.[1]

The warriors also helped repulse attacks near Nacimiento. For example, on August 11, 1853, thirteen Seminoles and seven inhabitants of Muzquiz intercepted five marauders. After killing three, they took not only their booty but also their personal property and horses.

The unit's commander was Isidro Neco. According to Black Seminole oral tradition, he was a Biloxi Indian. His father, Juan Antonio Neco, also participated in the action. The two men and Isidro's sisters, Laura (or Nadra) and María, were probably refugees from Texas who had settled in Muzquiz. They eventually intermarried with both Mexicans and Mascogos from Nacimiento.[2]

The blacks and tribespeople continued to be periodically accused of stealing. In early 1854 both Wild Cat and John Horse were summoned to account for a cow and a calf that allegedly had been stolen. But Wild Cat could not be immediately located. On April 27, 1854, he had ridden against the Mescalero Apaches and Comanches on his own initiative. The Mexican authorities, while recognizing the need for such action, quickly forbade him from repeating it without prior approval.[3] Nevertheless, during the following year, chaotic Seminole expeditions still bothered the Mexican officials: "The continuous disturbances in the villages caused by their unforeseen appearances" were troublesome. In one instance, four Seminoles hunting in the *agostaderos* (summer pastures) of the village of Sardinas were mistaken for hostiles, prompting the nearby community of Santa Buenaventura to send fifteen men to intercept them.

To prevent such problems, the authorities told the colonists not to leave their camps without permission or deviate from their prescribed route. Although this order was laudable, it greatly impeded the Seminoles in their pursuit of the enemy. Not surprisingly, they tended to disregard it and continued to disrupt the villages they rode by.[4]

Early in 1854 Wild Cat and his followers were accused of entering Texas to steal cattle. The accusation led to increased attention on the group and to several widely varying reports of their numbers. In August 1854 Second Lieutenant Holabird estimated that the Seminoles in Mexico had "about fifty warriors and a number of negroes." He also said: "These Indians are under the immediate control of Wild Cat . . . and . . . subject to the military orders of Colonel Castaneda, the inspector general of the neighboring colonies. I look upon the Seminoles as a military colony, under Wild Cat, and his warriors are colonial troops."

Two months later, Colonel Joseph Plympton reported that the entire group numbered 318, 183 of them warriors and 82 regularly enlisted under their own officers. The men included "between 50 and 60 negroes who are on terms of perfect equality. . . . They are armed, and almost invariably accompany . . . [the tribesmen] in their depredating excursions. . . . One company, composed entirely of Indians, is commanded by Wild Cat; the other, made up of negroes only, was, until a few days past, under the command of a negro known as Gopher John."[5]

A year later, there was another report from an independent source:

Among the Seminoles there are two hundred and twenty odd negroes.
Some of these went to Mexico before these Indians and have since
intermarried with negroes who came in with them and are, therefore,
identified with the Seminoles in every way. Fifty or more of these negroes
are well armed and are good fighters. . . . There are negroes in Santa Rosa
and vicinity, who have not been incorporated with the Seminole negroes.
They are designated "State raised." The Seminole darkies has as little to
do with them as possible because they say the white folks wish to retake
them and they may thus become entangled, in their difficulties. Negroes
arrive frequently from the U.S. . . . [and] fully three thousand negroes
have entered Mexico since 1848.[6]

The unnamed source, identified only as a "gentleman," evidently was a keen
observer. His mention of those who "went to Mexico before these Indians
and have since intermarried with negroes who came in with them" merits
further comment.

Black Seminole oral history, in both Texas and Mexico, stresses that there
were at least three separate groups that formed their community. The first
were the Black Seminoles proper—those who originally followed Wild Cat
and John Horse to Mexico. They also included a few Black Creeks, notably
the Graysons and Perrymans.

The second element came from individuals who joined the colonists independently, primarily blacks already in Mexico. Most were runaway slaves from
Texas (the state-raised blacks mentioned in the previous quotation). But this
category also included Mexicans and Indians, such as the Neco family,
who were said to be Biloxi. Those who intermarried with the Black Seminoles were gradually assimilated and eventually became regarded as part of
the Mascogos.

The last group included the majority of the Black Creeks, such as the
Wilsons, Warriors, and Daniels, who emigrated to Mexico independently and
later joined the Wild Cat–John Horse band. For a considerable period of time,
they constituted a separate faction. Oral traditions that have passed into the
twentieth century explain how the Black Creeks first reached Mexico. Apparently, Tony Warrior had been there long enough before the Seminoles and

Mascogos to be able to "speak a little Mexican." Johnny Wilson and Caro, or Kelly (also known as Carolina and Kelina), Wilson evidently came with him.[7]

Among the state-raised blacks who joined the Seminoles in Mexico were various members of the Shields family, including brothers Benjamin, Archibald, and William. By 1858 they were already living near Muzquiz. Archibald later married Roselle Kibbitts, daughter of subchief John Kibbitts. Benjamin had a daughter with Kitty Johnson, the little girl whom Wild Cat almost sold for whiskey in Fredericksburg.[8]

Life at Nacimiento for all the colonists, no matter what their origins, could be dangerous. On July 15, 1854, seven Lipan Apaches attacked four Seminoles working in their fields. After showering them with arrows, the marauders temporarily forced the colonists to retreat to their houses. They soon emerged, however, and forced the enemy to flee. Then, on August 7, fifteen Lipan warriors ambushed a Seminole hunting party.[9]

Besides the danger from hostiles, the colonists had to deal with threats from across the Rio Grande. In early August 1854 they were ordered to muster fifty armed men to repel possible invaders from the Texas. Thirteen blacks under John Horse and twenty-two tribesmen under Wild Cat turned out, but the alarm proved to be false.[10]

At the beginning of 1855 the Seminoles were accused of attacking a peaceful band of Mescalero Apaches and killing not only many men but also some women and children. Wild Cat retorted that he was only protecting himself and his warriors from a band of thieving Indians who had threatened them. Among the baggage they seized were some dried human hearts.[11]

In May 1855 the governor of Coahuila ordered fifty Seminoles and Mascogos to ride to the capital for purposes unknown. When Wild Cat was summoned along with John Horse, only the Seminole chief appeared. He politely but firmly refused to go. The chief contended that his people were laboriously clearing and planting corn without proper tools. Although his explanation may have been true, John Horse's policy of maintaining neutrality in conflicts among the Mexicans might also have influenced him.[12]

Although the cry "filibusters on the border!" was often a false alarm, that was not the case in late 1855. Years later, elderly Black Seminoles asserted that their people had thwarted three attacks by Texan slavers in Mexico. Probably two were connected with the Carvajal invasions. The third must have been the Callahan raid in October 1855.

On August 25 some Americans in San Antonio had demanded that Colonel Langberg, the commander stationed on the frontier of Coahuila, return runaway blacks in Mexico. They offered to pay him for his cooperation but threatened unilateral action if he refused. Langberg quickly suggested a reciprocal exchange of the escaped slaves and fugitive Mexican *peones* living in Texas. But after word of the negotiations leaked out, the citizens of Coahuila opposed the agreement.[13]

The San Antonio group then approached James H. Callahan, a Texas Ranger captain with a reputation for ruthlessness in border warfare. The relentless Marcellus Duval, recently dismissed from his duties as Seminole subagent, apparently promised Callahan a share in any Black Seminoles he might capture. Callahan evidently had a similar arrangement with the Texas slaveowners.

By early September, all the necessary preparations had been made. Now the invasion needed only a plausible excuse to begin, which a Lipan raid soon furnished. On September 18, 1855, Callahan left Bandera Pass to pursue the hostiles. Before the filibusters reached the border, a group led by William R. Henry joined them. On October 2, 1855, more than one hundred men rode into Mexico.[14] After crossing the Rio Grande, Callahan's command went straight to Nacimiento. On October 3 a Mexican force soundly defeated them; and the invaders then withdrew to Piedras Negras.

While Callahan appealed to Texas for help, his men fortified Piedras Negras to salvage the expedition. But soon they were trapped in the little border town, besieged by a Mexican force that included the Seminoles and Mascogos. With their retreat to Texas hampered by the swollen Rio Grande, the filibusters reportedly torched Piedras Negras to cover their withdrawal. Then they returned to Texas.[15]

The border confusion continued throughout October and into November. The arrival of yet another band of American "volunteers" caused Colonel Langberg to order twenty men from Muzquiz, together with the Seminoles, to ride to Nava. Wild Cat led the tribesmen, and John Kibbitts commanded the blacks. But the Mascogos were missing several of their warriors, including John Horse. He had ridden to Lampazos with a pass to collect more men. Twelve blacks had already declined to participate in the campaign. Half had pleaded old age and other infirmities, while the rest had flatly refused to go. Possibly they were reluctant to obey Langberg because he had tacitly encouraged the Callahan expedition. Although the insubordinate six were threatened with expulsion from the colony, what actually happened to them is unknown.[16]

Despite this small mutiny, the Mexican authorities were pleased with the immigrants' overall performance. They found them "industrious, warlike and desirous of education and religious instruction for their families." In late November 1855 Juan Nepomuceno Vidaurri was appointed to teach them religion and help them farm. Then early in May 1856 authorities made Juan Francisco Valdez "preceptor of the Seminole and Mascogo tribes." The job initially paid ten pesos monthly and gave him a bodyguard to accompany him over "eight leagues through a solitary and dangerous region" between Muzquiz and Nacimiento. His salary was soon increased to forty pesos; but after a year and a half, when he had failed to teach even one of his charges to read or write, it was reduced to twenty-five.[17]

Although they appreciated the services of both Vidaurri and Valdez, the colonists probably were even more pleased when Pedro Saens was appointed armorer in May 1856. When he died, it was hard to replace him. After his death the colonists frequently lacked regular facilities to repair their firearms and make tools and implements.[18]

Santiago Vidaurri, the able but unscrupulous governor of Nuevo Leon, apparently provided the two instructors and the armorer for the Seminoles. He had just annexed Coahuila by force and ruled both states essentially independently of the central government. The ambitious Vidaurri paid greater attention to the colonists, which included supporting their families during campaigns, than his predecessors had. He evidently recognized how valuable a border defense corps they were and attempted to keep them contented and well equipped.

Vidaurri decided to clarify the relationship between the Seminoles and Mascogos and among the various leaders of the two groups. He apparently wanted the chain of command clearly defined so that responsibility could be fixed. By now, the Seminole Captain Coyote was prominent enough to challenge Wild Cat's authority. The government of Coahuila accordingly recognized him as second in command, in charge when Wild Cat was absent.[19]

The blacks' situation was considered even more troubling. After the Mexicans again accused them of unspecified bad conduct, authorities ordered the

Mascogos and other black fugitives from the United States to be "subordi-nated to Captain Catamount [Wild Cat]." The runaways were especially ex-horted to live honestly and industriously.

But the Black Seminoles balked at this order, declaring that they had al-ways acknowledged John Horse as their superior. In his absence, they recog-nized Captain Cofe. Unaccustomed to such disobedience, Vidaurri issued an order on May 24, 1856, approving "the election of the Mascogo blacks of Nacimiento in favor of John Horse as captain." Still, Vidaurri insisted that Wild Cat be recognized as the "Supreme Chief" of the two groups. Further-more, he expressed his concern about the dissension between the bands. In his opinion, "the blacks . . . [were] vicious and of bad customs and the Semi-nole [were] much more honorable men."[20]

This reference is the first piece of documented evidence demonstrating discord between the Indians and the blacks in Mexico. Perhaps it marked the beginning of a deliberate campaign to split them and ultimately remove one or both peoples from Nacimiento in order to return the land to private hands. This scenario seems plausible because the Muzquiz area had been relatively pacified, in part because of the Seminole presence.

Late in November, the Mascogos reemphasized their subordination to "Captain Juan de Dios Vidaurri (a) Caballo [John Horse] to whom they will lend blind obedience." Vidaurri apparently had nothing personal against John. In fact, in April 1856 he ordered that the family of "captain Juan de Dios Caballo" should receive fifteen pesos; and the government also promised him a cart, a plow, and oxen. The stubborn resistance of the blacks, including John Horse, to an imposed leadership had likely prompted Governor Vidaurri to influence them with gifts rather than threats.[21]

Throughout 1856 the colonists rode against the "wild Indians." But in October twenty Seminoles and fourteen Mascogos were ordered to Monterey to assist Vidaurri's Army of the North. Vidaurri had revolted against the cen-tral government for disavowing his annexation of Coahuila. The blacks, true to John Horse's policy of nonintervention in Mexican internal affairs, refused to participate. But eventually John Horse and four of his men agreed to go, accompanying twenty-one Seminole warriors led by Captain Coyote. John's trip to Monterey probably gave him the opportunity to explain his position to the authorities.[22]

Then, early in 1857, an enemy worse than any marauding hostile or Texan slaver swooped down on the Seminoles at Nacimiento: *la viruela negra*—small-pox. The disease first attacked some tribespeople camped at Alto, north of Muzquiz on the road to Nacimiento, and then spread to the Seminole village at Nacimiento. By late January 1857 the terrified Indians were fleeing into the hills, vainly searching for safety. The epidemic ended among the Semi-noles a month later. By that time, twenty-eight women and twenty-five men— including nineteen warriors and the two principal chiefs, Wild Cat and Coy-ote—had perished.[23]

The blacks were not spared; only two members of the group were not in-fected. But the Mascogos, as contemporary reports claimed, "suffered less because of being more regular in the observance of curative methods and of the diet which the disease demands." In truth, while the smallpox was devas-tating to the more susceptible Indians, the blacks had inherited resistance from their ancestors. The disease killed comparatively few, if any, of them.

By mid-March 1857 the plague had spent itself among both peoples, and those who had fled returned to Nacimiento. Nevertheless, the epidemic's ul-timate effects were far-reaching and permanent. The loss of Wild Cat and Coyote left the Seminoles without official leadership, a situation quickly rec-tified by the election of the previously unknown León (Lion) as captain.[24]

Despite the death of so many warriors and the two principal leaders, the Seminoles undertook even more expeditions than usual in 1857. Perhaps the hostiles were aware of their weakened numbers and became bolder, or the new chief wished to show his mettle. On February 20, even before the small-pox had run its course, "the Seminole and Mascogos being experienced in this type of war," were ordered to pursue some marauders who recently had killed a traveler. They returned by April 13 without having encountered the attackers, but John Horse brought back five ponies with unknown brands that he and his men were allowed to keep for future campaigns.[25]

During July and August the Seminoles fought the Lipan Apaches three times, killing six hostiles, including a chief. They also battled the Comanches, wounding one warrior and capturing more than one hundred horses and sixteen mules. The murder of four shepherds early in December 1857 pro-voked another expedition. Nokosimala and thirty Seminoles successfully at-tacked the Lipan and Tonkawa settlements in the Cañón de Nataje. Seven-teen Mexicans accompanied them, but the Mascogos did not cooperate in the campaign.[26]

Complaints about their lack of participation was only one charge in yet another controversy among the blacks, the tribespeople, and the Mexican authorities that had been escalating since Wild Cat's death. Seminole captain Felipe criticized the Mascogos for using too much water for irrigation; and the Mexicans again accused them, especially the runaways from the United States, of cattle rustling. In response, John Horse went to Governor Vidaurri. He claimed that the Muzquiz officials did not adequately supply his men for their campaigns. After warning John and his followers to behave, Vidaurri gave him some money and gunpowder.

But more complaints about the blacks' conduct followed in September 1857. Governor Vidaurri subsequently reminded them that they were fully subject to the same laws as the Mexicans were. Thus, they should obey both their chief and the local authorities. He also told John Horse to separate himself from the *cuarterones* (quadroons, as the non-Mascogo blacks were called), who were again charged with stealing cattle. John was advised to tell them to leave the community.[27]

Still, these measures did not keep the peace. A year later, the principal Seminole leaders—Captain León, Manuel Flores, and Nokosimala—appeared in Monterey. They stated that, after the smallpox had killed many of their kin, the Mascogos had impeded their irrigation in Nacimiento. Therefore, they asked that a Mexican be appointed to regulate the water rights. Furthermore, they wanted the blacks to "subject themselves to the care and command of the Seminole chief as they were previously under the command of the Cat [Wild Cat]." The Indians complained that, because the Mascogos preferred farming to pursuing hostiles, they owned more horses and property than the tribespeople did.[28]

Indeed, the blacks quite possibly used more water for irrigation than the Seminoles thought they were entitled to. The Mascogos were primarily agriculturalists, although they hunted occasionally and fought hard when necessary. In contrast, the Indians were primarily hunters and warriors. They were only incidental farmers. Moreover, many of them had died in the smallpox epidemic. Because the blacks were now more numerous, they cultivated more land, which needed additional water.

At this point, the Seminoles were probably more useful militarily than the Mascogos were, so more Indians than blacks went on campaigns. In fact, there is no record of an expedition including Mascogos for nearly a year after the spring of 1857. It is also very likely that runaway slaves occasionally killed cattle for food. But in view of later events, the conflicts between the Seminoles and Mascogos were probably encouraged by parties interested in their land at Nacimiento.

The Nacimiento area had remained relatively safe after the colonists had pacified it. But at midnight on March 2, 1858, marauders believed to be Mescalero Apaches appeared. They swept down over the fields from the Buena Vista hill, where the black village was located, to the headwaters of the Sabinas, where the tribespeople lived. The hostiles stole thirty Mascogo horses and six Seminole ones.

Problems about water rights were quickly forgotten. Twenty warriors from each tribe were issued ammunition, provisions, and a passport to pursue the raiders. Information about the expedition was sent to various points along the way, and local officials were asked to cooperate with the campaigners.

The group departed on March 6. For three weeks afterward there was silence. Then on the twenty-eighth, the Muzquiz authorities announced that ten days previously the unit had encountered the enemy at the Rio Grande. Before routing them, they killed two hostiles and recaptured all the animals taken from Nacimiento plus seventy additional horses, two mules, and some equipment. The only casualty was a minor arrow wound to Seminole chief Juan Flores. The governor praised the colonists and gave them the captured animals.[29]

Despite such success on the battlefield, some of the Seminole tribespeople wanted to relocate permanently to the United States. Wild Cat's death in early 1857 had weakened Mexico's hold on his surviving followers; and in 1856 the Seminoles had finally been declared independent of the Creeks, making Indian Territory more attractive to them. In addition, they had never received final title to the Nacimiento land and were involved in disputes over water with the Mascogos.

In the fall of 1858 a nephew of Wild Cat led a party to the Territory to investigate the possibility of relocating. The group temporarily returned to Nacimiento in January 1859. They intended to go back to the United States and take any others who wanted to leave.[30]

The inhabitants of Muzquiz, upset about losing their protectors, attempted to dissuade them, promising to provide equipment and provisions for another campaign, with the hope that the warriors might decide to stay for more action and loot. Despite the offer, the first contingent of Seminoles, under the command of Lion and Juan Flores, departed for the Territory in February 1859. Those who remained behind would leave soon.[31]

Meanwhile, a filibustering alarm, which had not been sounded since just after Callahan's raid of October 1855, was heard again. In March 1859 Lieutenant F. A. Washington from Fort Duncan warned the Mexican authorities that men were preparing to cross the Rio Grande solely to steal blacks.

The Mexicans responded immediately. They ordered blacks living in the border area, including the Mascogos at Nacimiento, to move inland for safety. In addition, the National Guard was mobilized and deployed at strategic points along the Rio Grande.[32] The invasion never materialized, possibly because of the swift Mexican response. Still, it furnished a pretext for the removal of the Black Seminoles farther south—ostensibly for their protection.

CHAPTER THIRTEEN

⊠   Adrift in the Laguna

They went down to the Laguna to work. . . . They settled in little groups,
wherever they could find food, but they got together when there was anything
important to decide. . . . They were always having trouble with the Indians.
The Lipans were the worst.

BILL DANIELS

On March 23, 1859, the secretariat of government of the state of Nuevo
Leon and Coahuila politely but firmly ordered John Horse's people to leave
Nacimiento. They were to go to Laguna de Parras in southwestern Coahuila.
Because the Black Seminoles were the filibusters' principal objective, the authorities felt that the colonists would be safer there. State authorities promised to supply the Mascogos with lands, water, and other assistance. In return,
as in Nacimiento, the Black Seminoles would help "to repel the aggressions
of the barbarians."[1]

In reality, only the central government could order the blacks or the tribespeople to leave Nacimiento. But the War of the Reform (1858–61) was rag-
ing, and conservative reactionaries controlled Mexico City. Furthermore,
Santiago Vidaurri, then supporting liberal leader Benito Juárez, was too powerful to offend.[2]

The official rationale for the transfer to Parras became part of Black Seminole oral history. "They went to the Laguna, because they were afraid the
enemy would carry them off. . . . [T]he enemy were the white people." Years
later, one of the elderly blacks still recalled the timing of the removal: "The
Mexican government sent . . . John Horse to go [to the] Lagun' and fight

Indians. They were planting corn when the word came; it was so high." Documentary evidence confirms this statement. The order to depart came in late March when the corn would have already been planted.[3]

Their destination was announced as the Hacienda de los Hornos district of Viesca. The travelers required several caravans for their trip, each under the leadership of a prominent citizen. According to Black Seminole oral tradition, "the Mexicans gave them wagons to go to the Laguna." Again, official records support oral history. In April local authorities had obtained four carts for transporting the baggage of the first group and sought two more wagons for non-Mascogo blacks.

The first party left Nacimiento on May 21, 1859. Then, with other blacks from the Rancho del Rincón, they set out from Muzquiz several days later. Felipe Alvarez led the some eighty persons, who were supplied with a scanty amount of ammunition and one cow for their journey.[4]

The few remaining Seminole tribespeople remained at Nacimiento under Nokosimala until August 1861, when they finally returned to the United States. Thereafter, the only Seminoles in Mexico were the Mascogos at Parras, although ten cuarterones and their families stayed in Nacimiento.[5]

The story of the Mascogos in the Laguna de Parras region is vague and fragmentary. Unfortunately, in early 1911 the Parras municipal archives were used as fuel during the Mexican Revolution. Therefore, nearly all the documentary record of the Laguna chapter of Black Seminole history is gone. Even memories and traditions from this period are scant because most of the Mascogos were at Parras for only five years. By the 1940s a few travelers' accounts and memories were all that remained of this part of Mascogo history. Nevertheless, we can draw a broad picture.[6]

The Mascogos had been promised watered lands, but oral tradition holds that they never got them. At first, the colonists settled on the Hacienda de los Hornos. Later, another group stayed at the Hacienda de San Marcos, where they were seen in 1869. But the principal community apparently was established at the Hacienda El Burro, halfway between the lake and the city of Parras.

The Black Seminoles never received a formal land grant in the Laguna. Instead, they "settled in little groups, wherever they could find food, but they got together when there was anything important to decide." John Horse must have constantly visited the scattered communities looking after his people.

He was described as "wandering around, like an Indian, hunting for a home—he was always doing that."[7]

The Laguna area, although "a very prosperous agricultural country," was ravaged by hostiles. As before, the Mascogos tilled the soil and hunted; but now they were mainly professional warriors in campaigns against Apaches. Unlike the situation in Nacimiento, where their chief profit—apart from use of the hacienda lands—came from recaptured horses, they were now paid a scalp bounty.

A Texas unionist fleeing across Mexico to California was at Parras in early November 1861. "One evening," he reported, "a dozen Negroes, once of the Seminole tribe, rode up to the Government house opposite our quarters; they had a scalp, and reported a fight they had with the Indians only a little distance from the town, right on our road. These Negroes are employed by the Mexicans to fight the Indians and are very successful."[8] Although they lacked the comparative prosperity and security of Nacimiento, the Mascogos were highly respected and favored in the Laguna, at least for their military skills; and they apparently operated independently.

An ex-Texas Ranger investigating local mineral resources encountered John Horse about 1861. He described him as "a stalwart negro, sometimes called Juan Caballo . . . or more commonly *Juan Vidaurri*." John was then leading two hundred soldiers, both Mexican and black. At Nacimiento he had been subordinate to both the Seminole chief and the Mexicans while campaigning. But he was now an officer, probably with the rank of colonel, and reportedly wore a uniform.[9]

Despite the respect accorded to their leader, the Black Seminoles longed for their Nacimiento lands. Probably in late spring of 1861, they appealed through the *alcalde* of Muzquiz for permission to return to Nacimiento. Governor Vidaurri, however, refused the request for the same reasons that had originally led to their relocation. As 1861 ended, the Mascogos, "numbering 40 to 60 persons" (*persons* in Mexican usage usually meant heads of family), were still at Parras.[10]

Not all the colonists came to the Laguna at the same time and under John Horse. Elijah Daniels, a Black Creek, reportedly became part of the group at the Laguna. He was born around 1830, probably in Georgia before the Creek removal to Indian Territory. Daniels eventually married Melinda Wilson, who was from another Black Creek family that had joined the Mascogos.

Daniels apparently was an unusual man for his time. He stood five feet, ten inches tall; wore gold earrings; and spoke several languages. A carpenter by trade, he could also write, as a few surviving handwritten letters, readable but filled with colorful misspellings and grammatical errors, attest. Along with Caesar Payne, Daniels seems to have become John Horse's second in command at the Laguna.[11]

Besides welcoming people such as Elijah Daniels, the Black Seminoles had always allowed runaways to join them. Three who did so were the Gordon brothers: Albert (the oldest), Henry, and Isaac. Albert was the first of the trio to flee into Mexico. After reaching the Laguna, he found the Mascogos living in freedom and was so impressed that he returned to Texas to retrieve his brothers. Although captured at Eagle Pass, they escaped and eventually found John Horse's band. Henry Gordon became so "Seminole" that, in the 1880s, when a group of Black Seminoles returned to Indian Territory, he and his family went along.[12]

Hostiles constantly threatened the group at the Laguna. According to one vivid recollection, "they'd ride up at 12 o'clock noon, kill people plowing the fields, fill their oxen with arrows, cut steaks off them while they were still alive." Thomas Factor was a victim of such an ambush. He was a brother of July, John Horse's father-in-law, who had been killed in Florida while serving as a guide. Thomas had adopted the surname of the Seminole Indian Nelly Factor, who had claimed him as her property. As his daughter later recalled, Thomas Factor was wounded during a raid and lingered several months before dying.[13] During a different attack, Friday and Jack Bowlegs lost all their family members.

Another raid, against Dick Grayson's camp, resulted in the capture of his young son, Dick Jr., and led to a major encounter with the hostiles—known in Black Seminole oral history as "the big fight."[14] Always known for their swift retaliation, the Mascogos were particularly vengeful now that a small child had been seized. As express riders carried the news to the scattered black communities, the men gathered at a central point under their subchiefs. John Horse commanded the thirty or forty fighters, while a score or so were left behind to guard the families.

Presently, the strike force rode to the nearest Mexican town to get more ammunition and provisions. At about the same time, a troop of Mexican soldiers (National Guardsmen) joined them. Several days after the raid, they were finally ready to hunt. A few Mascogo scouts preceded the group as they departed. John Horse was at the head of his heavily armed and well-mounted men, while the Mexicans brought up the rear.

The scouts, who were renowned for their tracking skills, found that the trail, although old, was remarkably plain. They kept their mounts at a brisk walk, constantly turning in their saddles to wave on the main body. They followed the spoor for several days. When it became even clearer, the outriders no longer rode far in advance and closed with the others.[15]

The cavalcade emerged from a stand of mesquite onto a small, stony plain. On the other side of the plain, a rifle shot away, was more mesquite, with cottonwoods and willows in the distance suggesting water. In the midst of this open space stood a large cleft rock. When they reached it, John Horse suddenly reined up and lifted his hand to signal a halt. Gesturing the subchiefs to his side, John said that the pursuit had been "too easy," the trail "too clear." He believed the hostiles they were tracking wanted to be followed, and he wanted to send the scouts ahead. After the men reported back, they would all "take counsel" and decide what to do. The others agreed, and three Mascogos galloped off.

The more experienced warriors realized that danger was near and needed no orders to prepare for it. The younger ones followed their example. All swung into a semicircle resembling a fully bent bow, with their convex side toward the more distant mesquite. Those on well-trained horses and equipped with rifles kept to their saddles, but the men with more ponderous weapons or on skittish animals dismounted. They fixed the points of two stakes, looped together with rawhide, into the hard earth. After adjusting the staves to their proper height, they rested their heavy muskets on them and prepared the firearms for action. Those taking part in their first war party held the riderless mounts in the middle of the semicircle.

John Horse rode forward to the point on the bow where an arrow would have rested and gazed intently toward the mesquite. Suddenly, a rifle shot rang out, then two more in rapid succession. The blacks gripped their weapons more tightly. John Horse looked around the semicircle, held up his hand both to warn and calm his men, and focused again on the mesquite. Soon two scouts burst out of the thicket, lying low on their lathered horse's necks. They were closely followed by their comrade.

Gathered around John Horse, the trio breathlessly described a big Indian camp they had stumbled upon. One scout thought the tribespeople were Comanches, while the other two identified some as Lipan and Mescalero Apaches. But all three scouts agreed that there were many warriors right behind them. John immediately ordered his men to prepare to fight.[16]

An ominous hum soon became a faint yelling that increased in volume and menace. Suddenly, a hard-riding horde burst from the scrub all along the front of the assembled blacks. The hostiles whooped triumphantly when they saw the tiny semicircle facing them. They quickly discharged a few random shots and arrows that hummed harmlessly overhead or curved and fell short.

The Mexican officer stared in momentary disbelief. Then he jerked around his mount and quirted him frantically through the ranks of his startled followers down the back trail. His troopers spurred after him.

John Horse continued to calm his nervous men, ordering them to stand firm as the enemy bore down on their thin ranks. Then he deliberately lifted his rifle to his shoulder, aiming carefully at a Comanche warrior riding a length ahead of the other hostiles. As the attackers drew near, John pulled the trigger. The leading tribesman toppled from his saddle.

"Yo-ho-ee-hee!" John's exultant yell, reminiscent of the Seminole war cry in Florida, accompanied an irregular crackle of fire as his riflemen picked their targets and discharged their weapons. Attackers fell off their speeding mounts or clutched frantically at manes. Some horses went down, throwing the riders over their heads, while others bucked and reared. Several hostiles, faced with murderous fire, pulled up sharply, throwing their ponies to their haunches, then jerked them around and forced the animals back through the oncoming ranks. The more daring Indians swept on from behind, lying low on their horses' necks and flogging them ahead. The Mascogos began firing muskets and *escopetas* (shotguns) that had been kept in reserve. Still more warriors went down. Even the most courageous now swung to the left and right of their mounts for protection as they rode around the semicircle. The Black Seminoles instinctively formed a ring as they were surrounded.

For a few minutes, uncertainty reigned. The tribesmen had lost heavily but could still overrun the little band if sufficiently determined to push the charge home—and John Horse knew it. In order to stop the initial attack, his men had maintained such heavy fire that all their weapons, except for a few pistols, were now empty. Another hostile charge before they reloaded their firearms would be fatal.

Suddenly, one chief whooped and galloped forward, an inspired rush that could galvanize the others to act. But when John boldly raised his empty rifle and leveled it, the leader and his few followers veered off. John quickly ordered his horsemen to point their spent weapons while those on foot reloaded. This bluff, plus the many casualties lying between the mesquite and the blacks, made the Indians hesitate. When the Mascogos on the ground had reloaded, John and the other riflemen slid from their horses. Sheltered by the animals' bodies, they reloaded their own weapons.

Deliberately and ominously, the attackers began to circle the small band. At first, they circled just beyond easy rifle shot, but they soon drew closer. Hanging against their ponies' far sides, the warriors only occasionally exposed themselves, a maneuver intended to wear down their enemy. But John Horse, familiar with the tactic, coolly ordered his men to hold their fire until the hostiles moved closer.[17]

Presently, Indian muskets begin to bang sporadically. But even their best marksmen were inaccurate while shooting from under the necks of their speeding mounts. Nevertheless, even a random bullet will sometimes hit a mark. About this time, elderly Squash Grayson was wounded. Despite his advanced age, he had joined the expedition to rescue his grandson. The bullet, fortunately, inflicted only a flesh wound.

The warriors were now close enough for the black sharpshooters to display their skill again. Although the attackers were using their ponies for cover, it was possible for one rifleman to drop an animal while another targeted its rider before he could reach cover. But even as more horses and tribesmen went down, the moving circle continued to narrow.

Scores of arrows began stitching the air in vicious curves, finding marks within the small ring of defenders. But the attackers did not launch their arrows directly at the blacks; they wanted to avoid injuring the animals protecting the Mascogos. Rather, they arched them over the rampart of horseflesh to strike the defenders on the circle's far side.

Two sons of John Wilson were the first casualties. A shaft struck Adam in the hip and sank above its barbs. His brother Peter turned as Adam cried out. Peter seized the arrow's end—disregarding warning shouts and frantic gestures of veterans who saw his intent—and yanked it out. Then he stared in horrified anguish at the bloody crater left in his brother's body. Moments later, a shaft struck Peter's hip almost exactly where Adam had been hit. He reeled but did not fall. Supporting his wounded brother, he staggered with him out of the fighting line and collapsed.

It was a bad hour for the Wilson family. Another arrow completely tore through subchief John Wilson's chest. He turned silently to a companion, who drew his knife. Steadying the shaft, his friend sawed its head off, jerked it out, and wrapped a dressing tightly about the wound. An arrow also pierced Cato Wilson through the groin and hip. Bristow, young brother of John Wilson's wife, Phyllis Bruner (but known as Wilson because his brother-in-law had adopted him), fell dead or mortally wounded; and John Wilson, Jr., also died.

Within a few minutes, at least one Mascogo had been killed and a half-dozen wounded, one mortally. John Horse had lost at least one-fifth of his command. Although they must have inflicted a much larger loss on the enemy, the blacks were greatly outnumbered. They were simply unable to swap casualties at such a rate. The defenders who were still standing desperately blazed away at the circling Indians.

John repeatedly loaded and fired from behind his horse while anxiously watching the attackers. Without warning, the hostiles charged again. One chief swung his pony about and, screaming his war cry, headed straight for the blacks. John vaulted into the saddle with an answering shout. He ordered his men to remount and fight their foe hand to hand. From all sides, the hostiles poured in; and the blacks jumped on their horses to meet the attack.

The Mascogos, whether on horseback or on foot, battled the tribesmen in their best fighting tradition. Some of the stronger men used their muskets as clubs. They beat down buffalo-hide shields, splintered lance shafts, and rammed iron-shod stocks into their enemies' astonished faces. Others used cold steel. Hacking off spear points, they maneuvered inside their opponents' guard and decapitated them with murderous precision. Handsome, smooth-faced Dick Grayson, Sr., fought his son's captors with reckless fury. But while grappling with a knife-wielding adversary, he was mortally wounded.

At this point John Horse made a bold decision. He ordered his men to regroup and reload their weapons but not to fire until told. Then he screamed his terrifying Seminole war cry, rallying the defenders into a mounted circle. They fought almost shoulder to shoulder, desperately trying to repel the attack. Those kneeling within the ring—virtually under the plunging hooves—

prepared their firearms for action. The Mascogo horsemen's machetes swept in wider and fiercer circles, and musket butts clubbed with redoubled force.

But the small band of blacks was inexorably compressed by the clubs and spear thrusts assailing them from all sides. Annihilation seemed inevitable, when a pistol was suddenly shoved into John Horse's hand. As one of the subchiefs shouted that all the guns were loaded, John gave the order to fire.

The blast seemed to lift some of the hostiles out of their saddles. Virtually their entire first rank fell from their ponies or pulled out of the melee. John saw his chance and ordered a charge. The mounted Black Seminoles rushed the dazed survivors, who abruptly turned their horses and galloped off in full flight, knowing the clash was lost. The Mascogos who still had loaded weapons fired until the Indians disappeared into the mesquite.[18]

John ordered his men to pursue the fleeing warriors, chase them into their camp, and search for young Dick Grayson. He spurred after the hostiles, and his best-mounted men followed him. They overtook and killed a few tribesmen on lame or wounded animals. Soon all the Mascogos, except for those seriously wounded and the young horse holders, dashed along the plainly marked trail toward the enemy encampment. Although a few warriors rallied among their buffalo-hide tepees and quickly died there, most fled into the surrounding mesquite. Dick Grayson, Jr., was found in one of the lodges, apparently forgotten by his captors. After rescuing the boy, John Horse ordered his men to burn the camp.

Burying their dead, the weary Black Seminoles then rode back to the Laguna. Although it had been a long trail and a tough fight, the Mascogos had successfully battled an entire camp of Comanches and Apaches. They had fought them hard and "whupped them out!"

During the time that the Black Seminoles lived in the Laguna, Mexico remained in constant turmoil. The War of the Reform between Benito Juarez's liberals and the conservatives lasted until 1861. Then the victorious but tired Juaristas had to fight the French. Their emperor, Louis Napoleon Bonaparte, longed for an empire like that of his famous uncle, Napoleon. With Mexico in disarray and the Americans embroiled in their own civil war, French timing was perfect. The War of the Intervention began in December 1861.

For a while, the fighting directly impacted only the coastal and southern areas of Mexico. But as the defending Juaristas were pushed back, the conflict eventually spread north and engulfed the region where the Mascogos were located. In mid-1863 President Juárez had to withdraw to Monterey, Coahuila. Out of favor with Juárez, Santiago Vidaurri quickly fled to Texas. In August the Franco-Imperialist forces advanced again. They captured Monterey and Saltillo, forcing Juárez to flee again, first to Parras and then to Chihuahua.[19]

During this time, Juárez evidently met John Horse. According to a knowledgeable source, "John Hoss . . . applied to President Juarez for permission to return to the Nacimiento." The Mexican leader gave him "a verbal right to go there and occupy two leagues of the land." But "apparently no written title or paper is on record of said transaction."[20]

Before the Mascogos could leave for Nacimiento, involvement in the war thwarted them. Early in 1865 the Laguna rose against the invaders, driving them out of Saltillo and Monterey. But their triumph was short-lived; enemy forces soon reoccupied the two cities. Using Parras as a base, they operated extensively in the vicinity.

About this time John's people apparently encountered the French. Enraged by the hostility of the local population, the French soldiers retaliated by destroying the small communities of the Laguna, including El Burro where the blacks lived. Rosa Fay was a little girl "running around" when French troops attacked her town. "My brother Toby," she said, "was in bed with the smallpox when they were burning the house next to us. The soldiers were just running from one house to the next with torches, putting them to the thatch . . . but they didn't burn our house."

According to available evidence, John Horse, true to his principle of nonintervention in Mexican political disputes, had not taken up arms either for or against Maximilian. So when the French entered the town and—apparently unopposed—began to burn it, he went out to meet them. His son, Joe Coon, and David Bowlegs accompanied him. But when John tried to speak to the French commander, he was so nervous that his stuttering made him unintelligible. His two companions quickly intervened and identified themselves. The French officer acknowledged that he knew about them and advised them to return to Nacimiento. He reportedly ordered that their houses be spared.[21]

Maximilian was also aware of the Black Seminoles. Don Jacobo Sanchez Navarro, one of his principal supporters, still claimed Nacimiento, and the emperor had reportedly paid Don Jacobo "a large sum for these four sitios and other lands at Nacimiento." Maximilian wanted the property for the Mascogos. His arrangement with Don Jacobo might have resulted from the Sanchez Navarro family's offer of 2 million acres in Coahuila, including Nacimiento, for Maximilian's use in a proposed colonization scheme.[22]

By late June 1866 the Juaristas again possessed Parras, and later that year the French began withdrawing from Mexico. Maximilian was forced to surrender in May 1867 and was soon court-martialed. On June 19 a firing squad executed him. A few days later, Santiago Vidaurri was captured and shot dead.[23]

Meanwhile, due either to Juárez's verbal permission, a suggestion from the French officer who had spared their houses at El Burro, or a direct order from Maximilian, some Mascogos did return to Nacimiento in 1865. They traveled under the leadership of John Kibbitts. According to oral tradition, John Horse gave him "a paper . . . to hold Nacimiento against white or red— or green, or any other color, for that matter!" John Horse and the rest of his followers stayed at the Laguna.

One of those who went to Nacimiento in 1865 was a little girl named Julia, daughter of Benjamin Shields and Kitty Johnson. The child, then about two or three years old, had been given to her grandparents, John and Nancy Kibbitts, to be raised. In return, she was expected to help them as they aged. She rode to Nacimiento on horseback, sitting in front of her grandmother.[24]

The Mascogos, who had been unable to keep together at the Laguna, now split even further apart. Some groups had already drifted so far from the main body that, for a time, the rest of the Black Seminoles lost contact with them. With the American Civil War over and slavery abolished in the United States, a few had even returned to Texas. Elijah Daniels and some others were now on the Nueces River in Uvalde County, some seventy miles east of Del Rio. The group included his own family, his brothers-in-law Peter and Tony Wilson with their families, and probably other members of the large Wilson clan. Tony Warrior and his wife and children were also there.

Other Black Seminoles who left the Laguna went to Matamoros, across the border from Brownsville, Texas. By 1870 Joe Coon; Friday, Aleck, Jacob, and Julio Bowlegs; and Dick Johnson and his stepchildren, Peter and Monday Bruner, had moved across the border to Brownsville. They worked there as farm laborers.[25]

When the Mascogos under John Kibbitts arrived in Nacimiento in 1865, they found a large band of Kickapoos staying there. Trying to avoid involvement in the American Civil War, the tribespeople had left the Indian Territory for Mexico in the winter of 1864. They had come at the suggestion of a few of their kin, who had remained in Mexico after the main body returned to the U.S. in 1851. But during their journey, a Confederate Texas force had ambushed the Kickapoos at Dove Creek in Tom Green County. The warriors routed the soldiers, who sustained heavy losses. One authority said that it was "the most disastrous defeat ever suffered by the Texans in their long history of Indian wars . . . ; considering the attack at Dove Creek to be a declaration of war . . . the Kickapoos were able to rationalize their merciless campaign along the Rio Grande until the 1880's."

The Indians eventually reached Muzquiz and finally settled in Nacimiento, probably with the consent of the local authorities. Six white families, most likely unionist refugees from Texas, and eight or ten black families were also living at Nacimiento. According to the Kickapoo chief, No-ho-aht, "the whites left in the spring of 1866."[26] The blacks possibly were the vanguard of the Mascogos returning from the Laguna, but more likely they were individual black settlers who had managed to avoid being deported earlier.

In 1861 the alcalde in Muzquiz had been ordered to expel the cuarterones from Nacimiento. No evidence has been found, however, that he actually did. In fact, in 1863 four cuarterones—Benjamin, Hache or Archie, Walter, and Marcos—with their wives and a Mexican vaquero reportedly defended Nacimiento from an attack by two hundred Lipan Apaches. Undoubtedly, Benjamin and Hache were Benjamin and Archibald Shields, who had intermarried with the Mascogos.[27]

With the Seminoles and most of the blacks gone, the Lipans had apparently decided to destroy the settlement to avenge all the successful expeditions that had come from there. One evening, a vaquero named Ysobel Rubio was camped in the valley of the Sabinas. Suddenly he noticed that his horse, Listón, was nickering nervously and looking toward Nacimiento. The Mexican decided to ride cautiously in that direction. Presently, he saw a raiding party headed for the settlement, so he frantically quirted his mount to reach Nacimiento before the Apaches did.

In the early dawn, when the warriors swept down on what they presumed would be an easy target, the four black men and Rubio were waiting. From the loop-holed houses, they greeted the invaders with accurate fire. The settler's wives, and probably the grown children, kept their weapons loaded. Perhaps the women also fired when the charges came particularly close to the palisade that linked the houses to each other and enclosed the village square. Still, the few defenders would have eventually been overwhelmed if Rubio had not again intervened. He mounted Listón, then somehow slipped through the encircling hostiles and galloped for Muzquiz. He soon returned with sixty men to end the siege.[28]

After returning to Nacimiento, the Mascogos resettled in their previous location, a few miles below the headwaters of the Sabinas. The Kickapoos had the more attractive but more exposed site formerly occupied by the Seminole tribespeople. According to oral tradition, the Kickapoos and John Horse formalized the arrangement. If, indeed, John went north to Nacimiento to negotiate with the Kickapoos, he quickly returned to the Laguna. Of the three hundred or so Black Seminoles then in Mexico (except for the few who had moved to Matamoros and into Texas), the main body stayed in the Laguna until late 1870 under the leadership of John Horse.[29]

His subchief, John Kibbitts, was not idle in Nacimiento. He soon appeared before the authorities at Monclova. After identifying himself as his people's leader, Kibbitts complained that Santiago Vidaurri had deprived them of their lands. He convinced the Mexican officials that "the Seminole and particularly the Mascogos have lent very important services to the State . . . and it is necessary that they continue to live there." On January 11, 1866, the Muzquiz authorities ordered the return of two of the four sitios de ganado mayor that had originally been given to the Seminoles and Mascogos in 1851. President Benito Juárez confirmed the grant in November 1866.[30]

PART FOUR

The Seminole Negro Indian Scouts, Texas, 1870–1914

CHAPTER FOURTEEN

⊠ Black Watch on the Rio Grande

These scouts were a mixture of Indian and the negro and were such cunning trailers and fearless fighters Lieutenant Bullis was nearly always successful when he went after a band of Indians.
DAVID W. BARNHILL

The 1866 Nacimiento land grant evidently failed to satisfy John Horse's restless people. Soon after they resettled in their former home, John Kibbitts complained that "the Mexicans stole horses and robbed them." Moreover, relations with the Kickapoos apparently were strained because the Indians considered their black neighbors to be squatters.[1]

At this time Mexico was constantly racked by revolution. But the American Civil War was over, and slavery had been abolished in the United States. Not surprisingly, the Mascogos yearned to return. Communication between those Black Seminoles who had never left Indian Territory and the ones who had moved to Mexico in 1850 had never entirely ended. When Robert Kibbitts, son of John Kibbitts, visited the Territory in 1869, he learned that some Seminoles, who had been Union loyalists, would welcome the blacks.

American officials also wanted the Black Seminoles back in the Territory. They felt that the Indian groups who had migrated to Mexico—including the Black Seminoles—constantly threatened Texas. So in 1869 the commissioner of Indian affairs suggested that John Horse's people be removed to the Territory where they could be better monitored.[2] In addition, beleaguered U.S. Army officers, their thin forces inadequate to protect the long, porous Rio Grande border, evidently respected the black warriors' fighting and tracking abilities, crafts they had mastered during some twenty years of service to the Mexican government. The Mascogos could provide the scouting skills that the American military sorely needed.

John Kibbitts was formally invited to visit Fort Duncan at Eagle Pass, Texas, to discuss relocating his followers. On March 17, 1870, the subchief conferred with Captain Jacob C. DeGress, then commanding the post. During their meeting, DeGress presented Kibbitts with rations and a safe-conduct pass that allowed his band "to cross the Rio Grande and camp . . . [at] Fort Duncan until their request to move to Arkansas [Indian Territory] . . . [could] be considered." DeGress reported that the Kickapoos were also "anxious to move back to their Reservation in the United States."³ After Kibbitts left, the officer's initiative was quickly approved by the Department of Texas.

On March 30 Captain Frank W. Perry replaced DeGress. In early June, Perry and U.S. Consular Agent William Schuchardt traveled to Mexico to determine if the Kickapoos were really "anxious to move back to . . . the United States." After reaching Santa Rosa, they sent a messenger inviting both the Kickapoos and John Kibbitts to parley. The two officials were especially interested in relocating the tribespeople, who regularly launched crossborder raids from their Mexican sanctuary with the active support of the local authorities.

Although the Kickapoo chief never appeared, Kibbitts did. During the interview he stated that he was now "ready with part of his people to leave Mexico . . . and come to Fort Duncan, receiving rations and being employed as scouts until removed to the reservation designated to them."⁴ His offer to help suppress the hostiles running amok in Texas was well received by Captain Perry. The experienced officer knew how difficult it was for regular troops to locate and engage the swift-moving raiders who terrorized the frontier. As U.S. Army Inspector General Randolph B. Marcy wrote in 1871, "this . . . sector [of southwest Texas] does not contain today so many white people as it did when I visited it eighteen years ago, and if the Indian marauders are not punished, the whole country . . . [will] become totally depopulated."⁵

The tenor of subsequent negotiations between the Black Seminole leadership and the military is obscure. Years later, Julia Payne, John Kibbitts's step-granddaughter, remembered that "an American officer and some soldiers rode up to grandfather's home at Nacimiento. He was on a mule, and [had] a [white] flag to show he was a fren'." She recalled that the man wanted her people's help in fighting "Injuns . . . in Texas." The officer promised the men "$25 in silver every month and everybody, women, and children, too, [would get] plenty rations . . . good rations."

If Captain Perry ever did visit Nacimiento, no official record of it has been found; and because he died in June 1876, he was unavailable to comment on the matter in later years. Still, there is no question about how the Black Seminoles perceived their arrangement with the U.S. Army. First, they believed that Perry and Kibbitts had made a formal agreement, which they often referred to as "the treaty." Under it, they were to return to Texas where the able-bodied men would serve in the military. In turn, the government would pay their relocation expenses and "furnish . . . provisions . . . land . . . horses, plows, farming equipment, etc." When their scouting services were no longer needed, they would then be transported to land granted to them for permanent occupancy, presumably in Indian Territory.

Interestingly, John Horse did not directly participate in the negotiations. He was probably still at the Laguna de Parras in southwestern Coahuila. But Kibbitts apparently communicated with him and received his tentative approval. When the arrangement was actually concluded, John Horse was reportedly in Mexico City, shrewdly obtaining the Mexican government's consent for his people's removal to Texas. He never burned his bridges.[6]

The Mexican authorities reluctantly accepted John's request, stipulating, however, that the United States assume full responsibility for the Black Seminoles' future welfare. Reports state that a copy of the pact between the blacks and the Americans was sent to Mexico City to satisfy the Mexican government's concern, but it has never been located. The Mexicans also said that the blacks could reclaim their Nacimiento lands if they returned within five years. If not, their property would be forfeited.

On July 4, 1870, the first group of relocated Black Seminoles—one hundred men, women, and children—splashed across the Rio Grande and arrived at Fort Duncan. John Kibbitts led them. There was a stark contrast between this orderly event and the chaotic one they had experienced twenty years earlier, crossing at night in separate parties to avoid persecution. Now the Black Seminoles were both welcomed and needed in the United States.[7]

After meeting John Kibbitts, Major Zenas R. Bliss, who would shortly become Fort Duncan's commanding officer, described him as "very smart and reliable." During their talk, Kibbitts told the officer that "Gopher John . . . is living about two hundred miles southwest of Santa Rosa, Mexico, and has with him about one hundred and fifty negroes. There is also a party of these negroes near Matamoros, but how many Kibbitt does not know. . . . Gopher John told Kibbitt that he would join him . . . at Santa Rosa, and come here . . . but in case he did not arrive in time, Kibbitt was to come over, and the others would join him here. Gopher John and his party . . . will come soon."[8]

The blacks soon obtained permission to settle on Elm Creek, five miles from Fort Duncan. The able-bodied men were authorized to become scouts for six-month periods and paid the same wages as privates. John Kibbitts was to have a sergeant's rank and pay.

The first contingent of the unit officially known as the "Detachment of Seminole Negro Indian Scouts" was enlisted at Fort Duncan on August 16, 1870. Sergeant John Kibbitts proudly gave his Indian name as "Sit-tee-tas-to-nachy" (Sittee Tustenuggee or Snake Warrior). His ten privates included his son Robert (Bobby); Hardy Factor, John Horse's old and trusted aide, also known as "Yah-ha-tas-to-nocky" (Yaha Tustenuggee or Wolf Warrior); Hardy's sons Pompey and Dindie Factor; Adam Fay; Tony Warrior's son, John Ward; John Thompson; John Horse's nephew, George Washington; John Dixie or Dixon; and elderly John Wood (Picayune John), who had been Wild Cat's personal aide.[9]

On December 14, 1870, Major Bliss reported that "Gopher John, the chief of the Seminole Negroes, has come in, and reports that the rest of the tribe are on the road, and will soon be in." Shortly after he arrived, John Horse returned to Mexico, where he served as an interpreter for Bliss in his attempts to persuade the Kickapoos to relocate to the United States. Most, however, refused to move back.[10]

During the Black Seminoles' first few months at Fort Duncan, Major Bliss had plenty of opportunity to observe them. In his memoirs, he described them as "negroes [having] all the habits of the Indians. They were excellent hunters and trailers, and splendid fighters." Another officer wrote about their "ebony faces, flat noses and full lips, but [with] the characteristic high cheek-bones of the Indian, [and] . . . long black, crinkly hair." Probably there was a considerable range of physical traits in the group, from full-blooded blacks to those with strong Native American strains.

Their trailing skill was almost uncanny. Once, when Major Bliss was scouting with Robert Kibbitts, the officer spotted an old campfire with horse tracks nearby. Bliss immediately declared that Indians had been there. Kibbitts replied, "No, mustangs." He explained that "the fire had been built before the last rain" because the ashes were damp. But the wild animals "had passed after the rain, for there was mud spattered on the grass." Furthermore, the prints indicated hooves flatter and rounder than those of shod horses. Sure enough, the following morning the two men came upon seven riderless mustangs.

Captain Orsemus Bronson Boyd related an even more impressive example of the Seminole scouts' tracking ability. He wrote:

> At four o'clock one morning, a Seminole Indian, attached to the command, brought me intelligence that six hours previously six horses, four lodges, one sick Indian, five squaws, and several children had descended into the cañon one mile above us, and were then lost to sight. I asked:
> "Had they provisions?"
> "Yes; corn and buffalo meat."
> "How do you know?"
> "Because I saw corn scattered upon one side of the trail, and flies had gathered upon a piece of buffalo meat on the other."
> "How do you know that one of the Indians is sick?"
> "Because the lodge poles were formed into a travois, that was drawn by a horse blind in one eye."
> "How do you know the horse was half blind?"
> "Because, while all the other horses grazed upon both sides of the trail, this one ate only the grass that grew upon one side."
> "How do you know the sick one was a man?"
> "Because when a halt was made all the women gathered around him."
> "Of what tribe are they?"
> "Of a Kiowa tribe."
> And thus, with no ray of intelligence upon his stolid face, the Seminole Indian stood before me and told all I wished to know concerning our new neighbors, whom he had never seen.

Two hours later, Boyd found a small band of Kiowas. They were just as the unidentified scout had described them.[11]

The U.S. Army supplied the blacks, including the trackers, with arms and rations. Their slow-firing muzzle loaders were replaced first by Sharps and then by Spencer carbines that were short-barreled, accurate repeaters.

The scouts had to furnish their own mounts for which they received compensation.

The men usually dressed as they had while living in Florida and Mexico. A report dated December 31, 1871, describes their clothing as "good enough for Indians." Some of them were, of course, much more "Indian" than others. In later years, one man sported a buffalo-horn war bonnet like the ones worn by Plains tribesmen.

Because only routine military activity occurred on the border for several months after the enlistment of the first scout contingent, no additional Black Seminoles were needed.[12] By the fall of 1871, however, twenty more men were recruited. Nearly all were from the Elijah Daniels band of Black Creeks, who had been living and working at the Griffin ranch on the Nueces River in Uvalde County. Daniels and Caesar Payne, his second in command, joined the unit mostly because they had been working "for people . . . [who did] not pay" them. A few of the new recruits were Black Seminoles from the Matamoros/ Brownsville group.[13]

The scouts' initial months at Fort Duncan were fondly remembered by two daughters of Kitty Johnson, John Kibbitts's step-daughter. Julia Payne, the elder of the pair, was about seven or eight years old when her step-grandfather joined the military. In the early 1940s, she recalled that "at Fort Duncan they gave us nice wall tents on the hill until we could move down into the bottom and build mud houses . . . ; we never lacked for rations in those days; [we] had so much food we had to throw it away. Every eight days they'd drive up two or three beeves and kill them right there."

Molly Perryman, Julia's younger half-sister, recollected that the "Seminoles lived at first in tents at Ft. Duncan where the trestle of the railroad bridge [now] crosses." She also remembered helping Juana, John Horse's sister, draw water from the nearby Rio Grande.[14]

About this time, probably due to friction with the "pure Seminole" Kibbitts band, Daniels's independent-minded mixed Seminole and Creek group requested a transfer from Fort Duncan to Fort Clark, located about forty miles to the north in Brackettville, Texas. On August 3, 1872, three Daniels, six Wilsons, four Paynes, Renty Grayson, two Bruners, and John Ward (Warrior) arrived at their new post, exchanging the barren banks of the Rio Grande for the spring-fed, ever-flowing Las Moras Creek. The Black Seminoles soon established homes on both sides of the stream, which coursed through the Fort Clark reservation.[15]

In 1873 the combat era of the "Detachment of Seminole Negro Indian Scouts" began. Their previous activities had been largely routine—for example, guarding livestock and performing escort duties. But under the able, battle-hardened John Lapham Bullis, to whom many of them were assigned in March 1873, they would participate in nearly a decade of savage border warfare. The officer eventually commanded all the Seminole scouts.

In 1862 twenty-one-year-old Bullis first entered the military as a corporal in Company H, 126th New York Volunteer Infantry. After being captured at Gettysburg and later released, he was commissioned a captain in Company A, 118th United States Colored Troops in August 1864. Mustered out of the service in 1866, he quickly reenlisted in the regular army as a second lieutenant and was eventually attached to the Twenty-fourth Infantry—one of two black infantry regiments in the U.S. military. "Thin and spare . . . , [a] small, wiry man with a black mustache . . . [and] his face burned red as an Indian," Bullis soon demonstrated his leadership abilities.

On September 1, 1871, Bullis and four black troopers (or "buffalo soldiers") of the Ninth Cavalry's M Company encountered a group of "some (25) or so indians driving several herds of cattle, near Fort McKavett, Texas." After a fierce firefight with the hostiles, who held the high ground, Bullis found it "impossible to dislodge them with the number of men" he had with him. Nevertheless, they recovered two hundred of the stolen livestock. He ended his report of the action by saying, "My men done well."

Because of his experience with black soldiers, both in the Civil War and in Texas, Bullis was well suited to command the Black Seminoles for eight years during the 1870s. A real "snake eater" like his scouts, he also respected and trusted them. They felt the same about him. As Joe Phillips, who served under Bullis said, "he was a good man . . . he look after his men. . . . He didn't stan' back and say 'Go yonder'; he would say, 'Come on, boys, let's go get 'em.'"[16]

It is a credit to Bullis's ability and the Black Seminoles' skills that, in a dozen or so documented clashes from 1873 to 1881, they never lost a man or suffered a serious injury, even when greatly outnumbered. Furthermore, Bullis's men, who never numbered more than fifty, received four of the sixteen Medals of Honor awarded to the several thousand Native Americans who scouted for the U.S. Army in the West.[17]

In early 1873, as the Black Seminoles settled themselves along Las Moras Creek, the military brass debated about how to end the costly cross-border raiding by hostiles who lived in Mexico. Of greatest concern were the Kickapoos, but Lipan and Mescalero Apaches were also considered a menace. With Mexican authorities either unwilling or unable to prevent the tribesmen from attacking Texans and stealing their livestock, Colonel Ranald S. Mackenzie was selected to stop the border incursions.

In his memoirs, Ulysses S. Grant called Mackenzie "the most promising young officer in the army." Grant also said: "Graduating at West Point, as he did, during the second year of the [Civil] war, he had won his way up to the command of a corps before its close. This he did upon his own merits." Unlike Custer, the other "Boy General" of the Civil War, the intense and ascetic Mackenzie was no glory hound. He also won all his battles in the West. Mackenzie appreciated the value of effective units like that of Bullis and his men.[18]

After his transfer to Fort Clark on April 1, 1873, Mackenzie drilled his troops daily to increase their combat readiness. On April 11, 1873, Secretary of War W. W. Belknap and General Philip H. Sheridan visited the post. Sheridan ordered Mackenzie to carry out "a campaign of annihilation, obliteration and complete destruction" of the Mexico-based marauders. Interestingly, there was no written authorization for the expedition. When Mackenzie asked about written orders, Sheridan allegedly retorted: "Damn the orders! Damn the authority! You are to go ahead on your own plan of action, and your authority shall be Gen. Grant [then the president] and myself."[19]

On May 17 Colonel Mackenzie's command crossed the Rio Grande. He led six companies of his crack Fourth Cavalry regiment, eighteen Black Seminole scouts from Fort Clark under First Lieutenant Leopold Parker, and sixteen more from Fort Duncan under Bullis. The Black Seminoles rode immediately behind Mackenzie and his aides.

After a forced march of approximately eighty miles, traveling all night at a "killing pace," the four hundred or so men struck the Lipan, Mescalero, and Kickapoo settlements near Remolino, Mexico, early the next morning. According to Black Seminole oral history, the expedition's targets should have been only the Lipans and Mescaleros, not the Mascogos' former Kickapoo neighbors. But because the three bands were camped so near one another, Mackenzie's troops erroneously attacked the Kickapoos. Black Seminole opinion about this event is not confirmed by official reports. The Kickapoos' record of pillage and murder in Texas justified, at least to the American officials, their punishment.

When Mackenzie ordered the charge, the raiders poured into the villages in successive waves. Later, a descendant of one of the Kickapoo survivors said that the villagers "ran together like ants." After realizing that it was the U.S. Army attacking them, the Kickapoos quit resisting. Moreover, most of their warriors had left to hunt deer two days before. But the Lipans, both male and female, had been bred in the tradition of no-quarter warfare against the United States; and many fought fiercely. The Mescaleros, whose settlement was most distant from the killing field, melted into the brush.

The orders were to spare women and children. As the battle raged about him, Seminole scout Tony Wilson had a Lipan in his sights. Just as he squeezed the trigger, his target threw up an arm and revealed that she was female. But her gesture came too late. The black's carbine cracked, and the woman fell dead. Wilson was reportedly haunted for the rest of his life by this error in judgment. It eventually made him insane.

The short one-sided clash destroyed the three villages, killed at least nineteen Indians, and resulted in the capture of forty women and children. Sixty-five ponies were taken, some marked with Texas brands. The troops had one mortally wounded and two less seriously injured. The only adult male Lipan seized was elderly Costilietos, the principal chief, who was lassoed by Black Seminole Renty Grayson. Costilietos's daughter was also among the prisoners. Under the name of Marcia, she later married scout James Perryman. The ceremony was performed "with a Bible" by Lieutenant Bullis himself.

After the action, the victorious expeditionary force laboriously returned to Texas, their progress slowed by the captives and their wounded. The Seminole scouts served as flankers, guarding the column's rear during the long, difficult withdrawal to the Rio Grande.

Black Seminole oral tradition holds that the Kickapoo prisoners—several of them possibly acquainted with Bullis's men—were not outraged by the attack. They probably accepted it as part of border warfare. The Black Seminoles were very solicitous to them during the slow trip back to Texas, even giving the Kickapoos water from their own canteens. By the time the group reached Fort Clark, the two factions "were just like brothers."[20]

In his official report of the mission, Colonel Mackenzie praised "Liet. Bullis with the Seminole Scouts, who charged under the command of that gallant officer very well." The Remolino raid was applauded by Americans in general, but particularly by those in Texas. Mackenzie's ruthless strike largely ended crossborder incursions by Mexico-based hostiles for the next few years. Although Mexican public opinion condemned the invasion, the weak central government of President Lerdo de Tejada protested it only mildly.[21]

On July 10, 1873, the commanding officer of Fort Clark reported: "There are in the band [of Black Seminoles] here twenty seven (27) enlisted men, and Eighty two (82) old men, women, and children, and about the same number at [Fort] Duncan." He did not, however, say how frustrated the two hundred or so people at both posts were. The blacks wanted the land that they thought had been promised to them. They expected that it would be in the Indian Territory, where their families could stay while the men fulfilled their military obligation to the U.S. government.

On June 28, 1873, Elijah Daniels, more articulate than his brethren, had applied for a "Track of Land in the state of . . . Arkansaw Where we can have a home for Life Time." (The Black Seminoles always referred to the Territory as Arkansas.) He also requested rations and equipment while the families were getting settled. His petition eventually caused the relocation issue to be considered by two special commissioners who were advising the Bureau of Indian Affairs in mid-1874. The pair was attempting to bring the few Kickapoos, still in Mexico, back to the Territory. The officials wanted them to join their kin who, albeit reluctantly, had gone there shortly after the Remolino raid.[22]

At this point, rations were being distributed only to men on active duty and to the Black Seminole women working as laundresses. This practice was justified in order to pressure the scouts into reenlisting. But three-fourths of the people were women, children, old men, and others not able to serve in the military. Thus, the blacks had to subsist on the wages of the few enlisted scouts. Because they were unable to grow enough food for everyone along either Elm Creek or Las Moras Creek, their plight worsened. On one occasion, Fort Duncan's commanding officer, Lieutenant Colonel William R. Shafter, visited the Black Seminole camp located near his post. He reported that "several . . . persons had eaten nothing that day and none of them had more than a little refuse corn," which they had scavenged at the fort's warehouse.[23]

Meanwhile, since his people had returned to the United States, John Horse's position was an anomalous one. Late in 1873 John Kibbitts claimed that, sometime after they had gone to Mexico, "John Horse was removed from the head of the tribe and I was put in his place . . . for several years." Kibbitts also stated that the Black Seminoles in Texas had voted for headman and that he had "received the vote by 17." But years later an elderly Black Seminole woman had another recollection: "John Horse was the only chief of the Seminole after Wild Cat. John Kibbitts was chief only from Nacimiento to Texas. . . . If John Kibbitts was ever elected chief it was because only his followers were voting!"

Apparently, the blacks' separation into two main factions while in Mexico— one at Laguna de Parras under John Horse and the other at Nacimiento under John Kibbitts—had weakened John Horse's authority over the entire group. After Kibbitts negotiated the relocation to Texas and became a sergeant in the first scout unit, John's power was further undermined. John Horse never enlisted in the scouts, which probably diluted his influence as well. Although men of his age such as Hardy Factor did enlist, John may have refused to serve under a former subordinate. Nevertheless, he possibly had some say in the detachment's affairs. "John Kibbitts led the scouts," stated Curly Jefferson, "and John Horse gave advice."[24]

Perhaps, all things considered, he deliberately avoided official ties to the U.S. Army, assuming that his people's respect for him would maintain his prestige. In fact, some sixty years after his death, John Horse was still regarded with awe and affection by those who had known him as children. His powerful frame, handsome features, and erect carriage were clearly remembered. One person said, "He was a tall man, big, stout, proud; he walked proud." They described the attention he gave to his clothing. He sometimes dressed "like an Indian" and other times as a white man.[25]

In late 1873 John Horse reasserted his leadership and, once again, acted as his people's champion. He decided to go to Washington and directly ask the president of the United States to help them. Black Seminole oral tradition holds that John rode on horseback to San Antonio and then continued his journey by train. But he did not achieve his goal of obtaining a permanent home for the blacks. So while returning from Washington, John stopped at San Antonio to talk with Brigadier General C. C. Augur, the Department of Texas commander. John Kibbitts joined him there. On December 10, 1873, they formally petitioned Augur for the land that Captain Perry had allegedly promised them.

John Horse urged that the government "give us a home for the sake of our children." It could be located in Florida or the Indian Territory so "that they [the children] may learn something and get schooling." He further requested "full rations for my people" and that "the Mexicans who are intermarried with my people, and which are with us, and good men, may be enlisted for scouting."[26]

The two men impressed Augur. About six weeks after the interview, he wrote to the U.S. Army adjutant general in Washington: "In December last . . . John Horse, a very old man and former Headman of this band, together with John Kibbitts the present Headman, came here to see me. . . . John Horse is, with his friends, anxious to go to the Seminole Agency." General Augur expressed his concern about the blacks' dilemma. He worried about what would happen if John Horse's people were not helped and was concerned that "they . . . [would], in sheer desperation to prevent starving, have to resort to steal-ing and preying upon the white settlers. This . . . [would] beg retaliation, and in a short time it . . . [would] cost vastly more to restore peace, than . . . to give them the desired support." But regretfully Augur had to tell John Horse and Kibbitts what they already knew—that the Indian Department would not as-sist them, and the "War Department could do nothing beyond enlisting all who were fit for service."[27]

As a consequence, some Black Seminoles returned to Mexico, primarily to maintain their rights to the Nacimiento land. But most remained in Texas, stubbornly believing that the American government would eventually grant them justice.[28]

CHAPTER FIFTEEN

⊠ Blood on the Saddle

The old people in those days were so loving with one another. That's why things went the way they did in the fighting—none killed and few wounded. The old people were doing some powerful praying.

PENNY FACTOR

A detachment of Black Seminoles—Titus Payne, George Washington, Adam Payne, Aaron Payne, and two others—saw action the very day that John Horse and John Kibbitts were vainly pleading for their rights in San Antonio.

On December 10, 1873, forty-one men of the Fourth Cavalry, under Lieutenant Charles L. Hudson, and the six scouts based at Fort Clark encountered a raiding party of nine Kiowas and twenty-one Comanches near Kickapoo Springs, Texas. The warriors, who lived on a reservation near Fort Sill, Indian Territory, had been marauding on both sides of the border. In the ensuing battle, nine hostiles, including the favorite son of Kiowa chief Lone Wolf, were killed. The dead also included one of his nephews. Eighty-one horses were captured, and only one soldier was slightly wounded.[1]

Despite all the problems the Black Seminoles faced, new recruits continued to join the scouts in late 1873 and during the next two years. The most prominent of them belonged to the July family. They included the father, Sampson, son of Chief July from Peliklakaha, Florida, and his eldest children—Carolina, John, and Charles—all of whom enlisted at Fort Duncan in 1874 and 1875. The Julys were the last Mascogo family to come from Mexico.[2]

In early 1874 General Augur granted one of John Horse's minor requests, to allow Mexicans married to Black Seminole women to become scouts. On

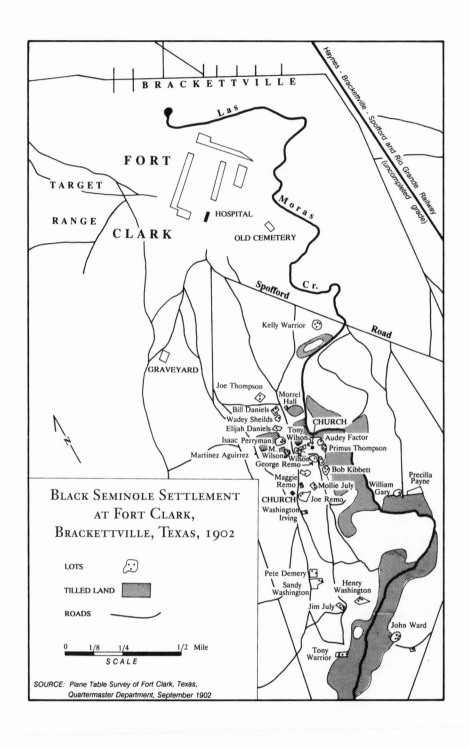

BRACKETTVILLE

Las

FORT

TARGET

Moras

RANGE

CLARK

HOSPITAL

OLD CEMETERY

Haynes · Brackettville · Spofford and Rio Grande Railway

(uncompleted grade)

Spofford Cr.

Road

Kelly Warrior

GRAVEYARD

Joe Thompson

Morrel Hall

Bill Daniels

Wadey Sheilds

CHURCH

Elijah Daniels

Tony Wilson

Audey Factor

Isaac Perryman

M. Wilson

Primus Thompson

Martinez Aguirrez

Wilson

George Remo

Bob Kibbett

Maggie Remo

Precilla Payne

Mollie July

William Gary

CHURCH

Joe Remo

Washington Irving

Pete Demery

Sandy Washington

Henry Washington

Jim July

John Ward

Tony Warrior

BLACK SEMINOLE SETTLEMENT
AT FORT CLARK,
BRACKETTVILLE, TEXAS, 1902

LOTS

TILLED LAND

ROADS

0   1/8   1/4   1/2 Mile
SCALE

SOURCE: *Plane Table Survey of Fort Clark, Texas,
Quartermaster Department, September 1902*

January 12 Trinidad Mariscal, a Mexican married to a Black Seminole, joined the scouts. Other non-Seminole recruits were Lewis White, an American black married to Dolly Bowlegs; Morrel Hall, a black ex-infantryman who later became pastor of the Seminole Baptist Church in Brackettville; and William Miller, son of a German father and a mulatto mother. Miller, who "looked like a white man and acted like an Indian," became a most daring and success-ful scout. Like Miller, another recruit, John F. (Joe) Remo, was not a Black Seminole but a Black Cherokee or a Choctaw. Remo himself claimed to have been born either in Louisiana or the Indian Territory. He had been a slave and was a Union Army veteran.[3]

The next important action for the Seminole scouts was in Colonel Macken-zie's campaign against the Southern Plains Indians (the Kiowas, Comanches, and southern Cheyennes) in the Red River War. In 1874 warriors from the three tribes left their hated reservations in Indian Territory and returned to their old hunting grounds in the Texas panhandle. They caused so much may-hem there that the U.S. Army sent a sizable force to track them down and herd them back to their reservations. Nearly three thousand troops, in six separate commands, were deployed to surround the tribesmen and end their uprising.

Mackenzie's southern column, the largest of the six units, marched north-westward from Fort Concho on August 23, 1874. Fifteen scouts from Fort Clark and six more from Fort Duncan rode with the soldiers. Lieutenant Bullis did not accompany them; he was sick and remained behind at Fort Concho.[4]

On the evening of September 19 three Black Seminoles—Sergeant James Bruner, Corporal George Washington (John Horse's nephew), and Private Adam Payne (or Paine)—were dispatched to locate hostiles. Two Tonkawa scouts, Johnson and John Willum, accompanied them. Operating as Mac-kenzie's spies, they were only to find the enemy and not engage them unless absolutely necessary. Therefore, the group traveled light.

Washington and, especially, Bruner were considered excellent trackers. Adam Payne's best quality was his aggressiveness; the other Black Seminoles admiringly called him a "bad man." He carried a Colt pistol, a double-bar-reled shotgun, and a large hunting knife. He also wore headgear adorned with buffalo horns, stood almost six feet tall, and weighed nearly two hundred pounds. He was so impressive-looking that one of the troopers, J. A. Magruder, later said: "I shall never forget . . . a big black . . . wearing horns."

The five men left their base camp, each leading a spare mount. After riding for several hours, the scouts stopped around midnight. Sometime after breaking camp the next day, they "found themselves surrounded by about forty (40) Kiowas . . . a hunting party . . . with their families. . . . A hot fight ensued. Only two (2) of the scouts, seminoles, named Adam Payne and George Washington, managed to shift their saddles and equipment from their riding to their [reserve] lead horses."

Although the precise details of the encounter are unclear, Payne apparently positioned himself between the warriors and his companions to defend them while they hurriedly switched to their fresh mounts. Then the five scouts, all but Payne now riding bareback, quirted their animals through the ring of attackers. They galloped southwest in the general direction of Mackenzie's command and "were obliged to run for their lives."

Several hostiles chased them and "a running fight followed for fifteen (15) miles." Adam Payne lagged behind the others because he rode a saddled horse laden with all his gear. Immediately in front of him was Private Washington. He had caught up with his saddled animal and was frantically trying to transfer its equipment to his fresh mount.

To protect Washington, Payne turned around and fired his shotgun at the closing warriors. The blast momentarily slowed them. Suddenly Payne's horse was "shot from under him." He rapidly stripped his gear from the dead animal and crouched behind it as the Indians charged.

When they drew nearer, Payne killed the closest attacker. While the others milled about in momentary confusion, he grabbed the slain man's riderless pony, which had continued to head toward him. Quickly saddling the animal, he leaped on its back and spurred after his comrades.

George Washington, meanwhile, had saddled his fresh horse and was galloping just ahead of him. Payne apparently covered Washington's and the other men's retreat by periodically slowing and firing at their pursuers.

At about two o'clock in the afternoon, the two Tonkawas reached the scouts' base camp. They were closely followed by Bruner and then Washington. As they slid off their lathered mounts, the exhausted men gasped, "Commanche Commanche, he gotta my saddle and my pony; come quick." Payne soon appeared with the hostiles right on his heels. But the "bunch of indians . . . withdrew in sight of . . . [the] camp." For his gallantry, Adam Payne was eventually awarded the Medal of Honor. Colonel Mackenzie wrote that he deserved such recognition for his "habitual courage. This man has, I believe, more cool daring than any scout I have known."[5]

About a week after Payne's daring exploit, 200–250 warriors struck Mackenzie's base near Boehm's Canyon, Texas, late on September 26. They hoped to stop the column's advance by stealing the soldiers' horses, but the frontier-wise officer had anticipated such a raid and had ordered that the animals be staked and hobbled. In addition, he had told "everyone . . . [to lie] down to sleep with his clothes on." The frustrated attackers, withdrawing just beyond pistol range, "kept up a desultory fire until daylight."

At dawn, Company E of the Fourth Cavalry and Lieutenant William H. Thompson's scouts (including both Black Seminoles and Tonkawas) routed the besiegers, chasing them for three miles and killing two of them. One of the warriors "was going up the side of an *arroyo* when a Seminole jumped down from his saddle, and taking deliberate aim, killed the Comanche's horse." A Tonkawa scout then shot the dismounted man. The troops sustained no casualties.[6]

The command's next target was Palo Duro Canyon in the Texas panhandle, the hostiles' stronghold. Comanchero Jose Tafoya guided U.S. forces there— but only after Mackenzie reportedly "propped up the tongue of a wagon and hanged Tafoya to the end [of it] until he was glad to talk." The troops reached the canyon on September 29, 1874, noting that it was so deep that the Indian ponies far below seemed no larger than "chickens."

At daybreak, an advance party of six white guides, thirteen Black Seminoles, and twelve Tonkawas descended into the gorge by a narrow goat path. The Fourth Cavalry, with Mackenzie in the lead, followed them. The tribespeople scrambled up the canyon walls, offering little resistance. The strike force killed three warriors; one soldier was wounded. Mackenzie's men also seized 1,400 horses. Most of them were destroyed the next morning to prevent their recapture.[7]

It was probably during the Palo Duro campaign that Costilietos's captor at Remolino, Renty Grayson, distinguished himself in a hand-to-hand fight with the enemy. As he told the story in 1927, some Seminole scouts were pursuing a war party up a hill when Grayson realized that his companions had vanished. He backtracked to find out why. During his descent, he spotted a hostile. Grayson darted behind a tree and began observing the Indian, who also concealed himself and watched the scout.

Grayson decided to lure the warrior into firing by showing his cap on the tip of his ramrod. The man obliged and shot it. Then, without reloading, certain his target had been dropped, he boldly emerged from his hiding place.

Grayson jumped up and snapped off two quick rounds. The tribesman fell. The scout ran over, pinned him down, and snarled in "Mexican," the frontier lingua franca: "I am goin' to kill you." The captive replied: "What are you goin' to kill me for?" The answer undoubtedly startled him: "Because you kill my father." The Black Seminole was referring to the death of his father, Dick Grayson, who had been knifed years before in Mexico during the "big fight" with hostiles who had kidnapped his eldest son, Dick, Jr.

The wounded man begged for mercy, but Renty Grayson ignored his pleas. He had already decided to slay him in the same way his father had died, "with a butcher knife." The scout holstered his revolver, took out his machete, and "went into him." The prisoner, however, facing sure death, began battling for his life.

A half hour of fierce combat followed in which the physically mismatched opponents fought on the ground and grappled while standing up. The diminutive Grayson recalled: "If he not got shot he would got the best of me. He was big and heavy . . . ; he could raise me up but I never could raise him up."

At one point, the warrior, weakened by his wounds, desperately grabbed his foe's machete blade. The black jerked the knife and "cut nearly all those fingers off." After he finally finished off the Indian, Grayson sat down and "thought [he had] . . . lived one thousand years."[8]

The Black Seminoles, including Renty Grayson, participated in two more engagements during Mackenzie's campaign. The first was on November 3, 1874, near Laguna Cuarto, when the scouts helped attack a hostile camp. The troops killed two warriors and captured nineteen women and children. They also seized 144 horses.

The second encounter took place on November 5 near Tahoka, Texas. Lieutenant Thompson, "with nine scouts, discovered a small herd of horses and, charging it, succeeded in cutting one Indian off from the herd; another, who mounted, was killed after a long chase . . . [and] the third escaped after being pursued several miles."

During November 1874, Colonel Mackenzie reiterated his respect for the Black Seminoles' capabilities. He wrote: "Three parties of spies were sent out on the 25th: one, consisting of two Mexicans and three seminole negroes, to look about certain hiding places in the Staked plains. . . . These men, of course, take great risks. . . . The Mexicans in one case before, I feel sure, laid up and came back and reported nothing, but they have with them now a Seminole negro, who is a very determined man on a scout, and they will be afraid not to go."[9]

By about New Year's Day 1875, Mackenzie had returned to Fort Concho; and the Black Seminoles were back at either Fort Clark or Fort Duncan. The remaining troops relentlessly harried the beleaguered hostiles throughout the bitterly cold winter. As a result, the warriors increasingly drifted back to their reservations. By early 1875 mass surrenders were commonplace, and the Red River War was over. The Kiowas, Comanches, and southern Cheyennes never seriously challenged the U.S. government again.[10]

On April 25, 1875, the most distinguished and best-remembered exploit of the Seminole scouts took place. Early that day, Lieutenant Bullis—with Sergeant John Ward, Private Pompey Factor, and Trumpeter Isaac Payne—struck a fresh trail made by about seventy-five horses. They followed it to the Eagle's Nest Crossing of the Pecos and spotted a raiding party just as the hostiles were fording the river to the western side.

After tethering their mounts and creeping to within seventy-five yards of the Indians, the little detachment opened fire. They kept up their blazing for about three-quarters of an hour, killing three warriors and wounding a fourth. Twice, the four scouts drove off the stolen horses. Eventually, the hostiles, "some 25 to 30" armed with Winchester repeaters, realized how few their attackers were. As Bullis later wrote, "we were at last compelled to give way, as they were about to get around us and cut us off from our horses."

The four men scrambled for their lives. Leaping onto their horses, the three scouts were galloping away when Sergeant Ward glanced back. He saw that Bullis's mount was extremely "frighten[ed] and he [Bullis] could noe [not] get on." The officer was left on foot in front of the rapidly closing warriors.

Ward shouted, "Boys don't lets us leave him." Wheeling his horse, he dashed back to Bullis with his two comrades close behind. The tribesmen unleashed a tremendous volley on the scouts, particularly Ward. A bullet cut his carbine sling just as he reached the lieutenant. Then, while he was pulling Bullis up on his horse's rear, another round shattered his weapon's stock. Throughout the rescue, Factor and Payne provided heavy covering fire.

The three Black Seminoles, with the officer on his "sergeant's horse, back of him," galloped to safety. In Bullis's words, they "saved my hair." They rode fifty-six miles that same day to reach Fort Clark. For their gallantry, all three scouts received the Congressional Medal of Honor on May 28, 1875.[11]

With Ranald Mackenzie now at Fort Sill closely monitoring the nearby Comanche and Kiowa reservations, Lieutenant Colonel William R. Shafter, (or "Pecos Bill," as his troops called him) became responsible for ridding western Texas of hostiles, especially renegade Apaches and Comanches. Like Mackenzie, Shafter used Bullis and his men to gather intelligence and operate as a mobile strike force. A detachment of Seminole scouts accompanied Shafter's column into the Staked Plains of northwestern Texas in the summer of 1875. The expedition's mission was both to clear the area of Indians and explore it, looking particularly for water sources.

On September 12, the Black Seminoles were part of a unit that was attacked by Apaches near Dug Spring, New Mexico Territory. Although the troops sustained no casualties, the raiders chased off four horses. The next day's pursuit was fruitless.

On the night of October 16 Lieutenant Bullis, Corporal Miller (the white-looking but Indian-acting mixed-blood scout), and two others crept into an Apache camp at Laguna Sabinas (now Cedar Lake). They stole some thirty-five horses and mules without being detected. Two days later, Shafter's troops destroyed the camp, although the hostiles escaped.

The last Black Seminole action with Shafter's command was on November 2, 1875. Troops led by Lieutenant Andrew Geddes and including Black Seminole scouts and buffalo soldiers from Companies G and L of the Tenth Cavalry, struck some hostiles camped approximately sixty miles above the mouth of the Rio Grande at a place called Shafter's Crossing. After killing one warrior, they captured four Apache women and one boy.[12]

But while the scouts were with Shafter, the conditions for their families at Forts Clark and Duncan worsened. On November 16, 1874, a U.S. special commissioner advised that the federal government was obligated to remove the blacks to the Indian Territory and provide for them. Lieutenant Bullis also tried to help his men and their families. On May 14, 1875, he reported that there were "151 Seminole Negro Indians" at Fort Clark, including sixty-seven children. He said that some of the elderly people, women, and children wanted to go to Indian Territory or Mexico; but he suggested that the government should obtain land for them in Texas near the posts where the scouts were serving.[13]

On May 9, 1875, a census of the Black Seminole community at Fort Duncan was taken. It revealed that out of a total of 106 people, more than one-fourth were old men (including John Horse), women, children, or disabled persons. They had nobody to support them regularly because most of the post's nineteen scouts had their own families to provide for.

One of the disabled at Fort Duncan was George Washington, John Horse's nephew. About Christmastime 1874, he had been injured in an altercation with the notorious King Fisher gang in an Eagle Pass saloon. Fisher himself was creased in the scalp by a bullet, while Washington suffered a stomach wound that eventually killed him. Although the outlaw was indicted for the attack, he was cleared of the charges. Fisher reportedly hated the Black Seminoles thereafter.[14]

Meanwhile, Lieutenant Bullis continued writing on his men's behalf. On May 28, 1875, he stated that "a few weeks ago, they [all] packed up and were about to return to Mexico, and were with difficulty prevented by the very old ones." He added that "their destitute condition has driven them to stealing." In his letter, Bullis emphasized that the scouts were "fine trailers and good marksmen." Colonel Edward Hatch of the Ninth Cavalry also praised them, writing on August 9 that they were "brave and daring, superior to the Indians of this region in fighting qualities."

Finally, the commissioner of Indian affairs recommended that Congress appropriate funds for removing the blacks from Forts Duncan and Clark. Their number was estimated at five hundred, a sum undoubtedly greatly exaggerated. Nevertheless, the seriousness of their plight was not.[15]

On March 7, 1876, after Congress had failed to act, Elijah Daniels again requested a "good Treaty" for his people. Both Colonel Mackenzie and General Philip H. Sheridan supported his petition. Mackenzie wrote that the scouts were "hard working and industrious . . . and . . . have rendered much assistance to [our] troops." He further stated that the Department of the Interior should grant "proper proportion of land in the Seminole country" to them. Sheridan, in his endorsement, said: "I have a great deal of sympathy with these Seminole Indians, who I feel have been unfairly dealt with. . . . I . . . now urgently recommend that immediate steps be taken to carry out the proposition made by Colonel Mackenzie." As before, however, their pleas were ignored.[16]

By 1876 most of the Black Seminoles, including John Horse and his family, were living at Fort Clark. The few remaining at Fort Duncan were transferred there on February 8, 1877. The black settlement extended along both sides of Las Moras Creek, from near the present-day site of the Seminole cemetery (located upstream) to the Spofford Road near the post. John Horse lived at the lower camp just above the fort's graveyard. He was on the same side of the creek as the post buildings.[17]

Some local citizens viewed the burgeoning Black Seminole community with increasing hostility. On April 24, 1876, a petition signed by thirty-four residents asserted that the blacks were settled on private land and "constantly preying on the property of citizens." In fact, the government had not yet purchased the Fort Clark reservation, which was then located on leased acreage. Moreover, the hungry blacks' butchering of stray cattle had made them understandably unpopular among the neighboring ranchers.

Ironically, however, another group of Kinney County citizens was asking that Lieutenant Bullis be allowed to recruit seventy-five scouts and have an independent command. Presumably, this group did not include any of the angry petitioners calling for removal of the Black Seminoles from Fort Clark. In any case, the military authorities rejected their request.[18]

At this point, some of the local residents apparently decided to take matters into their own hands. On Friday, May 19, 1876, John Horse was returning from Brackettville after visiting a saloon. Shortly after riding onto the Fort Clark grounds, he encountered former scout Titus Payne, who had just been to the commissary. He had received rations, undoubtedly due to an indulgent officer's kindness, and carried a bag of food slung over his shoulder and a gun in his other hand.

The two walked together slowly, Payne on foot and John on horseback. As they passed southeast of the post hospital, near the fort's cemetery, several shots rang out. Titus Payne fell dead. John was hit four times, and his horse American was struck in the neck. But due to the animal's strength and loyalty as well as John's horsemanship, the two safely reached the nearby Seminole camp. Although severely wounded, John Horse eventually recovered.

Payne's body was removed from the scene and hidden in the bushes thirty or forty yards away. It was located three days later after scout Morrel Hall noted buzzards circling overhead. The killers had laid him out with "his gun placed across his chest."

Although the ambushers were never caught, a black outlaw called King Fisher (after the white gunslinger who was shot by George Washington) later told Tony Wilson that he had been hired to murder John Horse. He did not name his employer and said that Titus Payne was killed by mistake.

If the attack was meant to drive the blacks from Fort Clark, it did not work. It did, however, precipitate yet another spasmodic effort by the military authorities to find them a permanent home. Brigadier General E. O. C. Ord supported their relocation. He wrote, "They would be a real God sent [sic] with their simple manners and religious tendency, to some of the agencies where the wild Sioux or Apaches defy the most earnest appeals of our missionaries." But as before, nothing happened.[19]

Meanwhile, throughout 1876 John Bullis and his men continued to play an integral part in the U.S. Army's campaign to quell the problems along the Rio Grande. With the Kickapoos largely cowed by Mackenzie's 1873 Remolino strike and the southern plains tribespeople mostly confined to their Fort Sill reservations, the scouts' main foes were now Apaches. General Crook called them the "Tigers of the Human Species."

Of the various Apache bands, the Lipans and Mescaleros troubled Bullis and his men the most. The Lipans were based in Mexico, while the Mescaleros alternated between their New Mexico reservation and the Lipans' territory. Both bands enjoyed easy access, both coming and going, across the border. Mexico's weak central government was unable to stop their raids; but Mexican authorities became outraged when American forces repeatedly invaded their country, chasing hostiles who preyed on Texas.

In early February 1876, Sergeant William Miller boldly infiltrated a camp "of Comanches, Apaches, Mescaleros, and Lipans" in Mexico. The mixed-blood Seminole scout stayed with them for five days to learn their plans. Then he slipped away and returned to Fort Clark.[20] After Miller's daring exploit, Lieutenant Bullis and his men were almost continually on the march or in action. They entered Mexico several times in 1876 in pursuit of marauders. Their July and August operations were particularly effective.

On July 19 the scouts left their base camp on the Pecos River. They were part of an expedition, commanded by Lieutenant Colonel Shafter, sent across the border to punish Lipan warriors who had killed twelve Texans during raids in April and May. The troops entered Mexico on the twenty-fifth. Four days later, Bullis and twenty Black Seminoles with twenty buffalo soldiers from Company B, Tenth Cavalry, under Lieutenant George H. Evans, separated from the main column. They headed south, following the hostiles' trail. After riding fifty-five miles in about twelve hours, the unit reached the San Antonio River near the Mexican town of Zaragoza at three o'clock in the morning. At daybreak on July 30 they located the Lipan village of twenty-three lodges.

"We struck 'em bout five in [the] mornin'," recalled Black Seminole Charles Daniels, who participated in the engagement. Although the scouts and cavalrymen were outnumbered, the element of surprise proved decisive in the ensuing fight. After their first volley, the attackers were involved in a wild, confused melee. They avoided heavy casualties largely because the stunned warriors attempted to break through their lines and flee. According to Daniels, his companions did not have time to reload. The fight was "hand to hand" with clubbed carbines countered by long Lipan lances.

The struggle lasted for "about fifteen minutes." According to one report, twelve Indians died and four women were captured. Two other accounts stated, respectively, that ten and fourteen tribesmen were slain. But Daniels stated that there were "thirty two dead and wounded . . . de killin' were large, de killin' were large." Ninety-four horses were seized and the camp destroyed. Despite the fierce, close-quarters combat, only three men from the detachment—all scouts—sustained light injuries.

The strike force rejoined Shafter's command on July 31. They had been in the saddle for twenty-five hours, ridden more than one hundred miles, and fought a pitched battle. During the trip back, the command was chased by many Mexican regulars, who withdrew after Shafter's superior numbers intimidated them. The soldiers returned to Texas on August 4.[21]

While the scouts were campaigning in the field, John Horse remained at the Fort Clark reservation slowly recovering from his wounds. Later reports said that an "herb doctor" tended him. As he healed, the relations between the Kinney County residents and the Black Seminole community continued to deteriorate. Soon matters drastically worsened, primarily because of a situation involving former scout Adam Payne, the Medal of Honor recipient in the 1874 Red River War.[22]

Payne had fatally stabbed a white man, Private John Bradley of the Eighth Cavalry, on Christmas Eve 1875 in Brownsville, Texas. According to his people's oral history, Payne was arrested. But because there was no place to confine him, he was placed in the town's bull ring with a Mexican prisoner. When a cyclone allegedly wrecked their temporary prison, the two men escaped unharmed.

After this miraculous escape, Adam Payne sought refuge in the small Black Seminole community at Matamoros, Mexico. By late 1876, he was riding with the notorious border bandit Frank Enoch. Payne and Enoch eventually went to Brackettville, probably to stay in the nearby Black Seminole settlement at Fort Clark.

One day, the former scout reportedly was drinking in a Brackettville saloon. Sheriff L. C. Crowell appeared at one door, his deputy Claron Windus at the other. Payne, glass in hand, elbows on the bar, coolly sized up the situation and announced: "If you want a drink, come up to the bar and have one with me; if you don't, give me one of the doors!" According to reports, they gave him both doors.[23]

This episode, if true, might explain why the next time the two lawmen met Payne, they gave him no chance to defend himself. Late on December 31, 1876, Crowell, Deputy Windus, a man named James Thomas, and teamster Jonathan May rode to the Black Seminole camp to arrest Adam Payne and Frank Enoch on felony warrants. They also sought Isaac Payne and Dallas Griner, who had been "indicted by a Kinney County Grand Jury for the theft of a prized gelding" belonging to Claron Windus.[24]

Shortly after midnight, Adam Payne was dancing at a New Year's Eve party in the Bowlegs's yard at the Black Seminole settlement. Suddenly someone called out his name. As Payne turned toward the man, he was gunned down with a shotgun at such close range that his clothes reportedly caught on fire. He died instantly. Ironically, the man who blasted him was Claron Windus, who himself had received a Medal of Honor in 1870. This is the only known incident in which one Medal of Honor recipient killed another.

After the shooting, Robert Kibbitts attacked Windus but was overpowered by Crowell and Thomas. Meanwhile, about the time Adam Payne was gunned down, Enoch had also been shot. Severely wounded, he died in jail several days later.[25]

During the confusion, Isaac Payne fled to his house. Sixty-five years later, his wife Julia remembered: "We like to go crazy the night Adam was killed. There was a frolic . . . but I didn't want to go. Along about midnight I heard the shooting, and then I heard a horse galloping, and my husband fell off—he was drunk—and said, 'Julia they've killed Adam!'"

Presently, a judge was called to perform an inquest. Enoch was eventually removed from the scene; but Adam Payne's body was surrendered, most likely to his family. Kibbitts was later indicted for the attempted murder of Deputy Windus. A jury, however, ultimately found him innocent.

Several Black Seminoles were so exasperated by this second killing in less than a year that they returned to Mexico. Scout Pompey Factor, another Medal of Honor recipient, departed on January 1. He was subsequently listed as a deserter. Scouts Pleasant McCallip and Joe Philips were recorded as deserters on January 7, 1877. Dindie Factor, Dallas Griner, and Medal of Honor recipient Isaac Payne also left but were not then on active duty. The six men reportedly later fought Indians under Colonel Pedro Avincular Valdez for the Mexican government.[26]

Still, the majority of the scouts remained loyal—if not to the United States, then at least to John Bullis. Shortly after Adam Payne's death, the officer left Fort Clark with twenty Black Seminoles in pursuit of marauding Apaches. He and his men supported two units of buffalo soldiers under Captain Alexander S. B. Keyes. The troops trailed the warriors for more than two weeks in January. They covered two hundred miles, penetrating deep into Mexico. Although the men found and destroyed a "hastily abandoned camp in the Santa Rosa Mountains," they returned to Texas empty handed.

During March 1877 Bullis and the scouts tracked and located several bands of hostiles. Then in April they "fought a party of Indians at the Rio Grande about ten miles above the mouth of Devil's River." The Black Seminoles "run [sic] them over the Rio Grande."[27]

The next encounter occurred two months later, on June 29, 1877. While returning from a grueling two-month-long expedition, during which they were once without water for forty-two hours and "our animals suffered terribly," Bullis and thirty-seven scouts spotted a fresh trail about seventy miles above the mouth of the Pecos River. The next day, they followed the tracks for fifteen miles west to the Rio Grande. Bullis and his men quickly found where the Lipan raiding party had forded the "very high" river during the previous night.

Using the boat-building skills that had been so useful in crossing the Rio Grande in search of freedom twenty-seven years before, the Black Seminoles made a raft from logs strewn along the shore. They crossed the swollen river that evening and camped on the opposite side. Two horses drowned during the crossing.

The unit continued their hunt for the next two days. But with twenty of their mounts no longer able to travel, Bullis left the horses with thirteen scouts hidden near a water hole. On July 2 the reduced command found the hostiles' camp and promptly attacked it. Three warriors were wounded, one mortally. As usual, the Black Seminoles had no casualties.

Bullis decided not to pursue the hostiles because both his men and their animals were exhausted. Still, they recaptured some twenty stolen horses, which Lieutenant Colonel Shafter later gave to the scouts to reward their performance (pending claims by their legitimate owners). On July 4 the tired detachment recrossed the Rio Grande on their crude raft. Bullis, despite his fatigue, wanted to file his report quickly; so he rode to Fort Clark ahead of his men. He arrived on July 7 at two o'clock in the morning, having covered 140 miles in thirty-six hours. On July 12 the Department of Texas commander, Brigadier General E. O. C. Ord, praised "the perseverance and luck exhibited by Lieutenant Bullis and his little command, [and] this is only one of several instances of the same sort shown by them."[28]

It was early fall before the Black Seminoles saw action again. On September 26, 1877 three guides reported that hostiles were camped twenty miles west of Zaragoza, Mexico. Two days later, Bullis and Shafter crossed the Rio Grande with about four hundred men, including Seminole scouts, Tenth Cavalry buffalo soldiers, and Eighth Cavalry troopers.

The unit waited all day for a Mexican trader who had been paid to lead them to the Indians. But he never appeared. So at eleven o'clock that night, Shafter divided his command. While most of the soldiers stayed with him, he dispatched Bullis with ninety-one men, including about thirty Black Seminoles, to find the enemy camp.

At seven the next morning, Bullis and his unit attacked a "band of Lipans and Apaches" near the Perdido River. The hostiles had been alerted and were going to Zaragoza to seek refuge. They fled with the troops in hot pursuit. During the running fight, three women, two children, and some livestock were captured. As Bullis and his unit rode back to rejoin Shafter's forces, Mexican cavalry trailed them but withdrew when Shafter maneuvered his men into battle formations. The column returned to Fort Clark on October 4.[29]

The second Zaragoza raid caused great consternation on both sides of the Rio Grande and figured prominently in the congressional decision to investigate the Texas border troubles formally, including their impact on U.S.–Mexico relations. Both Bullis and Shafter were called to testify in December 1877.

Lieutenant Frederick E. Phelps had been on the September expedition to Zaragoza. He described the Black Seminoles as "quite orderly and excellent soldiers." He also said that Bullis "was a tireless marcher, thin and spare . . . ; he and his men could go longer on half rations than any body of men that I have ever seen."[30]

The scouts' next targets were Mescalero Apaches, well known to them from their Coahuila days. The Indians had been launching raids from their reservation at Fort Stanton, New Mexico Territory. They often sought sanctuary and a market for their stolen livestock in Mexico.

In mid-October 1877 Bullis left Fort Clark with thirty-seven men to hunt the renegades. The unit rode along the Rio Grande to the Pecos River. On the twenty-first, two Seminole scouts reported that they had found a recently deserted camp with many tracks going south. On October 28 Bullis's force crossed into Mexico and followed the fresh trail for the next three days.

On November 1, while laboriously climbing a rough, stony, path up a deep gorge, they encountered their enemy. The warriors were driving a large horse herd along the canyon rim. During the ensuing fight, the greatly outnumbered scouts were surrounded by Apaches concealed behind large boulders. The hostiles "severely handled" them, with Bullis "only getting his men out [with no casualties] by his skill and courage, but losing several animals and all his rations."

Lieutenant Phelps, who saw the battleground soon after the hot action, said: "The sides of the mountain were very precipitous; we passed the place where Bullis had been . . . which was a narrow ledge not more than ten or twelve feet wide, with a mountain towering above and the river hundreds of feet below; how he ever got his men out of there, with Indians on both sides, was a mystery to us all."[31]

Such harrowing escapades later prompted Frederick Remington to remark: "I have no doubt that he [Bullis] pays high life insurance premiums. . . . The Indians regard him as almost supernatural and speak of the 'Whirlwind' with . . . admiration as they narrate his wonderful achievements." Unfortunately, what the Indians said about his black warriors is unknown. Given the scouts' impressive combat capabilities, their adversaries probably used unprintable epithets in any case.[32]

After returning to Texas, Bullis dispatched two men on November 5 to ask Shafter for assistance. On November 13 Captain S. B. M. Young—with a detachment of the Eighth Cavalry, some Tenth Cavalry buffalo soldiers, and more Seminole scouts—joined Bullis at Pecan Springs near the headwaters of the Devils River. The 162-man force reentered Mexico and followed the Apaches' trail, now twenty-three days old.

Because of the Black Seminoles' exceptional tracking ability, the command, "which suffered greatly from [the] cold . . . ; [their] water in canteens frozen solid, [the] men only [had] summer allowances of clothing, and Company C 10th Cavalry were without great-coats," located the hostiles on November 29. They were camped near the Carmen Mountains. Hoping to trap their quarry, Young had his troops dismount and left sixty of them to guard the horses. The rest slowly "walked over a mountain nearly a mile in height."

During a sharp, running fight, with the scouts in the vanguard, Young's men killed two tribesmen and wounded three others. The soldiers captured twenty-three horses and mules, one of which belonged to Bullis. An officer and a sergeant were slightly injured.

Amid the action, three Black Seminoles (apparently including the intrepid Sergeant William Miller) were rescued. They had been ambushed earlier that morning while scouting the advance. Captain Young said that the men "took shelter in a deep and rocky ravine, and for some hours defended themselves against heavy odds, with loss of one horse."

Nevertheless, because one of Young's three columns did not get into position in time to surround the enemy, the warriors escaped. They abandoned a variety of supplies, including "dried deer, horse and mule meat, all of which was divided equally among the men and officers, but it only gave us about two or three ounces each." Even so, the food was appreciated because rations were very low. In fact, one of the campaign participants believed that Bullis and his men survived by eating rattlesnake.

The force recrossed the Rio Grande on December 3 and arrived at Fort Clark on the sixteenth. Bullis and his men had been in the field for nearly two long months.[33]

CHAPTER SIXTEEN

⌧ The End of the Scouts

We now have orders, (after serving the government for . . . [many] years) that
we must all move off. . . . Some are old and blind, some are old and crippled. . . .
We have no other home.

MEDAL OF HONOR RECIPIENT JOHN WARD
AND TWENTY-SIX OTHER BLACK SEMINOLES

After the May 1876 attack on John Horse and Titus Payne and Adam Payne's murder on January 1, 1877, the composition of the scouts began to change. Before long, fewer than half of those who joined the unit were true Black Seminoles. Some were state-raised (non-Seminole) blacks; they were usually discharged soldiers. Others were Mexican. In fact, between 1878 and 1880, twelve of the fourteen recruits had Mexican names—one of them was the comanchero Jose Tafoya, whom Mackenzie had allegedly nearly hung just before the Palo Duro rout. In addition, three Apaches were attached to the scouts in October 1878.

There were three distinct periods in the unit's personnel history during its active combat years (1870–81). From 1870 to 1872, almost all were Black Seminoles or Black Creeks recently arrived from Mexico. From 1873 through 1877, about half of those who enlisted were state-raised blacks. From 1878 to 1880, most who joined had Mexican names.[1] Nevertheless, of the one hundred or so men serving at one time or another from 1870 to 1881, about two-thirds were either Black Seminoles or Black Creeks, as compared to one-sixth state-raised blacks and one-seventh Mexicans. Overall, the unit's makeup justified its official title: the Detachment of Seminole Negro Indian Scouts.

But the golden age of the Seminole scouts was drawing to a close. Their punishing campaigns of 1876 and 1877, some of them deep into Mexico, apparently convinced the hostiles to confine their mayhem south of the Rio Grande. Although Bullis and his men continued to go on expeditions as usual (including one under Colonel Mackenzie into Mexico in June 1878), no clashes with warriors occurred until 1881.

Before the Black Seminoles fought their last Indian battle, they performed their greatest feat of tracking and endurance. On January 31, 1879, Lieutenant Bullis—with fifteen cavalrymen; twelve civilian packers; and thirty-nine Seminole scouts, including José Tafoya and three Lipans—rode after some renegade Mescalero Apaches. After stealing some stock near Fredericksburg, the hostiles were heading back to their reservation at Fort Stanton, New Mexico Territory.

The column relentlessly trailed them for thirty-four days, moving west across the barren desert. The men and horses suffered severely from thirst. At one point nearly all perished. But on February 28 Sergeant David Bowlegs displayed uncanny desert craft: he discovered a sleeping spring. With great care and skill, he successfully made the water flow freely again. Bullis gratefully named the place Salvation Spring.

Although the troops traced the raiders to within two miles of their reservation, the Indian agent was unable to locate the guilty parties and refused to allow Bullis to search for them on the reservation. So the unit returned to Fort Clark empty-handed, having been gone for eighty days and covering 1,266 miles.[2]

Among their other duties, Bullis and the Black Seminoles sometimes escorted civilian prospecting parties. During one such expedition in early 1880, he and his thirty men were closely observed by Burr G. Duval, who kept a diary of the trip to the Big Bend area. Duval wrote: "Bullis has made quite a reputation on the frontier as a scout. . . . I was much impressed with his quiet determined look and would consider him a man who, as the Texans say, would 'do to tie to.'" Duval noted that the Black Seminoles' "religious element [was] highly developed. Every night they have a sort of camp meeting, singing prayer and reading the Bible, which among these lonely hills sounds weird and peculiar."[3]

A year later, the Seminole scouts fought their last Indian battle, marking the final significant hostile raid in Texas. On April 14, 1881, a small Lipan band killed a woman and a boy at an isolated ranch at the head of the Rio Frio. The warriors also robbed other houses in the area and stole horses. Almost two weeks after the attack, Lieutenant Bullis was ordered to pursue them. He immediately left Fort Clark with thirty-two scouts.

"The Indians did their dirt at Uvalde," declared Julia Payne some sixty years later. Then "they killed a horse and made shoes out of the rawhide [for their ponies' hooves] so they wouldn't make tracks." Despite this device and the time that had elapsed, the Black Seminoles located the Lipan spoor on April 27. They tracked them "over the rugged, precipitous mountains and canyons of Devil's River, where the marauders killed thirty of their horses, as they could not drive them through this terrible country."

After the hostiles crossed the Rio Grande, the scouts followed them into the Burro Mountains in Mexico. On May 2 Bullis and his men discovered the Lipan camp, observing it until after sundown. Then, with seven scouts left behind to guard their mounts, the rest moved on foot and surrounded the tribespeople. They attacked at daybreak, killing four warriors and a woman. They captured another woman, who was wounded, and a child. Twenty-one animals were seized. Only the chief, San Da Ve, escaped; but he was mortally wounded. As usual, the strike force had no casualties. The men returned to Texas on May 5.

For this action and the July 1876 Zaragoza raid, Bullis, who had advanced to captain in 1886, was breveted a major in 1890. Significantly, he received this honorary rank during the first year that Congress authorized it for Indian War veterans. He was later promoted to the regular rank of major in 1897.[4]

The Burro Mountain raid ended the Black Seminoles' Indian fighting for the U.S. Army. The Comanches and Mescalero Apaches were finally on their reservations, and the Lipans had at last learned their lesson. In 1882 twelve expeditions originating from Texas posts covered 3,662 miles and found no signs of hostiles. The Texas Indian wars were over; and Bullis's men, appropriately, had fought the last battle.

Obviously, the Seminole scouts were not wholly responsible for pacifying West Texas. U.S. regulars, including the all-black regiments of the Twenty-fourth and Twenty-fifth Infantry and the Ninth and Tenth Cavalry buffalo soldiers, played major roles in the campaign. But without the scouts (and Bullis's able leadership), much of the troopers' work would have been futile. Unlike the soldiers, the Black Seminoles could follow an old trail across hundreds of miles of barren deserts and rough mountains. They could consistently locate and then attack their quarry or could guide the regular troops and situate them favorably to fight the enemy. West Texas owed much of its final exemption from Indian depredations to the scouts' tracking skills, horsemanship, marksmanship, endurance, desert craft, and—above all—fearsome fighting ability.

Lieutenant John L. Bullis's connection with his men terminated in June 1881, much to their regret. None of his replacements would duplicate the relationship of mutual trust and friendship that existed between him and the Black Seminole community. It was said that, within a few days after any of his men had a child, Bullis would inspect the infant. If male, he would take the newborn into his arms and announce with great relish: "Fine baby! Fine baby! Going to be mighty fine scout some day—mighty fine scout!"

Bullis went on to receive great recognition for his services, but much of the acclaim was due to his long association with the Black Seminoles. The grateful citizens of West Texas dubbed him "Friend of the Frontier" and presented him with two handsome swords. In 1882 the Texas legislature passed a resolution thanking him "for his gallant and efficient services." Brigadier General David S. Stanley called him "the most successful of any Indian fighter in the history of the United States Army." In 1905 President Theodore Roosevelt promoted him, on merit alone, from major to brigadier general—apparently the first instance of a three-grade advancement in U.S. Army history.

In stark contrast, the Seminole scouts and their families were eventually evicted from Fort Clark when their services were no longer needed. Already, as the hostile activity diminished and then ceased, the military had begun gradually to reduce the number of Black Seminoles on active duty.[5]

Meanwhile, John Horse had returned to Mexico by at least 1877. Subchief John Kibbitts had died in 1878. Elijah Daniels, who reportedly took over after Kibbitts's death, probably exerted little authority except over the Black Creeks, who were primarily his own family and the Warriors, Wilsons, and Graysons.

Daniels was evidently not on the best of terms with Bullis. When the scout was discharged for the last time in November 1876, Bullis rated his character as "good, but is old and not a good scout." Shortly after his discharge, Daniels tried to have himself and his group transferred to Fort Concho to circumvent Bullis, who had apparently refused to reenlist him. The effort failed.[6]

Those who now served as sergeants in the scouts seemed to have some claim to leadership of the Black Seminoles. One was First Sergeant David Bowlegs, who had found Salvation Spring in 1879. In 1880 he was seriously considering Indian Territory, not Mexico, as a possible home for his people. Bullis requested permission for Bowlegs and four other scouts—Sergeants Sampson July and Robert Kibbitts; Privates Isaac Payne and Pompey Perryman—to visit the Territory to inspect it and ascertain what rights they had there. Bowlegs finally went during the summer of 1881. He was favorably impressed. Upon his return, he told the commanding officer at Fort Clark: "If I had no one but myself and my wife, I would rather soldier than do anything else I know of, but I have a large family growing up, and we are here where we own nothing, and can get no work. My children will grow up idle and become criminals on this frontier. I have been raised like an Indian, but want to go to my people and settle in a home and teach my children to work, and most of my people are like me."[7]

Bowlegs requested transportation to the Territory for one hundred people. The Fort Clark commander passed his petition along to Lieutenant General Philip H. Sheridan, who heartily endorsed it: "I have known these Indians for many years, and they are in every way worthy of having their wish complied with. They should long since have been sent to the Indian Territory to join their people."

David Bowlegs also visited Mexico to induce the Black Seminoles in Nacimiento to return. Apparently, he was not very successful. Meanwhile, the number ready to leave Fort Clark in the summer of 1882 had decreased to fifty-seven; and the Black Seminoles now asked for only "four Army Wagons" and some rations.

Whether or not those items were furnished is not clear, but Bowlegs and his followers eventually left for the Territory. His band included several of the independent-minded Bruners (Jake, Jim, and Joe and their families) and Black Creeks Cato and Johnny Wilson. Henry Gordon was also part of the group. He was the ex-slave from Georgia who had joined the Black Seminoles in Mexico.

Retracing the steps that some of them had taken more than thirty years earlier, the Bowlegs party reached Indian Territory around December 1882. Dolly Bowlegs White, David's sister, and her family followed them in 1883.[8] Despite efforts by the Seminole tribal leadership to evict them and an order to leave from the commissioner of Indian Affairs in 1885, the Bowlegs band settled near Nobletown. Welcomed by the local Black Seminole community, they still never received a land allotment. Their tales of scouting and Indian warfare were still remembered in Wewoka, Seminole County, Oklahoma, many years later.[9]

Shortly after news of the group's safe arrival filtered back to Texas, the scouts on active duty announced that they wished to join the Bowlegs group in the Territory when their next enlistment ended. At this point, the old matter of the treaty allegedly negotiated with the late Captain Perry reemerged. Lieutenant F. H. French, the unit's current commanding officer, reported that the blacks had been promised land in the Territory as soon as their services were no longer required but "the copy of the agreement furnished them has been lost. The records of Ft. Duncan . . . show that an agreement was made and was forwarded to Department Headquarters in the Spring of 1870 by Lieutenant Col. Z. R. Bliss . . . then Major 25th Infantry."

Meanwhile, John Jumper, principal chief of the Indian Territory Seminoles and a former Confederate officer, firmly rejected the idea of allowing more blacks to rejoin his tribe. He said: "We are . . . informed . . . by the report of Genl Sheridan . . . that these negroes are a turbulent lawless band." Sheridan, however, promptly rebuked Jumper: "I have never made any such . . . statement. These people, on the contrary, are in my opinion, law abiding, well disposed and worthy of consideration." Still, his strong endorsement did not advance their prospects for acquiring land in the Territory or elsewhere.[10]

In 1884 the scouts were about to be discharged en masse. Lieutenant Colonel Bliss, who knew them well, advised his superiors about their plight, claiming that they were "in an almost helpless condition, with many widows and orphans." The Black Seminoles again asserted that Captain Perry had assured them that land would be made available when their tour of duty was completed. (Interestingly, Bliss remarked: "I presume he had authority for what he promised.") They also reminded the officer that they had proposed returning to Mexico in 1879, but Ranald Mackenzie had told them to stay because they would be given a reservation.

Second Lieutenant Edward B. Ives, the unit's new commander, asked that the order discharging thirty-four scouts be carried out gradually. He made this request because 194 people, including many women and children, depended upon the men's wages. But the detachment was still reduced to just six individuals. On 27 December 1884, however, their authorized strength was increased to twenty at the request of several experienced, frontier-wise officers who feared renewed border problems.[11]

In 1885 Sergeant Robert Kibbitts and former Sergeant Sampson July visited the Department of Texas commander to discuss their troubles. Although the two men convinced him that to call the blacks "outlaws . . . is a calumny and very easily refuted," nothing was done about their reservation. But Kibbitts was not discouraged. In 1886 he requested a furlough and went to Washington at his own expense to plead their case. Like John Horse before him, Kibbitts visited the office of the commissioner of Indian Affairs in March 1886. He presented several documents and asked for "a home in the Seminole Country."

Kibbitts also petitioned the Senate committee on Indian affairs, where he "made a favorable impression . . . as a man of intelligence." Senator H. L. Dawes, the committee chairman, subsequently requested information from the secretary of the interior about the rights of the Black Seminoles in Texas to Indian Territory lands. But despite Dawes's interest in their case, nothing came of the inquiry. Kibbitts returned to Texas empty-handed.[12]

In 1888 his people made yet another attempt to obtain a permanent home. But well aware that they would not be permitted to go to the Territory, their leaders now requested land on and around Fort Clark. At that time, forty-eight families were reportedly living there. Dembo Factor, by then eighty-six years old, signed the petition at the top of eight names. The other signers included prominent subchiefs such as John Wilson, Caesar Payne, and Hardy Factor. Claiming to be the Black Seminoles' current leader, Dembo Factor evoked his participation at the Dade massacre and the Battle of Okeechobee in Florida. As before, however, their application was denied; and they remained squatters on government land.[13]

For almost another generation, the U.S. Army continued to deploy a small scout unit on the border. But now the military sent them against smugglers and cattle thieves instead of hostile warriors. From 1886 to 1892, the number of those on active duty varied from fifteen to twenty men. Then, primarily because of renewed civil war in Mexico, the whole detachment was transferred from Fort Clark to Fort Ringgold, on the border at Rio Grande City.

One sergeant, two corporals, and twelve privates, commanded by Second Lieutenant Charles E. Hays, arrived there on October 5, 1892. Most of their families remained at Fort Clark.[14]

From their new post, the scouts participated in operations against Mexican revolutionaries based in Texas. During November, they scoured the countryside for insurrectionists who followed Catarino Garza. Then on December 10 a large group of his supporters hit a small Mexican outpost opposite San Ignacio, Texas. The U.S. war secretary's official report of the raid stated that several wounded Mexican soldiers, including their captain, had been thrown into burning buildings (which the bandits had set on fire) and burned alive. Shortly thereafter, the rebels returned to Texas with fifty stolen horses.

Thirteen Seminole scouts, led by Hays, and Troop I, Third Cavalry, under First Lieutenant Parker W. West, were soon following "the trail of the bandits, now many days old . . . which duty was very difficult on account of the character of the country . . . a mass of dense chaparral and cactus."[15] On December 24 the command surprised and attacked some thirty rebels about twelve miles northwest of Roma, Texas, killing one and wounding two. The survivors fled. The soldiers chased the escaping rebels but soon lost them. Three horses, which later were given to the scouts, and other items stolen from the Mexican garrison were recaptured. The U.S. forces had no casualties.

The Black Seminole performance, as always, was exemplary. Obviously, the military still needed their tracking skills. So on December 28, 1892, Major A. S. B. Keyes of the Third Cavalry, commanding Fort Ringgold, recommended the enlistment of an additional twenty scouts. He added: "Officers now . . . speak of them in highest terms." His request was quickly approved.[16]

During January and February 1893, the unit continued to scour the border for the revolutionaries' camps. On February 23, 1893, two Black Seminoles—Corporal Billy July and Private Sam Gordon, under Lieutenant Percival G. Lowe—accompanied Sheriff Washington W. Shely to Las Mulas Ranch, Starr County, thirty miles north of Fort Ringgold. They were going to arrest Eusebio Martinez, also known as Mangas de Agua. He was "the most desperate of all the bandits" and "had stated that he never would be taken alive." Martinez was asleep with his gang when the men found him, but he woke up shooting. He was killed almost instantly, and his two companions fled. This incident probably was the last armed engagement of the Detachment of Seminole Negro Indian Scouts.

On March 12 a grateful official acknowledged "the work accomplished by Mr. Shely, Lieutenant Lowe and his scouts, in thus ridding the country of the most dangerous murderer, robber and thief on the border." On September 10, 1894, Brigadier General Frank Wheaton, then commanding Fort Ringgold, also praised the Black Seminoles. He described them as "intelligent, brave, and reliable trailers. Little or nothing was accomplished until they were utilized. . . . I felt under great obligations to them."[17]

But when the border area quieted down, the Seminole scouts were not so necessary. By about 1903 they had returned to Fort Clark to perform "extra and special duties in the Quartermaster's Department, care of the reservation and its fences and gates, and prevention of unauthorized wood cutting, hunting, fishing and grazing."[18]

During the first decade of the twentieth century, the unit's demobilization was again contemplated. Reportedly, General Bullis, then retired and living in San Antonio, was dismayed that his old organization, with its fine record of service, would be disbanded. According to Black Seminole oral tradition, the elderly officer was ill and at home in bed when he learned that his former command was being eliminated. He immediately arose, called for his clothes, and began to dress. Then he suddenly fell dead.

Bullis actually died on May 26, 1911, at the Fort Sam Houston Army Hospital in San Antonio. He had collapsed while watching a boxing match the previous evening. After hearing of his death, former scout Sandy Fay, who had served as Bullis's striker (or orderly), traveled from Fort Clark to San Antonio. He stood guard at the general's house all day and all night until Bullis was laid to rest.[19]

The final order to dissolve the detachment was issued three years after Bullis's death on July 10, 1914. With the unit's disbandment imminent, a new location had to be found for the people living along Las Moras Creek. Once again, the question of the treaty was revived. Where *was* the agreement that had allegedly promised the blacks land for their services as scouts?

One account stated that "Col. Shelby of the 13th Cavalry visited the reservation and asked to be shown the treaty papers. For some reason the treaty had been left at Santa Rosa, Mexico, and John Shields, First Sergeant, was sent to bring the treaty back to the United States . . . ; a Mexican revolution was in progress and before the treaty could be obtained, the courthouse was destroyed and the records lost."

But even if the document existed and was located, where could John Horse's people go? Even if they were welcomed back into the Indian Territory—which was definitely not the case—the Seminole tribal rolls were officially closed in 1907. "The Secretary of the Interior . . . [had] no power to add any names thereto." Moreover, "no allotments . . . [could] be made to them as Seminoles and, of course, there . . . [was] no provision of law for making allotments to them as Negroes."[20]

So on July 10, 1914, all the Black Seminoles had to leave their homes. The only exceptions were a few elderly ex-scouts and their families and widows of deceased scouts with their children. Just twenty-four people would be allowed to remain. The houses of those who left were to be destroyed after their forced removal.

At that time, 207 Black Seminoles lived on the Fort Clark grounds: 113 adults and 94 children divided into 52 families. Only twelve scouts remained on active duty. Four were discharged on the last day of July, four on the last day of August, four on the last day of September. Eventually, even those allowed to stay for humanitarian reasons were expelled.

Miss Charles Emily Wilson is the last living Black Seminole who was born on the Fort Clark reservation. Her great-aunt was Susan, John Horse's wife. Miss Wilson, remembering the trauma of the eviction, said: "I can still see those old ladies weeping, just weeping."[21]

Ironically, these courageous people, who had bested some of the fiercest tribespeople in the West—Kiowas, Comanches, Kickapoos, and Apaches— who themselves struggled unsuccessfully to be formally recognized as Indians, were finally treated as such. Following a pattern repeated with tribe after tribe, the U.S. government ejected them from their homes, ignoring their justifiable protests.

PART FIVE

Father of His People, Mexico, 1876–1882

CHAPTER SEVENTEEN

⌗ Farewell to John Horse

When the colored people heard that John Horse was dead they just howled.
MOLLY PERRYMAN

What had happened to John Horse and the Black Seminoles in Mexico? John, who remained vigorous well into his sixties, "was a young man all the time he was in Mexico [that is, during his first stay there]; he only began to age on this [the Texas] side." John had gone to Texas in 1870 when he was about fifty-eight years old.

In Texas, his advancing age may have occasionally bothered him. Perhaps the forced inactivity of a life in which John Kibbitts and Elijah Daniels led the campaigns took its toll. Still, John Horse probably stayed quite energetic until the ambush at Fort Clark in May 1876. Then about sixty-four years old, he never recovered completely from his four bullet wounds. As Dolly July said, "John Horse always walked straight until he was shot; then he was bent over and his feet all broke out. He was hurt mighty bad."[1]

After his wounds had largely healed, John immediately rode back to Nacimiento, where he reassumed his position as head chief of the Mascogos in Mexico. Apparently he never returned to the United States.

The elderly Black Seminoles' memories of him, some seventy years later, probably stemmed chiefly from this later period of his life. They remembered him primarily as a patriarch, sage, and healer but never as a warrior. Although only one of his children, Joe Coon, grew to adulthood, John used to say: "Every child is my child—all children and old people . . . are my own children and my own old parents." A "kind and generous" leader, he continually provided for those who were hungry. But he would not humiliate them by giving them food directly. Instead, "he would kill a fat beef or a big hog and cook it and invite everyone in to eat." Thus, all could eat their fill without shame.[2]

His medical skill was also freely given. "He was a 'regular doctor'—when people were sick he'd come to see them and unless Jesus was ready for them he'd save them. He was a doctor, Indian-style, gave them folk medicines— none of this stuff out of a bottle." Some of these herb remedies were powerful emetics and purgatives, probably akin to the famous "black drink" of the Seminole Indians of Florida. Two elderly black women reminisced: "[People] used to drink tea to make them vomit—it sho' scraped us both up and down!"[3]

One of his feats of healing was a technique apparently imported from Africa. Jane Phillips became very ill after her father, Joe Phillips, returned from a raid with a Comanche necklace of white bone beads—probably stripped from a slain warrior. Joe had draped the chain on his little daughter's neck and then promptly forgot about it. But the necklace's medicine beads would make anyone ill who wore them except their legitimate owner. Soon Jane became very sick and seemed ready to die.

When John Horse was summoned, he immediately saw the beads. Recognizing them for what they were, he yanked the chain from her neck and threw it away. From his medicine pouch he took a buffalo horn with the tip cut off. Kneeling down, John put the big end against Jane's chest and the small one in his mouth. He sucked and sucked until all the poison was drawn out. Then he blew into the horn until the little girl regained her strength. She recovered quickly and completely.[4]

According to those who knew him, John Horse's one weakness was his addiction to liquor. "He liked his whiskey"; or, more irreverently, "Old Man Gopher John was a 'drunker.'" Still, he "never got into trouble."

But inside this kind patriarch was the spirit of the fierce warrior of Florida days, the astute headman of the Indian Territory, and the dashing military leader of the Laguna de Parras. His audacious cunning still survived.[5]

The Black Seminoles interviewed in the early 1940s usually ascribed John Horse's success as chief of a fighting people for more than a generation to his matchless bravery, boldness, and skill with weapons. His grandson, John Jefferson, said: "John Horse wasn't afraid of anything, so when he meets up with the enemy he don't wait, he acts quickly; he just goes right into them and busts them wide open before they know what's happening!"[6] But to attack "wide open" implies that the foe has been located and the strike launched under favorable conditions. Sheer daring must be complemented with shrewd intelligence, as John, even late in his life, demonstrated.

The chaos in Mexico produced by a decade of civil war enabled the hostiles to begin raiding Coahuila with renewed ferocity. A magazine article in 1872 declared, probably with some exaggeration, that "Coahuila has been almost entirely abandoned to the hordes of savages that swarm over the plains and valleys of that distant territory."[7] But open warfare in Nacimiento was intermittent. Thus, during occasional uneasy truces, the Mascogos became acquainted with the Lipans and Comanches through trading and parleying.

Nevertheless, a closer relationship only intensified the dislike the Black Seminoles felt for their traditional enemies. An elderly woman later declared: "We seed a lot of . . . Comanche and Lipans . . . [and they were] ugly lookin'. Dey'd kill horses and take off fat . . . and eat it raw. . . . [They] smell bad. . . . [It was] like a polecat skunk."[8] Still, the Indians' dietary habits and odor could probably have been tolerated if not for their constant marauding. Often after they had been in Nacimiento on a friendly visit and "spied out the land," the Indians tried to steal the Mascogo herds.

In those days the houses in Nacimiento were still loopholed for rifle fire and connected by a palisade. Every night the colonists drove their horses into the sheltering village enclosure. But at daybreak the Mascogos occasionally found some animals riddled with arrows discharged by frustrated attackers who had been unable to catch them.[9]

One group was especially notorious for its regular and extensive raiding. From the earliest days of Black Seminole residence in Coahuila, the people of San Carlos, Chihuahua, had aided hostile Comanches, Lipans, and Mescaleros. In exchange for sharing the spoils with the village authorities, the warriors received their protection.[10]

Around 1878, a local Coahuila official, Don José María Garza Galán, decided to deal with the menace. A Mexican cautivo who had escaped from the band of hostiles told him that the Indians were staying in a remote area of the San Carlos Mountains with access to enough water to make them self-sufficient. He also said that the mayor of a nearby Mexican community protected them.

Garza Galán consulted with John Horse, who declared that peace would prevail only if every last marauder was killed or captured. Reportedly, the two men went to see Mexican president Porfirio Díaz. After hearing that the entire group had to be exterminated, Díaz replied that it was the settlers' responsibility to solve the problem. They should do whatever was necessary.

After returning to Muzquiz, Garza Galán collected the Mexican troops and John Horse the Mascogo warriors. They swiftly rode to the traitorous village and surrounded it. The posse seized the mayor and then posted sentries to prevent anyone from warning the Indians. Inspecting the steep trail to the enemy camp, John Horse observed that the troops could not approach the hostiles undetected. The only thing to do was to get the warriors drunk and then take them by surprise.

John forced the mayor—by threatening to kill his family—to ride to the hostiles with enough liquor to incapacitate them. As a signal that the camp was vulnerable, the mayor would release a mare whose nursing foal remained behind. The horse would trot back to her foal, and the attackers would know it was time to strike.

Things went as planned. After the mare returned, the Black Seminoles and the Mexicans climbed the steep trail. They found all the men in an alcoholic stupor and massacred them. The women and children were seized, taken to Muzquiz, and jailed. Two warriors who were away hunting soon went to Muzquiz to try to obtain their release, but all were eventually shipped south. Never again did the Indians of San Carlos trouble Coahuila.[11]

Other menaces, however, did threaten the community. In the early 1880s, despite 1866 confirmation of the Nacimiento grant by Mexico's highest authority, problems resurfaced concerning the Mascogo title to the land. Most likely, the settlers' property rights were now challenged because John's people had temporarily abandoned Nacimiento for the United States some ten years earlier. Fortunately, "a Mexican named Castillón, wrote to Texas to tell them [the Black Seminoles] they'd better come back and occupy their land at Nacimiento."[12]

"Every time the Mexicans surveyed . . . [Nacimiento,] they took a little more." But the Mascogos did not accept this mistreatment passively. Sampson July, next in authority to his brother-in-law John Horse, reportedly collected money to independently survey the property.[13]

By the end of 1881, the situation was critical. A man named A. E. Noble "bought" Nacimiento in 1879 from the heirs of the original owner, Sanchez Navarro. His agent was John Willett. In December 1881 Willett ordered the Black Seminoles to leave. The Mascogos defiantly declared that they would fight the eviction by "uniting themselves with the Indians from the Indian Nation of Arkansas and of Texas"—undoubtedly the Seminole and Kickapoo tribespeople from the Territory and the Black Seminoles from Fort Clark, Texas.

The governor of Coahuila asserted that their land had been abandoned, but the Mascogos countered that Benito Juárez had granted them a title. Moreover, they had never left the area except for short periods and "only when Superior Authority ordered that they intern themselves in the State of Durango." This statement probably referred to their transfer to the Laguna de Parras, which bordered Durango. Actually, nearly all the Black Seminoles had gone to Texas early in the 1870s. Still, a few of them may have remained behind.[14]

On March 8, 1882, a priest named Francisco de Paula Andrés formally protested the order of February 12 that the Kickapoos and Mascogos must leave Nacimiento. Father Andrés and the tribal leaders personally presented the written objection to the authorities.[15] The governor of Coahuila accepted the priest's statement that "only . . . the judiciary" could settle what was a private matter. On March 22, 1882, the government "informed the interested parties and the Municipal President of Muzquiz" that they should take their quarrel to the courts. The eviction order was thus rescinded.[16]

But the Mascogos were still not satisfied, especially when Noble took the matter to court. Because the Mexican central government had given Nacimiento to them and their Indian allies in 1852 and the grant had been confirmed in 1866, they believed they could again ask the federal authorities for help.[17]

So John Horse, despite his advanced age, once more prepared to speak for his people. He would personally petition the Mexican president. Obviously, because of his years and infirmities and the journey's dangers, John could not ride to Mexico City by himself. Still, as an elderly Black Seminole woman later commented, "he wouldn't have been afraid to go alone, he wasn't afraid of anything."[18]

Accounts differ about the number and identity of his traveling companions. One, certainly, was his brother-in-law (Picayune) John Wood, who had married John Horse's sister Juana in their old age. Some asserted that his long-time aide, Hardy Factor, also accompanied him. Others mentioned his only son, Joe Coon, who was then about forty.[19]

In the eyes of the Black Seminole community, John Horse was going on an important mission. Thus, there was a great celebration the evening before his departure. Even children went to say farewell to the old, beloved leader. They included Dolly July (then Dolly Ward), about twelve years old; her sister; and Jane Phillips, age seven, whom John had recently saved from the deadly Comanche necklace.[20]

The Kickapoos also came from their camp to say good-bye, for John Horse was to represent them in Mexico City as well. The chief and his principal warriors were arrayed in their ceremonial dress. With scalps at their belts and carrying drums, they assembled before John's house, where he received them courteously. The Kickapoos first honored John's horse, American, by braiding bright-stained eagle feathers into his mane and tail. They also painted his white flanks with symbolical designs. Then the Kickapoo chief spoke briefly but grimly: "John Horse, you are going to Mexico City to speak with the president, and we do not think you will return. So we have come to do you honor and bid you farewell." Although John replied, his words have not been preserved.

Then the drums signaled the celebration to begin. Although no one has mentioned that Kickapoo women participated in the festivities, the young Mascogo women joined in the dance with both the blacks and the Kickapoo warriors.

The next morning, John and his companions rode to Muzquiz, about twenty miles from Nacimiento and a good day's ride. They spent the night in the home of Don Manuel Iglesias. He had married a Biloxi Indian woman whose sister Nadra had married a Black Creek named Adam Wilson. Thus, Don Manuel was affiliated with the Mascogos of Nacimiento. Because John and his entourage lacked funds for the trip, Don Manuel collected money for them.[21]

The group left Muzquiz and rode south by way of Saltillo or Monterey. After many days, they reached Mexico City. John Horse had been there before and evidently had no difficulty arranging to see the Mexican president.

Black Seminole tradition holds that John saw Porfirio Díaz, but the president in 1882 was Manuel Gonzalez. Possibly, however, John did talk to Díaz rather than Gonzalez because Díaz was controlling the government at that time.

According to oral history, John Horse was ushered into a room in the palace of Chapultepec. After Don Porfirio Díaz welcomed him, he invited John to sit on an armless divan. Presently, the Mexican leader also sat down. Díaz courteously waited for the Black Seminole chief to state his business. When John said nothing, he asked him to speak. But John Horse, still silent, just moved closer to his host, who politely slid sideways down the couch. A pause ensued. Once more, Porfirio Díaz suggested that his guest should start the conversation. The Mascogo remained quiet and again shifted his position toward the Mexican. Bewildered, Díaz retreated.

Once again this process was repeated. John's host finally declared: "Capitán Caballo, what are you trying to do? Do you want to push me from the divan to the floor?"

"Just so, *mi presidente*," John Horse finally replied, "are the Mexicans and the white men pushing the Seminoles—they want to push us not merely from a divan but from the earth itself!" John went on to explain how his people and their Kickapoo allies had been mistreated through unfair surveys, the sale of their lands, and the recent expulsion order.[22]

There has been much justifiable criticism of Porfirio Díaz, for more than thirty years the president-dictator of Mexico. But the Mascogos remembered him with respect and fondness because he ordered that their property be returned to them. Perhaps his language then resembled that ascribed to him many years later, when a group of American businessmen petitioned him for a land grant, including the Nacimiento settlement. Díaz reportedly said: "Gentlemen, this land is not mine to be granted or sold, or any man's; it was bought with blood!"[23]

Unfortunately, the Kickapoos' words of farewell to John Horse were portentous. He would never return home. The traditions surrounding the circumstances of his death vary widely. But the most plausible is that he succumbed to pneumonia in the Military Hospital in Mexico City on August 10, 1882. He was buried in a sixth-class grave in the Dolores Cemetery the next day, according to Mexican custom.[24]

Thus, his journey ended, begun somewhere in the Alachua wilderness of Florida seventy years earlier. It had taken John through the Everglades, across rivers, over plains and deserts, and into mountains. He had traveled from Florida through the Indian Territory to Mexico, then to Texas, and back to Mexico again. Against great odds, John Horse had constantly sought freedom for himself and his people.

But his last trip was not in vain. The promise that the Black Seminoles should remain in Nacimiento was eventually fulfilled. On March 7, 1884, the Nacimiento land was ordered to be divided between the Mascogos and the Kickapoos. On September 6 "the citizen Juan Quivi, of the Mascogo tribe"— presumably a son and namesake of John Kibbitts—and Micanuta, representing the Kickapoos, petitioned the governor of Coahuila, asking him to survey their pastures and the area under cultivation. Their request was soon granted.[25]

There was prolonged mourning in Nacimiento and at the Fort Clark settlement when the Black Seminoles learned that John Horse had died. When his "people heard that John Horse was dead they just howled like Indians or Mexicans." The Kickapoos also grieved for him. They comforted his widow, Susan, and brought her venison and other offerings. The tribespeople also held a mourning ceremony, according to their own customs, in their camp.[26]

Joe Coon apparently went to investigate his father's death, which many, including his mother, considered suspicious. But Joe never came back. Reports say that he was either "knifed and killed in a saloon by Mexicans" or "tracked and killed in the desert by Mexican rangers—*rurales*." The loss of both her husband and her only son was too much for Susan, who soon became paralyzed. She did not survive them long.[27]

Shortly after John Horse's death and Joe Coon's disappearance, the Black Seminole property was threatened again. Their land was too fertile a spot in the barren hills and deserts of northern Coahuila not to be coveted. In 1885 José María Garza Galán, then governor of Coahuila, tried to take some land from the Mascogos and Kickapoos, "giving them in exchange others of inferior quality." The Mexican secretary of war supported Garza Galán. On March 17, 1886, he suggested that the blacks and the Indians should be removed. But the president of Mexico, now definitely Don Porfirio Díaz, protected their rights in a statement of June 23, 1887.[28]

Garza Galán did not give up. Five years later, in a letter dated 16 October 1891, he bitterly denounced the Black Seminoles as "vicious, indolent, and disobedient . . . occupied with robbery and pillage . . . deserters from the American Army."[29] This time the central government ignored his attack. Instead, they ordered that the Mascogo males, both in Mexico and Texas, be counted so that their individual claims to a share in the Nacimiento lands could be officially established. The census listed 123 males of all ages.[30]

In 1919 President Venustiano Carranza recognized, once more, the right of the Mascogos and Kickapoos to occupy their Nacimiento property: "It is recognized that these lands belong to the descendants of the original families, to whom the government donated the lands."[31] But this action evidently did not satisfy the Black Seminoles; perhaps their property had again been threatened with expropriation. On April 3, 1936, they requested yet another confirmation of the Nacimiento grant and restitution of lands that had been taken away from them.

A commission was established by the Departamento Agrario to study the matter. The officials reconfirmed the Mascogo rights to their Nacimiento holdings and allotted them an additional 2,892 hectares of pasture land because some of their property had been taken away by adjacent haciendas. On September 21, 1938, President Lázaro Cárdenas signed a decree that was published in the *Diário Oficial* of November 30, 1938, ratifying both the original grant and the extra hectares.

Thus, John Horse's long struggle to obtain land and a permanent refuge for his people finally bore fruit. Fifty-six years after his death, the Black Seminoles firmly possessed their Nacimiento property. They do so to this day.[32]

◈ Notes

Chapter One: Their Best Soldiers Are Black

1. McCall, 1974:164; Interview with Rosa Fay, 1942; Negroes who surrendered to General Taylor, "Seminole War 1837," Consolidated Files, Records of the Office of the Quartermaster General (QMGO), RG92, NA; Bonneville to Jesup, 10 June 1848, J102, Records of the Bureau of Indian Affairs (BIA), RG75, M234, 801/no frames, NA; Porter 1960.

2. Porter, 1971:184; Cox, 1925.

3. Wright, 1924.

4. Covington, 1968; Sturtevant, 1971; Mahon, 1985:1–10; Hancock, 1980:5.

5. Porter, 1949:362–84.

6. Swanton, 1970:262–63; Porter, 1971:187.

7. Simmons, 1973:41, 50, 76; *American State Papers: Military Affairs.* (*ASP.MA*), 6:533–34; Williams, 1962:240; Kennedy, 2, 1925:337–38; Morse, 1972:309–10.

8. *ASP.MA*, 7:427.

9. Simmons, 1973:76–77.

10. We have opted to designate as Black Seminoles those people of African origin who attached themselves voluntarily to the Seminoles or were purchased by them as slaves. Members of the Black Seminole communities of Brackettville, Texas, and Nacimiento de los Negros, Coahuila, Mexico, strongly support this decision. Personal interview of Alcione M. Amos with Charles Emily Wilson, Ethel Warrior, William Warrior, and Alice Fay Lozano, 1992.

11. Simmons, 1973:45, 76.

12. Boyd, 1958:84.

13. Porter, 1971:191.

14. *Niles Register* (*NR*), 23 January 1813, 330; 16 January, 1813, 311–12.

15. *State Papers and Publick Documents* (*SP&PD*), 9:182, 186.

16. Davis, 1930–31:111.

17. Ibid., 107.

18. *SP&PD*, 9:169; "East Florida Documents," 1929:154.

19. McClelan, 1931:11–13; Patrick, 1954:191–93; *SP&PD*, 9:175–77; Williams, 1962:197; Porter, 1971:194–95.

20. Davis, 1930–31:151.

21. Ibid., 155.

22. *NR*, 14 November 1812, 171; 12 December 1812, 235–37; Williams, 1962:198; Davis, 1930–31:146–55.

23. Davis, 1930–31:268; *SP&PD*, 9:156.

24. Rerick, 1902, 1:121; Patrick, 1954:231.

25. *NR*, 13 March 1813, 29; 20 March 1813, 48; 27 March 1813, 67; 17 April 1813, 116; Davis, 1930–31:271–74.

26. Patrick, 1954:259, 268–83.

27. Rerick, 1902, 1:122; Patrick, 1954: 282; *American State Papers: Indian Affairs (ASP.IA)*, 1:844, 845; Wyllys, 1929:445.

Chapter Two: This Savage and Black War

1. *American State Papers: Indian Affairs (ASP.IA)*, 1:851–55.

2. Rippy, 1964:45–48, 55; *ASP.IA*, 1:858–60.

3. Subject File HJ 1816, Naval Records Collection of the Office of Naval Records and Library, RG45, NA (hereafter cited as Subject File HJ).

4. 15th Cong., 2d Sess., H.D. 122; *American State Papers: Foreign Relations (ASP.FR)*, 4:499–500, 555–61; Forbes, 1821:200–205; Williams, 1962:96–102; Williams, 1976:201–3; *Army and Navy Chronicle (A&NC)*, 26 February 1836, 114–16; Subject File HJ; Innerarity to Innerarity, 13 August 1816, in "Letters," 1933.

5. *Niles Register (NR)*, 15 November 1817, 189–94; Woodward, 1939:153; *ASP.FR*, 4:596; *ASP.IA*, 2:155; *American State Papers: Military Affairs (ASP.MA)*, 1:682, 727.

6. Owsley, 1985; Wright, 1968:573–75.

7. *ASP.FR*, 4:585–86; *ASP.MA*, 1:723.

8. *ASP.MA*, 1:686.

9. Ibid., 686, 691.

10. Ibid., 691.

11. *ASP.FR*, 4:586–97, 577–78; *ASP.MA*, 1:686, 690–92, 695.

12. Gadsden, 1937:243–44.

13. *ASP.MA*, 1:722.

14. Ibid., 732.

15. Ibid., 682.

16. 27th Cong., 2d Sess., H.R. 723, 4.

17. 15th Cong., 2d sess., H.D. 14; *ASP. FR*, 4:599–600; *ASP.MA*, 1:689, 700–701, 703–4, 722, 727, 728, 731–32, 741, 749; *NR*, 6 June 1818, 247; *Concise Narrative*, 1819:30–31; Williams, 1962:204–6; Williams, 1976:96–102; Woodward, 1939:168; Young, 1934–35.

Chapter Three: The Gathering Storm

1. Swanton, 1970: 400–401, 404, 406–7, 409, 411; Hodge, 1960; Young, 1934–35:97.

2. Vignoles, 1977:135–36, *Territorial Papers of the United States*, 22:745; Goggin, 1939, 1946; Porter, 1945; Newton, n.d.

3. Mahon, 1985:27, 30–35.

4. Williams, 1962:214; Cohen, 1964:239.

5. Morse, 1972:310–11; *American State Papers: Indian Affairs* (*ASP.IA*), 2:412; Porter 1971:295–338.

6. Sprague, 1964:19; Foreman, 1972b:319; Kappler, 1903–41, 2:203–5; *ASP.IA*, 2:412, 429–42, esp. 432 and 439; Mahon, 1962a; Mahon, 1985:29–50.

7. Foreman, 1972b:319; *Niles Register* (*NR*), 18 March 1826, 27.

8. Sprague, 1964:19; Williams, 1962:33.

9. *ASP.IA*, 2:429, 689–94; Sprague, 1964:65–67.

10. Porter, 1960; interviews with Sarah Daniels and Molly Perryman, 1942, 1943; Julia Payne and Rosa Fay, 1942; Dolly July and Penny Factor, 1943.

11. McCall, 1974:164; Porter, 1943a.

12. John Cowaya alias Gopher John to Jesup, 24 March 1849, "John Cowaya," List of Articles Lost and Left in Florida by Seminole Negroes . . . ," 1 August 1846, "R. W. Kirkham," Consolidated Files, Records of the Office of the Quartermaster General (QMGO), RG92, NA; Taylor to Jesup, 7 December 1837, T275, Arbuckle to Jones, 12 September 1838, A818, M567, 157/83-85, Jones to Arbuckle, 17 October 1838, M565, 11/39-40, Records of the Adjutant General Office (AGO), RG94, NA.

13. Foreman, 1972b:21, 319–20.

14. Cohen, 1964:60.

15. Mahon, 1962b; Washburn, 1973:2443–45; Kappler, 1903–41, 2:249, 344–45; Foreman, 1972b:376–78n17.

16. Sprague, 1964:81, 100; Hitchcock, 1971:78; *NR*, 30 January 1836, 367; *American State Papers: Military Affairs* (*ASP.MA*), 6:454, 458, 464, 465; Porter, 1971:295–357.

17. Foreman, 1972b: 322–23.

18. Brevard, 1924, 1:118; Bemrose, 1966:19.

19. Sprague, 1964:86.

20. Porter, 1947; Hartley and Hartley, 1973:117–18.

21. *ASP.MA*, 6:56–80, 435–38; Cohen, 1964:56–63; Simmons; 1837:542–57; Sprague, 1964:73–86; Foreman, 1972b:322–26; Potter, 1966:96–97; Bemrose, 1966:29–35; Forry, 1928:46.

22. *ASP.MA*, 7:845; *Army and Navy Chronicle (A&NC)*, 7 March 1839, 154–55; *NR*, 25 March 1837, 49; 1 May 1841, 132; Childs, 1873:169, 280; Cohen, 1964:238, 239; Foreman, 1972b:328, 343, 345, 350n22, 364; Sprague, 1964:97–99; Simmons, 1837:542–57; Williams, 1962:272–74.

23. McCall, 1974:399–401; Sprague, 1964:300; interviews with John Jefferson and Dolly July, 1941; Bill Daniels, Rena July, Gregorio Frausto, and Fred Fletcher, 1943; Molly Perryman, 1941, 1942.

24. Sturtevant, 1962:51.

Chapter Four: From Dade's Massacre to the Siege of Camp Izard

1. The standard reference for the Second Seminole War is John K. Mahon, *History of the Second Seminole War*, 2d ed., 1985.

2. Porter, 1971:262–94; Mahon 1985:102.

3. Godfrey, 1977:9–12.

4. Porter, 1943b, 1943d.

5. *Army and Navy Chronicle (A&NC)*, 3 November 1836, 285.

6. Cohen, 1964:72. In 1888 Dembo Factor, then living in Texas, claimed that he had been a participant in the massacre. Petition of Florida Seminole Negroes, January 1888, 3565-1888, Letters Received by the Bureau of Indian Affairs (BIA), 1881–1907, RG75, NA.

7. Cohen, 1964:75.

8. Porter, 1943d:42.

9. *Niles Register (NR)*, 30 January 1836, 367–68; 20 August 1836, 419–20; 17 June 1837, 255–58; *American State Papers: Military Affairs (ASP.MA)*, 7:425; Cohen, 1964:69–76; Williams, 1962:218–19; Sprague, 1964:89–91; McCall, 1974:303–8.

10. Welch, 1977:34.

11. "Jacksonville," 1925:22–30.

12. Cohen, 1964:125–26.

13. Prince, n.d.:108.

14. Sprague, 1964:92–93, 106; Cohen, 1964:82–86, *NR*, 19 August 1837, 395–98; Giddings, 1964:115–18; *ASP.MA*, 6:562–63.

15. Hitchcock, 1971:88; Mahon, 1985:138–46.

16. Silver, 1949:167, 171–72.

17. Prince, n.d.:11.

18. Ibid., 15; Potter, 1966:143.

19. Mahon, 1985:147.

20. Prince, n.d.:91.

21. Hitchcock, 1971:93.

22. Potter, 1966:156; Silver, 1949:178.

23. Hitchcock, 1971:95; Prince, n.d.:30.

24. *ASP.MA*, 7:125–465 (esp. 367–77 and 459–60); *NR*, 30 January 1836, 369; 6

February 1836, 395; 2 April 1836, 85; 1 April 1837, 71–73; Barr, 1836:4, 16–17; Hitchcock, 1909:93–95; Sprague, 1964:107–13; Cohen, 1964:96–105; Giddings, 1964:120–24; Prince, n.d.:15–35.

25. Bemrose, 1966:77.

26. *A&NC*, 7 April 1836, 214.

Chapter Five: General Scott, Governor Call, and the Great Wahoo

1. Sprague, 1964:131; *American State Papers: Military Affairs* (*ASP.MA*), 7:279.

2. Potter, 1966:169–70, 178; Cohen, 1964:191–92.

3. Bemrose, 1966:91; Potter, 1966:171.

4. Cohen, 1964:166–67; Potter, 1966:172–73.

5. Cohen, 1964:174; Potter, 1966:173–74.

6. Cooper, 1884:[23]; Potter, 1966:176; Cohen, 1964:189; *ASP.MA*, 7:385.

7. *ASP.MA*, 7:385; Potter, 1964:176–78; Cohen, 1964:189–90.

8. Cohen, 1964:192–93; Potter, 1966:179–80.

9. Williams, 1962:234; Cohen, 1964:192.

10. Prince, n.d.:54–55; Cohen, 1964:194–95; *ASP.MA*, 7:286–89.

11. *ASP.MA*, 7:279; Giddings, 1964:131–32.

12. Porter, 1971:262–94; 26th Cong., 1st Sess., S.D. 278:62–63, 67–69, 75–77; Childs, 1873, 2:302–3; Sprague, 1964:158–59; Giddings, 1964:127–29.

13. Doherty, 1961:12; Martin, 1943:333.

14. Hollingsworth, 1942–43:349–57; *ASP.MA*, 6:994–95; Williams, 1962:256.

15. *ASP.MA*, 6:995; Hollingsworth, 1942–43:365.

16. 26th Cong., 1st Sess., S.D. 278:86-87; Hollingsworth, 1942–43:365–66; Guild, 1971:131.

17. Guild, 1971:131–32; Hollingsworth, 1942–43:61; *ASP.MA*, 6:996.

18. Hollingsworth, 1942–43:62; Guild, 1971:133.

19. Hollingsworth, 1942–43:61–62; *ASP.MA*, 6:998; Williams, 1962:257–58; Guild, 1971:132–33; 26th Cong., 1st Sess., S.D. 278:87.

20. Guild, 1971:133; Sprague, 1964:162; Giddings, 1964:129–31; Prince, n.d.:77.

21. Prince, n.d.:80.

22. 26th Cong., 1st Sess., S.D. 278:92; Williams, 1962:260–61; Sprague, 1964:162; Hollingsworth, 1942–43:169–70; *Niles Register* (*NR*), 24 December 1836, 260; Guild, 1971:132.

23. Guild, 1971:134.

24. Sprague, 1964:162; Williams, 1962:261–62; Hollingsworth, 1942–43: 176–77; 26th Cong., 1st Sess., S.D. 278:92–93; *NR*, 24 December 1836, 260–61.

25. 26th Cong., 1st Sess., S.D. 278:95.

26. Phelps, 1927:74; Childs, 1873, 2:372; *ASP.MA*, 7:833, 876; Sprague, 1964:112, 166.

27. Mahon, 1985:185; Heitman, 1903:719.

28. Williams, 1962:263; Giddings, 1964:133; Sprague, 1964:163–65; Hollingsworth, 1943:177–78; Guild, 1971:135–36; 26th Cong., 1st Sess., S.D. 278:92–98; *NR*, 24 December 1836, 261.

29. Sprague, 1964:166.

Chapter Six: There Is No Peace

1. Kieffer, 1979:126–50; *American State Papers: Military Affairs* (*ASP.MA*), 7:993.

2. *ASP.MA*, 7:820; *Army and Navy Chronicle* (*A&NC*), 5 January 1837, 12.

3. *ASP.MA*, 7:820–22.

4. *ASP.MA*, 7:877; *A&NC*, 5 January 1837, 12; 7 March 1839, 154.

5. Porter, 1950:180–82; Prince, n.d.:35, 89.

6. *ASP.MA*, 7:454, 825–26; *A&NC*, 2 February 1837, 79, 111; Sprague, 1964:167; Childs, 1873, 2:371.

7. *ASP.MA*, 7:827–28; Childs, 1873, 2:371–72; Sprague, 1964:170–71; Foreman, 1972b:343.

8. Sprague, 1964:174; Mahon, 1985:198.

9. *ASP.MA*, 7:829–30; Childs, 1873, 2:373; Sprague, 1964:171–77; *Niles Register* (*NR*), 11 March 1837, 30.

10. *ASP.MA*, 7:832.

11. *ASP.MA*, 7:828, 851; Sprague, 1964:172; Childs, 1873, 2:373; and *A&NC*, 7 March 1839, 154–55.

12. *ASP.MA*, 7:828; Childs, 1873, 2:374, 3:282–83; Foreman, 1972b:343; Porter, 1971:316–17.

13. Porter, 1971:262–94.

14. Ibid., 262–94, 339–56; Hernandez to Jesup, 16 March 1837, Jesup Papers, Records of the Adjutant General Office (AGO), RG94, NA, (hereafter cited as Jesup Papers).

15. Sprague, 1964:168–70, 325; Giddings, 1964:136–37.

16. *ASP.MA*, 7:827, 830–32.

17. *ASP.MA*, 7:833, 865–66; Childs, 1873, 3:170.

18. Sprague, 1964:172; John Cowaya alias Gopher John to Jesup, 24 March 1849; note from Lieutenant J. T. Sprague, no date, "John Cowaya"; Whitney to Mason, 7 August 1845, "Gopher John," Consolidated Files; Jesup to Belknap, 16 April 1849, M745, 24/358, Records of the Office of the Quartermaster General (QMGO), RG92, NA.

19. Sprague, 1964:177–78; *NR*, 25 March 1837, 49; *AN&C*, 30 March 1837, 215.

20. Childs, 1873, 3:280–82; *ASP.MA*, 7:835; Foreman, 1972b:345.

21. *ASP.MA*, 7:835; *NR*, 29 April 1837, 133; *A&NC*, 27 April 1837, 265; Giddings, 1964:148; Jesup to Poinsett, 9 April 1837, letterbook, 7 February–8 May 1837, Jesup Papers.

22. *ASP.MA*, 7:837; *NR*, 29 April 1837, 133; 3 June 1837, 213.

23. *NR*, 3 June 1837, 213.

24. Porter, 1971:278–79; *ASP.MA*, 7:838.

25. *ASP.MA*, 7:838–39; 25th Cong., 3d Sess., H.D. 225:18; *NR*, 21 June 1837, 261; Jesup to Jones, 21 October 1837, letterbook, 11 August–5 November 1837:239–41; Jesup to Cross, 17 November 1837, letterbook, 5 November 1837–3 January 1838:50–52, Jesup Papers.

26. *ASP.MA*, 7:840, 842, 846, 851–52.

Chapter Seven: Okeechobee!

1. Porter, 1950:174–82; Mahon, 1985:205–6.

2. *American State Papers: Military Affairs (ASP.MA)*, 7:849–50; Motte, 1953:116–18, 277–78n1.

3. *Army and Navy Chronicle (A&NC)*, 28 September 1837, 200, 203–4; Sprague, 1964:186–87; *ASP.MA*, 7:849–50; Motte, 1963:116–23; Forry, 1928:215.

4. *ASP.MA*, 7:882; Casey to Harris, 1 October 1837, Records of the Bureau of Indian Affairs (BIA), RG75, M234, 290/no frames, NA.

5. *A&NC*, 26 October 1837, 269–70.

6. Motte, 1953:138; Jesup to Cross, 17 November 1837, "Gen. Thomas Jesup," Consolidated Files, Records of the Office of the Quartermaster General (QMGO), RG92, NA (hereafter cited as Consolidated Files).

7. 25th Cong., 2d Sess., H.D. 327:5–6; *A&NC*, 26 July 1838, 50.

8. 25th Cong., 2d Sess., H.D. 327:5–8; Motte, 1953:138–39; Forry, 1928:90.

9. Jesup to Jones, 21 October 1837, Jesup Papers, Records of the Adjutant General Office (AGO), RG94, NA (hereafter cited as Jesup Papers); Motte, 1953:135.

10. *A&NC*, 23 November 1837, 328–29; Foreman, 1931:425.

11. Foreman, 1931:426; Foreman, 1972b:353; *A&NC*, 21 December 1837, 395.

12. Jesup to Cross, 3 December 1837, "Gen. Thomas Jesup," Consolidated Files.

13. Report by Gould, Dunn, and Capron, 30 November 1837; "List of prisoners who made their escape on the night of the 29th of November, 1837," Jesup Papers.

14. Foreman, 1931:428–36; Jesup to Cross, 30 November 1837, letterbook, 5 November 1837–3 January 1838:119, Jesup Papers; *ASP.MA*, 7:886–91.

15. Armistead to Chambers, 20 December 1837, Jesup Papers; McCall, 1974:161.

16. *ASP.MA*; 7:986; *Niles Register (NR)*, 10 February 1838, 383; statement by Tony Barnett, 14 May 1846, "R. W. Kirkham," Consolidated Files.

17. *ASP.MA*, 7:986–87.

18. Ibid., 987; Buchanan, 1950:145–46.

19. Sprague, 1964:213; Mahon, 1985:227.

20. *ASP.MA*, 7:987; Buchanan, 1950:146.

21. *NR*, 13 January 1838, 305; Buchanan, 1950:146.

22. *NR*, 13 January 1838, 305; 27 January 1838, 327; 3 February 1838, 353; *ASP.MA*, 7:987; Gentry, 1937:21.

23. *ASP.MA*, 7:987.

24. Monk, 1978:25; Sprague, 1964:213.

25. *ASP.MA*, 7:988; *NR*, 13 January 1838, 305.

26. *ASP.MA*, 7:988–89.

27. Motte, 1953:168, 182–85; *NR*, 17 February 1838, 388

28. *ASP.MA*, 7:193–96; 25th Cong., 2d Sess. H.D. 219:1–5.

Chapter Eight: From Suspicion to Responsibility

1. 25th Cong., 2d Sess., S.D. 507:8–9.

2. Ibid., 8; *Army and Navy Chronicle* (*A&NC*), 22 March 1838, 178, 190; Motte, 1953:210.

3. Freedom certificate of John Cohai and his wife, 30 April 1840, Old Books 9/10, Department of Florida, bound as book 4, Department of New Mexico, Ninth Military Department, Records of Army Continental Commands, RG393, NA (hereafter cited as Freedom Certificate).

4. Jesup to Poinsett, 18 March 1838, "Gen. Thomas Jesup"; statement by Tony Barnett, 14 May 1846, "R. W. Kirkham," Consolidated Files, Records of the Office of the Quartermaster General (QMGO), RG92, NA (hereafter cited as Consolidated Files); Jesup to Marcy, 3 April 1848, Jesup Papers, Records of the Adjutant General Office (AGO), RG94, NA (hereafter cited as Jesup Papers).

5. *A&NC*, 22 March 1838, 190; Jesup to Marcy, 3 April 1848, Jesup Papers; Jesup to Marcy, 1 July 1848, Records of the Bureau of Indian Affairs (BIA), RG75, M574, 13/101–4, NA (hereafter cited as BIA).

6. Jesup to Smith, 6 March 1838, letterbook, 3 January–7 May 1838, Jesup Papers; Bankhead to Jesup, 20 March 1838, J67, Records of the AGO, RG94, M567, 167/494-95, NA (hereafter cited as AGO).

7. Giddings, 1964:185; Jesup to Poinsett, 23 March 1838, J743, M567, 167/638–41, AGO.

8. *Niles Register* (*NR*), 5 May 1838, 145; Taylor to Jesup, 4 April 1838, J82, M567, 167/700–702, AGO; Jesup to Jones, 6 April 1838, letterbook, 3 January–7 May 1838:289, Jesup Papers.

9. Smith to Jesup, 8 April 1838; Smith to Chambers, 14 April 1838, Jesup Papers; Abraham to Jesup, 25 April 1838, Abraham Manuscript, P. K. Yonge Memorial Library of Florida History.

10. *A&NC*, 19 July 1838, 44–45; Foreman, 1972b:367–68; Morrison to Harris, 20 June 1838, M436, M234, 290/no frames, BIA.

11. Foreman, 1972b:364–70; Mahon, 1985:245.

12. Arbuckle to Jones, 12 September 1838, A818, M567, 157/83–85, AGO.

13. Jones to Arbuckle, 17 October 1838; Jones to Taylor, 17 October 1838, M565, 11/39–40; Taylor to Jones, 17 November 1838, T297, M567, 11/648–51, AGO; Masters, Jefferson Barracks, 10 January 1846, "Gopher John," Consolidated Files; Foreman, 1972b:370.

14. Mahon, 1985:255–57.

15. Sprague, 1964:233, 316–17; Adams, 1970:368–80.

16. *A&NC*, 28 March 1839, 205; *NR*, 27 April 1839, 131; 22 June 1839, 265; 14 September 1839, 44.

17. Wilhelm, 1873, 1:154, 156; McCall, 1974:399–401.

18. Payments list initialed J. C. C., 22 December 1845, "Gopher John," Consolidated Files; Wilhelm, 1873, 1:155; Jarvis, 1906–7:270.

19. Report of John Cavallo's activities as interpreter in Florida 1845, "Gopher John," Consolidated Files (hereafter cited as Record of Service).

20. Record of Service; *NR*, 9 May 1840, 146; *A&NC*, 21 October 1840, 268–69.

21. Mahon, 1985:274; Armistead to Adjutant General, 15 June 1840, A146, M567, 201/635–38, AGO.

22. Foreman, 1972b:374–75, 378; Sprague, 1964:312; Mahon, 1985:281–82.

23. Harney to Twiggs, 26 June 1840; Armistead to Adjutant General, 29 June 1840, A161, M567, 201/717–23, 724–27, AGO; Mahon, 1985:277–78.

24. Record of Service; Sprague, 1964:258–60.

25. Rodenbough, 1875:55–56; Hanna, 1936:76–77n26.

26. Sprague, 1964:260, 262–63, 277.

27. Ibid., 249–50, 252–53, 556.

28. Record of Service; Jesup to Commissioner of Indian Affairs, 2 April 1845, "Gopher John," Consolidated Files; Sprague, 1964:286–88; Mahon, 1985:287.

29. Record of Service; Sprague, 1964:286–88, 290–93.

30. Sprague, 1964:297–304; Record of Service.

31. Foreman, 1972b:378–80; Record of Service.

32. Record of Service; Sprague, 1964:459; Mahon, 1985:308.

33. Cooper to Kerr, 14 May 1842, Old Book 3, Department of Florida, bound as book 1, Department of New Mexico, vol. 2, Ninth Military Department, Records of the Army Continental Commands, RG393, NA; Freedom Certificate; Copy of endorsement made in Gofer [*sic*] John's freedom papers, A1282, M234, 291/no frames, BIA; Worth to Adjutant General, 14 July 1842, W331, M567, 262/632–34, AGO; Foreman, 1972b:380; Sprague, 1964:483.

34. *American State Papers: Military Affairs (ASP.MA)*, 7:820–22. For an analysis of the Second Seminole War's impact on all participants, see Mahon, 1985:321–22.

35. Porter, 1967, esp. 238; Mahon, 1985:316, 321; Covington, 1982.

Chapter Nine: Seven Lean Years

1. Foreman, 1972b:380; Foreman, 1972a:224–26; Worth to Adjutant General, 14 July 1842, W331, Records of the Adjutant General Office (AGO), RG94, M567, 262/632–34, NA (hereafter cited as AGO); *Niles Register (NR)*, 6 August 1842, 355; Canby to Crawford, 12 December 1842, C1846, Records of the Bureau of Indian Affairs (BIA), M234, 806/no frames, RG75, NA (hereafter cited as BIA).

2. Foreman, 1972a:223–25; *Annual Report of the Commissioner of Indian Affairs (ARCIA)*, 1842–43:77; Harris, 1932:235.

3. Harris, 1932:234; *ARCIA*, 1842–43:161; 1844–45:176; Gopher John to Jesup, 10 June 1848, J102, M234, 801/no frames, BIA; Copy of John Warrior's freedom papers, 16 February 1844, Headquarters Records, Fort Gibson, Letters Relating to Indian Affairs, Records of Continental Commands, RG393, M1466, 1/392, NA (hereafter cited as Fort Gibson Letters).

4. Harris, 1932:236–37; Foreman, 1972a:237; Hill to Judge, 14 April 1844, J1467; Complaint letter of Seminole Chiefs, 20 April 1844, M1941, M234, 800/no frames, BIA.

5. Foreman, 1972a:237; Porter, 1971:337; Petition signed by Alligator, Wild Cat, and others, 16 May 1844, A1680, M234, 800/no frames, BIA; Jesup to Wilkins, 30 May 1844, "Gopher John," Consolidated Files, Records of the Office of the Quartermaster General (QMGO), RG92, NA (hereafter cited as Consolidated Files); Douglass to Crawford, 10 September 1844, D970; Miccomut-char-sar to Gaines, 23 May 1849, J262, M234, 800 and 801/no frames, BIA.

6. Lancaster, 1986:81.

7. Gopher John to Jesup, 8 July 1844; Duval to Jesup, 4 July 1844, "Gopher John," Consolidated Files; Butler to Harris, 25 July 1845, B2558; Mason to Jones, 10 July 1844, with endorsements by Jesup and Wilkins, M1973, M234, 800/no frames, BIA.

8. John Cavallo to Jesup, 8 January 1845, "Gopher John," Consolidated Files; Judge to Boone, 31 August 1844, J1684, M234, 800/no frames, BIA.

9. Mason to Jones, 5 March 1845, "Fort Gibson"; John Cavallo to Jesup, 8 January 1845; Mason to Adjutant General, 5 February 1845, "Gopher John," Consolidated Files; Butler to Crawford, 16 April 1845, B2452; Butler to Harris, 25 July 1845, B2528, M234, 800/no frames, BIA.

10. Foreman, 1972a:242–43; Kappler, 1903–41, 2:407.

11. Statements by James Logan, 30 November 1847, William D. Shaw, 28 January 1848, and H. W. Wharton, 26 May 1848; Voucher in the amount of $180.00, J96, M234, 801/no frames, BIA.

12. Judge to Crawford, 27 April 1845, J1684, M234, 800/no frames; Arbuckle to Armstrong, 8 February 1845, R185, M234, 240/473-76, BIA.

13. Memo of expenses, board and lodging of Gopher John in Washington, D.C., from 18 May 1845 to 25 February 1846, "Gopher John," Consolidated Files; *Washington Directory*, 1846:43.

14. Writ of attachment against Gofer [*sic*] John (a free Seminole Negro), appearances 193 and 194, October term 1845, Circuit Court, District of Columbia, Case Papers 1802–63, Records of the District Courts of the United States, RG21, NRC; Marcy to Hoban, 8 August 1845, Records of the Office of the Secretary of War, RG107, M6, 26/45, NA.

15. Memo of expenses, board and lodging of Gopher John in Washington, 18 May 1845 to 25 February 1846; Extract of Hertzel to Collins, 8 April 1846; Whitney to Mason, 7 August 1845, "Gopher John"; Wharton to Jesup, 5 February 1848, "Fort Gibson"; John Cowaya to Jesup, 24 March 1849, "John Cowaya," Consolidated Files; Jesup to Belknap, 16 April 1849, Records of the QMGO, RG92, M745, 24/358, NA (hereafter cited as QMGO).

16. "Statement of John Cow-a-ya," 26 March 1846, "Fort Gibson," Consolidated Files.

17. John Horse to Augur, 10 December 1873, 488 M 1870, Records of the AGO, M619, RG94, NA.

18. Jesup to Arbuckle, 8 April 1846, M574, 13/91-92, BIA; John Cowaya's pass, 8 April 1846, M745, 20/209, QMGO.

19. Jesup to Marcy, 1 July 1848, M574, 13/101-104, BIA; and Foreman, 1972a:256. For more on the legal problems of the Black Seminoles in Indian Territory, see Littlefield, 1977, esp. chaps. 4, 5, and 6.

20. Loomis to Jesup, 21 January 1848, "Fort Gibson," Consolidated Files.

21. Foreman, 1972a:256–57.

22. Kirkham to Jesup, 20 August 1846, M1466, 1/402–3, Fort Gibson Letters; Kirkham to Jesup, 26 August 1846, statement made by Tony Barnett, 14 May 1846, "R. W. Kirkham," Consolidated Files; Jesup's endorsement to Cady to Jones, 18 March 1846, M567, 312/324–26, AGO.

23. Kirkham to Jesup, 1 and 26 August 1846, "R. W. Kirkham," Consolidated Files.

24. Brown, 1973:67.

25. Dean to Mannypenny, 24 June 1856, D180, M234, 802/no frames, BIA.

26. Duval to Medill, 2 June 1847, D38, M234, 801/no frames, BIA; Porter, 1971:324–26.

27. Arbuckle to Jesup, 19 June 1846, "Seminole War"; Kirkham to Jesup, 1 August 1846, "R. W. Kirkham," Consolidated Files.

28. Foreman, 1972a:244; *ARCIA*, 1846–47:66–70; Loomis to Flint, 10 July 1847, M1466, 1/406, Fort Gibson Letters; Duval to Medill, 15 October 1847, D65, M234, 801/no frames, BIA; Loomis to Jesup, 7 December 1847, "Fort Gibson," Consolidated Files.

29. Bonneville to Flint, 14 April 1848; Bonneville to Rutherford, 14 April 1848, B408, M567, 369/720-24, AGO; *Fort Smith Herald*, 7 June 1848; Gopher John to Jesup, 10 June 1848, J102, M234, 801/no frames, BIA.

Chapter Ten: The Exodus to Mexico

1. *Official Opinions*, 1852–70, 4:720–29.

2. Jesup to Bonneville, 28 July 1848, Headquarters Records, Fort Gibson, Letters Relating to Indian Affairs, Records of Continental Commands, RG393, M1466, 1/

412, NA (hereafter cited as Fort Gibson Letters); Private memo from Marcy to Jesup, 22 July 1848 and Jesup's reply of same date, "Gen. Thomas Jesup," Consolidated Files, Records of the Office of the Quartermaster General (QMGO), RG92, NA (hereafter cited as Consolidated Files).

3. Marcy to Arbuckle, 5 August 1848, Letters Sent by the Secretary of War, RG107, M6, 28/359-60, NA; Flint to Belknap, 19 December 1848, Records of the Bureau of Indian Affairs (BIA), RG75, M574, 13/155-58, NA (hereafter cited as BIA).

4. Flint to Belknap, 19 December 1848; List of negroes turned over to the Seminole Chiefs at Fort Gibson, 2 January 1849; Arbuckle to Jones, 8 January 1849, M574, 13/139-58, BIA; Belknap to Arbuckle, 3 January 1849, M1466, 1/415-16, Fort Gibson Letters; Foreman, 1971a:257-58.

5. Miller, 1988:130-31; Foreman, 1972a:258-59; 33d Cong., 2d Sess., H.D. 15:10; "I'm in the Wewoka Switch," 1963.

6. *War of the Rebellion*, ser. 4, 1:523; Foreman, 1971a:261; 33d Cong., 2d Sess., H.D. 15:22.

7. Duval to Belknap, 7 June 1849, M234, 801/no frames, BIA; 33d Cong., 2d Sess., H.D. 15:22-23.

8. 33d Cong., 2d Sess., H.D. 15:28.

9. Duval to Brown, 30 May 1850, D392, M234, 801/no frames, BIA; Interviews with John Jefferson, 1941, and Enrique Galán Long, 1942.

10. Foreman, 1972a:248; 31st Cong., 1st Sess. S.D. 49.

11. Raiford to Drennen, 15 November 1849, D274, M234, 924/no frames, BIA; Interviews with Rebecca Wilson, 1941, 1943; Rosa Fay and Julia Payne, 1942; William (Bill) Wilson, Penny Factor, Sarah Daniels, and Adam Payne, 1943; Molly Perryman, 1942, 1943.

12. Foreman, 1972a:262; *Memorial*, 1893:69-70; Duval to Brown, 30 May 1850, D392, M234, 801/no frames, BIA.

13. Rollins to Brown, 8 May 1850, R896, M234, 858/512-16, BIA; Foreman, 1972a:262; Webb, 1965:133; Banta, 1933:54-58; *Texas State Gazette*, 21 June 1851.

14. Interviews with Molly Perryman and Julia Payne, 1942; Penny Factor, 1943. All three were Kitty Johnson's daughters.

15. Interview with Penny Factor, 1943. In 1853, however, a Black Seminole identified only as Cofe [Cuffee] accused Wild Cat of having sold him into slavery in Texas for eighty pesos. Cuffee eventually escaped from San Antonio and returned to Mexico. Legajo 45, 1853, numero 1790, Archivo de la Secretaria de Gobierno, Saltillo, Coahuila, 1848-76, 44:185-91, M-A-10, Bancroft Library, University of California, Berkeley.

16. *Texas Republican*, 24 August 1850; *Texas Monument*, 7 Aug. 1850; Sumpter, 1969:4; Foster, 1978:42-43; Interviews with Curly Jefferson, John Jefferson, Adam McClain, 1941; Rosa Fay, 1942. Sprague's journal confirms most of the recollections of the Black

Seminoles, except the chase. Because other groups were pursued, however, it is possible that the informants were relating those episodes (Sprague, n.d.). The emigrants did stop at Eagle Pass, before entering Mexico (Montgomery, 1852:73–77).

17. Jauregui to Ministro de Guerra y Marina, 18 July 1850, *El Siglo Diez y Nueve*, 12 August 1850; Foster, 1978:42–43; "El Nacimiento," 1850, Porter Papers, Schomburg Center for Research in Black Culture (hereafter cited as Porter Papers). This is the first time that John Cavallo is listed as John Horse in the official record. We will use this name in subsequent chapters.

18. "El Nacimiento," informe, primera parte, anexo num. 2, Porter Papers; Webb, 1965:133; Smith, 1963:65–88; Tyler, 1972:1–12.

19. 33d Cong., 2d Sess., H.D. 15:12, 16–17; Dent to Flint, 15 July 1850, A135, Records of the Adjutant General Office (AGO), RG94, M567, 422/458–60, NA (hereafter cited as AGO); Bowlegs to Jim Jumper, 12 April 1850, Records of the Headquarters Army of the Southwestern Frontier, RG393, M1202, 7/566–69, NA.

20. Dent to Flint, 15 July 1850, A135, M567, 422/458–60, AGO; Foreman, 1972a:262–63.

21. Foreman, 1972a:262–63.

22. Duval to Brooke, 21 October 1850, M567, 434/746–49, AGO; Duval to Bell, 20 October 1850, M234, 801/no frames, BIA; Glisan, 1874:65; *Fort Smith Herald*, 8 November, 6 December 1850.

23. Foster, 1978:46; Interview with Curly Jefferson, 1941; Duval to Lea, 24 April 1851, D605, M234, 801/no frames, BIA.

24. Marcy, 1866:55–56; Marcy and McClellan, 1961:101–2.

25. Woodhull, 1937:119, 123.

26. Duval to Bell, 20 and 21 October 1850; Rollins to Bell, 30 October 1850; Brooke to Bell, 12 November 1850, Governors' Records, Texas State Library; *Fort Smith Herald*, 13 December 1850.

Chapter Eleven: This Land Was Bought with Blood

1. Interview with Rosa Fay, 1942.

2. Interviews with Curly Jefferson, 1941; Penny Factor and Teresa Wilson, 1942; Schoen, 1936:296, 299; Lundy, 1969:116.

3. *Reports of the Committee*, 1875:323; Brooke to Bell, 12 November 1850, Governors' Records, Texas State Library (hereafter cited as Governors' Records).

4. *Reports of the Committee*, 1875:303–4, 407–8; Maza, 1893:474–78; *Memoria*, 1852:17–18; Article 2, Agreement between President of Mexico and Wild Cat and Papicua, 26 July 1852 (hereafter cited as Agreement with President of Mexico); El Nacimiento, anexo num. 5, primera parte, 29–32, Departamento Agrario; Interview with Penny Factor, 1942.

5. Brooke to Jones, 21 November 1850, B707; Morris to Maldonado, 24 March

1851; Maldonado to Morris, 29 March 1851, H205, M567, 434/746–48, 447/480–86, Records of the Adjutant General Office (AGO), RG94, NA (hereafter cited as AGO); *Texas State Gazette*, 21 June 1851.

6. El Gobernador Interino del Estado de Coahuila a todos sus habitantes, 25 September 1850; El Nacimiento, anexo num. 5, informe primera parte, 24–32, Departamento Agrario.

7. 33d Cong., 2d Sess., H.D. 15:14; *Memoria*, 1852:49–51; *Reports of the Committee*, 1875:327, 408–9; *La Patria*, 12 July 1851; Glisan, 1874:93; Latorre and Latorre, 1976:14.

8. *Western Texan*, 18 September 1851.

9. Schwartz, 1974:iv; Fornell, 1956:411; Rippy, 1919; Rippy, 1922; Shearer, 1951b; Hughes, 1964:100–105; Ford, 1963:195–205.

10. Duval to Lea, 15 November 1852, Records of the Bureau of Indian Affairs (BIA), RG75, D223, M234, 801/no frames, NA (hereafter cited as BIA).

11. Maldonado to Comandante del Fuerte Duncan, 20 September 1851; Arredondo to Alcade Mayor del Condado de Bejar, 20 September 1851; Maldonado to Gobernador, 22 September 1851; English translation of Maldonado's letter of 22 September 1851; Official request of Governor Bell relative to certain runaway negro slaves, 17 September 1851, Governors' Records. When asked how Warren Adams was able to capture John Horse, Sarah Daniels stated simply, "Booze and Dave Town" (interview, 1942).

12. Sumpter, 1969:61.

13. *Reports of the Committee*, 1875:331; Maldonado to Jauregui, 2 November 1851; Langberg to Ministro de Guerra y Marina, 7 November 1851, Amagos de la invasión al Departamento de Rio Grande por fuerzas unidas de los EEUU Ano de 1851; Fuente to Ministro de Guerra y Marina, Archivo de la Secretaria de la Defensa; *La Patria*, 22 November 1851.

14. The chief sources of the history of the Seminoles in Mexico from 1852 to 1861 are the Guajardo Papers and the Muzquiz Records housed at the Beinecke Rare Book and Manuscript Library, Yale University (hereafter cited as GP and MR). Itinerario de la expedición San Carlos a Monclova El Viejo, GP; Huston to Lamotte, 10 February 1852, S324, M567, 472/101–3, AGO.

15. *Memoria*, 1852:39.

16. Article 3, Agreement with President of Mexico, 26 July 1852; Revere, 1872:206; Interviews with Curly Jefferson, 1941; Rosa Fay, 1942; Teresa C. Wilson and Penny Factor, 1943.

17. Froebel, 1859:351; Itinerario de la expedición San Carlos a Monclova el Viejo, GP; En la villa de Múzquiz a 10. de abril de 1852, MR; Interviews with Curly Jefferson and Dindie Factor, 1942, 1943.

18. R. A. to Al mismo, Sr., 5 July 1852, MR.

19. *El Siglo Diez y Nueve*, 30 April, 14 and 18 May, 18 and 29 July, 31 August 1852; Manero, 1878:30–31; Agreement with President of Mexico, 26 July 1852; Sesión

ordinaria del 2 de Septiembre de 1852, MR; *Reports of the Committee,* 1875:409; Latorre and Latorre, 1976:15.

20. Sesión ordinaria del 2 de Septiembre de 1852, MR.

21. June 1852, GP; En la villa de Múzquiz a 10. de julio de 1852; Fragoso to Múzquiz, 27 November 1852; Unknown to 10. Oficial, 20 November 1852; Alcadia to Nava, 21 December 1852, MR.

22. Tyler, 1968:60.

23. Múzquiz to Supremo Gobierno del Estado, 4 October 1852, MR; *Western Texan,* 18 November, 2 December 1852.

24. *Reports of the Committee,* 1875:409.

25. Interviews with Elsa Payne, Sarah Daniels, and Dindie Factor, 1943. Porter, who was not a linguist, was unaware of the existence of Black Seminole Creole during all the years he worked with the group. Professor Ian Hancock did the initial recording of the language in 1975 (Hancock, 1975).

26. Lista de los negros de la tribu Mascogo agraciada por el gobierno con terras de la Colonia del Nacimiento, Porter Papers, Schomburg Center for Research in Black Culture (hereafter cited as Porter Papers). The custom of having both American and Mexican names survives to this day. Personal observation of Alcione M. Amos, November 1976, Nacimiento de los Negros, Coahuila, Mexico, and interview with Alice Fay Lozano, 1993.

27. Despite the 1853 requirement that all infants should be baptized in the parish church, by 1891, out of 123 Mascogo males listed in a Mexican census, only seven were identified as Catholics. Gonzalez to Múzquiz, 7 December 1853, MR; Lista de negros, Porter Papers; Jones, 1976:453; *Festival,* 1993:59.

28. Botkin, 1989:65, 86, 91, and 124; Foster, 1978:51–52; Trout, 1909:84; David Bowlegs, Pension File, Application 1138416, Certificate XC946437; Jerry Daniels, Pension File, Application 1411757; Robert Kibbitts, Widow's Pension File, Application 856152, Certificate XC 2681380, Records of the Veterans Administration, RG15, NA.

Chapter Twelve: Perils on the Border

1. *Reports of the Committee,* 1875:408–9; June 1853, 15 August 1853, Guajardo Papers (hereafter cited as GP); Villarreal y Villarreal, to Juez de Paz de Santa Rosa, 13 September 1853; R. M. Comisaría to Sr. Prefecto del Districto, 9 September 1854 (121), Muzquiz Records (hereafter cited as MR); Porter, 1946b.

2. Múzquiz to Comisaría, 8 May 1854 (62), MR.

3. Santa Rosa to Sr. Prefecto, 28 April 1854; Comisaría to Rodrigues, 5 June 1854 (70); Ramirez to Comisario Municipal de la Villa de Múzquiz, 21 July 1854 (169), MR.

4. Ramirez to Como. Municipal de Múzquiz, 8 February (18); 27 February 1855 (26), MR.

5. 33d Cong., 2d Sess., H.D. 15:4, 6.

6. *Texas State Times*, 6 October 1855.

7. Interviews with Sarah Daniels and Julia Payne, 1942; Dolly July, 1941, 1943; Rena July, 1943.

8. Juan de la Garza, 18 August 1858, MR; Interview with Johnnie Mae Shields, 1943.

9. Prefecto del Districto to Comisaría, 17 July 1854 (92); Ramirez to Como. Municipal de Múzquiz, 2 August 1854 (174); Múzquiz to Sor. Prefecto del Distrito, 14 August 1854 (103), MR.

10. Ramirez to Como. Municipal de Múzquiz, 3 August 1854 (176); Castañeda to Sor. Comisario Municipal de la Villa de Santa Rosa, 15 August (186); 18 August 1854 (183); Comisaría to Prefecto del Distrito, 9 September 1854 (121), MR.

11. Comisario, Múzquiz, ca. 30 April 1855 (47); Ramirez to Como. Municipal de Múzquiz, 8 May 1855, MR; 1855, GP; Porter, 1971:440.

12. Serapio Fragoso to Comisario Municipal de la Villa de Múzquiz, 18 May 1855 (49); Mena to Comisario Municipal de la Villa de Múzquiz, 20 May 1855 (93); Múzquiz, 21 and 23 May 1855; San Miguel Al Mismo Señor, 19 June 1855 (79), MR.

13. Tyler, 1967:577; Tyler, 1972:7–8; *Reports of the Committee*, 1875:191–92.

14. Sumpter, 1969:61–62; Shearer, 1951a:436–39; *Reports of the Committee*, 1875:191–92; Duval to Lea, 15 November 1852, Records of the Bureau of Indian Affairs (BIA), RG75, D223, M234, 801/no frames; Brown, 1973:68.

15. Sumpter, 1969:61; Shearer, 1951a:439; *Texas Indian Papers*, 1960, 3:254–55; *Texas State Times*, 6 October, 17 November 1855; *San Antonio Texan*, 11, 18, and 25 October 1855.

16. Langberg to 1a. Autoridad de la Villa Múzquiz, 22 October 1855 (115); Múzquiz to Cmdte. la Sección de Coah., 24 Oct 1855; Múzquiz to Langberg, 25 October 1855, MR; *La Patria*, 17 May 1856.

17. *Reports of the Committee*, 1875:410; Galindo to 1a. Autoridad de la Villa de Múzquiz, 27 November 1855 (138); Garza Gonzalez to 1a. Autoridad Política de Múzquiz, 11 May 1856 (190); 6 December 1856 (393); 14 March 1857 (77); 22 September 1857 (204); 18 December 1857 (290); Garza Gonzalez to Alcalde 1o. de Múzquiz, 19 January 1858 (24), MR.

18. 24 May 1856, GP; Garza Gonzalez to 1a. Autoridad de Múzquiz, 24 May 1856 (171); 3 July 1857 (159); Garza Gonzalez to Sro. Alcalde 1o. de Múzquiz, 15 February 1858 (92), MR.

19. Flores Tapia, 1980:23; Moseley, 1963; 1856, GP.

20. 1856, GP; TT to Gobierno, 1 June, 25 April, and 24 May 1856; TT to Secretario de Gobierno, 19 May 1856; Garza Gonzalez to 1a. Autoridad Política de Múzquiz, 24 May 1856 (172), MR.

21. 9 April 1856, GP; Garza Gonzalez to 1a. Autoridad de Múzquiz, 27 November 1856, MP. John Horse was often mentioned after 1856 as "Juan de Dios Vidaurri (a)

Caballo," perhaps after he submitted himself to Catholic baptism. His sponsor probably was teacher Juan Nepomuceno Vidaurri. Wild Cat continued to be known exclusively as Gato del Monte, Gato de la Sierra, or simply Capitán Gato.

22. Moseley, 1963:230–31; Elizondo to Gobierno del Estado, 3 and 5 November 1856, MR.

23. *Reports of the Committee*, 1875:410; 20 January, 17 February 1857, GP.

24. Garza Gonzalez to 1a. Autoridad Política de Múzquiz, 24 March (77), 25 March (80), 21 April (149) 1857, MR; 28 May, 20 June 1857, GP.

25. Garza Gonzales to 1a. Autoridad Política de Múzquiz, 25 March (81), 21 April (102) 1857; Múzquiz de Avile to Garza Gonzalez, 7 April 1857, MR.

26. Garza Gonzalez to 1a. Autoridad Política de Múzquiz, 13 August, 8 September (195), 24 December (292), 27 December 1857, MR; 8 July; 3, 8, and 21 August; 8 September; 24 December 1857, GP.

27. Garza Gonzalez to 1a. Autoridad Política de Múzquiz, 27 August (183), 20 September 1857 (225); Garza Gonzalez to Alcalde 1o. de Muzquiz, 24 February 1858, MR; 28 September 1857, GP; *Reports of the Committee*, 1875:409; Interview with Sarah Daniels, 1943.

28. Ramón Múzquiz to Sr. Alcalde 1o. de Múzquiz, 13 September 1858 (170); Complaint of the Seminoles, 13 September 1858 (172), MR.

29. Espinoza to Alcalde Constitutional de la Villa de Múzquiz, 9 March 1858 (25); Múzquiz to Sro. Alcalde 1o. de Múzquiz, 18 March 1858 (107); Al Prefecto de Monclova, 22 March, 4 and 8 April 1858 (125), MR; 10 and 25 March 1858, GP.

30. *Annual Report of the Commissioner of Indian Affairs (ARCIA)*, 1858:328; *Reports of the Committee*, 1875:410; Bliss, n.d., 2:50–51; Múzquiz to Sr. Alcalde 1o. de Múzquiz, 17 February 1859 (27), MR; 9, 17, and 25 February 1859, GP.

31. *Reports of the Committee*, 1875:410.

32. Galindo to Alcalde 1o. Const. de la Villa de Múzquiz, 6 March (39), 8 March (41) 1859; Monclova, 9 March 1859 (42), MR; 6 and 31 March 1859, GP.

Chapter Thirteen: Adrift in the Laguna

1. *Reports of the Committee*, 1875:410; Múzquiz to Alcalde 1o. de la Villa de San Buenaventura, 31 March 1859, Archivo General del Estado de Coahuila (hereafter cited as Archivo de Coahuila).

2. Miller, 1985:235–37.

3. Interviews with Dindie Factor, 1943; Julia Payne, 1942.

4. Circa April 1859, Al Prefecto de Monclova, 21, 24, and 25 May 1859; Al Comandante del 1o. Cantón, 25 May 1859, Muzquiz Records (hereafter cited as MR); 14 April, 25 May 1859, Guajardo Papers (hereafter cited as GP).

5. *Reports of the Committee*, 1875:410; Rejón to Sor. Alcalde 1o. de la Villa de Múzquiz, 15 October 1860 (160); Múzquiz to Al Mismo, 4 November 1860, MR.

6. Alessio Robles, 1938:456–57.

7. Declaration by John Willett, 17 June 1895; "Notes by Gen'l John L. Bullis U.S. Army, retired commanded the scouts from 72 to 81, 9 yrs," Records of Cards and Correspondence Relating to Various Subjects, 1909–12, 28985, Records of the Department of Texas, Records of Army Continental Commands, RG393, NA (hereafter cited as Bullis's Notes); Interviews with Bill Daniels, Fred Fletcher, Gregorio Frausto, 1943; Rosa Fay, 1942; Dolly July, 1941.

8. Bullis's Notes; Newcomb, 1863:14–15.

9. Box, 1869:203–4; Interview with Bill Daniels, 1943; Bliss, n.d., 5:107.

10. Rejón to Sor. Alcalde 10. de Muzquiz, 6 July 1861 (175), MR; 6 July 1861, GP; *Reports of the Committee*, 1875:411.

11. Interview with Bill Daniels, 1943.

12. Interview with Priscilla Dixey, 1943; General Affidavit by August Bruner, 8 January 1913, Pension File of James Bruner, 1361661, Records of the Veterans Administration, RG15, NA.

13. Interview with Sarah Daniels, 1942, 1943.

14. Letters from John Jefferson to Porter, 22 March, 11 May, 12 and 24 July 1946; Interviews with Molly Perryman and John Jefferson, 1941; Julia Payne, 1942; Bill Daniels, Penny Factor, Elsa Payne, Adam McClain, and Bill Wilson, 1943; Dolly July, 1941, 1943.

15. Bliss, n.d., 5:126–27; Boyd, 1982:330–31; Fenley, 1939:187.

16. Interviews with Bill Daniels and Adam McClain, 1943. Although the Comanches and Apaches were hereditary enemies, they occasionally operated together against a common enemy. Fehrenbach, 1974:133; Wallace and Hoebel, 1952:8, 288; Newcomb, 1961:125; Myers, 1971:144; Sonnichsen, 1986:135, 169.

17. Fehrenbach, 1974:127–28.

18. Ford, 1963:135.

19. Meyer and Sherman, 1991:381–98; Scholes, 1969:104–7; Sinkin, 1979:105–9.

20. Declaration by John Willett, 17 June 1895.

21. Interviews with Rosa Fay, 1942; Sarah Daniels and Gregorio Frausto, 1943; Niox, 1874:469–73; Dabbs, 1963:99; Elton, 1867:48; Flores Tapia, 1980:92, 124.

22. C. Secretario, 30 May 1891, num. 44-12-60, Acervo Histórico Diplomático, Secretaria de Relaciones Exteriores (hereafter cited as Acervo Histórico Diplomático); 1867, GP; Anderson, 1959:xxiii–xxv.

23. Meyer and Sherman, 1991:397–40.

24. Interviews with Rosa Fay, 1942; Julia Payne, 1944.

25. Census taken by Second Lieutenant Patrick Kelliher, October 1971, Letters Received Related to Difficulties with Indians (Indian File), Department of Texas, 1870–1913, RG393, NA; United States Census, 1870, Cameron County, Texas, M593/1578:115–16; Uvalde County, Texas, M593/1597:1–2; Interview with John Jefferson, 1941.

26. Root, 1932:156; Latorre and Latorre, 1976:18–19; Gibson, 1963:193–207.

27. 1860, 1863, GP.

28. Guajardo, 1940:343–46; 1863, GP.

29. Interviews with Rosa Fay, 1942; Bill Daniels, 1943.

30. Ríos to C. Juez de 1a. Instancia de esta Villa, 20 February 1867; C. Secretario, 30 May 1891, Acervo Histórico Diplomático; Al Juzgado 10. Com. de Muzquiz, 20 February 1867, MR; *Diário Oficial*, 30 November 1938, 17.

Chapter Fourteen: Black Watch on the Rio Grande

1. Statement C, "Report upon the Indians and tribal profiles, Sept. 1st, 1868 attached to Reynolds to AGO," 19 September 1868, Records of the Adjutant General Office (AGO), M619, 642/171–73, 224–37, RG94, NA; 43d Cong., 1st Sess., H.D. 257:22; Foster, 1978:46. Much of the information about the Black Seminoles between 1870 and 1885 is included in file 488 M 1870 of the Records of the AGO, Letters Received, 1861–70, M619, Rolls 799–800, RG94, NA. Unfortunately, large portions of the microfilm are illegible. Because we had to consult the original documents, it was impossible to determine the frame numbers for this material. Citations will include only reference to file 488 M 1870, AGO.

2. *Annual Report of the Commissioner of Indian Affairs (ARCIA)*, 1868–69:87–88; Brief of papers relative to the subsistence, etc., at Fort Duncan, Texas, of Seminole (Negro) Indians from Mexico, 15 September 1884, 488 M 1870, AGO.

3. DeGress to Wood, 17 March 1870, Letters Sent, Fort Duncan June 1869–February 1872, 128–29, Records of Army Continental Commands, RG393, NA (hereafter cited as Letters Sent, Fort Duncan); To Whom It May Concern, 17 March 1870, File 488 M 1870, AGO.

4. Personal communication by Donald Swanson, 5 March 1993; Schuchardt to Fish, 25 June 1870, Records of the Department of State, Despatches from U.S. Consuls in Piedras Negras, 1868–1906, M299, 1/146–56, RG59, NA.

5. Wallace, 1964:29.

6. Brooks to Commissioner of Indian Affairs, 18 August 1932, 14308-1914-123, Classified Files, Records of the Bureau of Indian Affairs (BIA), RG75, NA; *ARCIA*, 1870:328; Interviews with Curly Jefferson, Dolly July, 1941; Julia Payne, 1942.

7. Interview with John Jefferson, 1941; Pratt to Post Adjutant, Fort Duncan, 4 July 1870, Letters Received, Fort Duncan, Records of Continental Commands, RG393, NA (hereafter cited as Letters Received, Fort Duncan).

8. *ARCIA*, 1870:328.

9. Ibid., 329; Muster roll of Detachment of Seminole Negro Indian Scouts, 16 August 1870, 103, Military Division of the Missouri, Special File, Seminole Negro Indians, 1872–76, Records of Army Continental Commands, RG393, NA (hereafter cited as Special File).

10. Bliss to Wood, 14 December 1870, Special File; Bliss to Assistant Adjutant General, Texas, 20 February and 28 March 1871, Letters Sent, Fort Duncan.

11. Bliss, n.d., 5:109, 126–27; Carter, 1961:437; Boyd, 1982:330–31.

12. Muster roll of Seminole Negro Indian Scouts, Fort Duncan, 31 October–31 December 1871, Regular Army Muster Rolls, Indian Scouts, Texas, Records of the AGO, RG94, NA; Record of medical history of post, Fort Duncan, April 1868–January 1875, Records of the AGO, RG94, NA; Carroll, 1971:553, n17–19.

13. Elijah Daniels and Caesar Payne to Commanding Officer, Fort Duncan, Texas, no date, Letters Received, Fort Duncan; Census taken by Second Lieutenant Patrick Kelliher, October 1871, Letters Received Related to Difficulties with Indians (Indian File), Department of Texas, 1870–1913, Records of Army Continental Commands, RG393, NA; 1870 Census of the United States, Uvalde County, M593/1597, NA.

14. Interviews with Julia Payne, 1942, 1944; Molly Perryman, 1942, 1943.

15. Interview with Rebecca Wilson, 1941; Merriam to Commanding Officer of Fort Clark, 18 July 1872, Letters Sent, Fort Duncan; Special Orders no. 96, 3 August 1872, 267, Special File.

16. Butler, 1935:358; Porter and Wallace, 1961:73–75; Reeve, 1950:203; Wallace, 1951:452–62, 76; Porter 1971:478; McCright, 1981:12–15; Woodhull, 1937:120; Clous to Post Adjutant, 16 September 1871; Bullis to Clous, 25 September 1871, Reports of Expeditions and Scouts, December 1870–May 1875, Fort McKavett, Texas, 98–105, Records of Continental Commands, RG393, NA.

17. Downey and Jacobsen, 1973:193–94; Mason, 1970:357.

18. Nohl, 1962:77–80; Grant, 1990:772.

19. Carter, 1961:423.

20. Rister, 1928:153–54; Utley, 1984:344–65; Carter, 1961:437; Nohl, 1962:77–101; Woodhull, 1937:121; Crimmins, 1926:20–21; Thompson, 1986; Thompson, 1992:423; Wallace and Anderson, 1965. Interviews with Julia Payne, 1942; Warren Perryman, 1941 (son of James Perryman and Costilietos's daughter); Bill Daniels, William (Bill) Wilson, and Penny Factor, 1943.

21. Wallace, 1967:169; Utley, 1984:347–49; Nohl, 1962:98.

22. Mackenzie to Assistant Adjutant General, Department of Texas, 10 July 1873; Petition by Eligah Daniel [sic]; John Warde [sic], and James Bruner, 28 June 1873, 2925, Special File; Utley, 1984:349.

23. Cowen to Secretary of War, 15 August 1874, 3893, Special File; Shafter to Assistant Adjutant General, Department of Texas, 10 May 1875, 38, Letters Sent, Fort Duncan.

24. John Kiveth [sic] to General Augur, 10 December 1873, 488 M 1870, AGO; Interviews with Curly Jefferson, 1941; Rosa Fay, 1942.

25. Interviews with Molly Perryman, 1941, 1942; Rosa Fay, 1942; Dindie Factor, 1942, 1943; John Jefferson and Dolly July, 1941; Bill Daniels and Rena July, 1943.

26. Interview with John Jefferson, 1941; John Kiveth [*sic*] to General Augur, 10 December 1873; John Horse to General Augur, 10 December 1873; 488 M 1870, AGO.

27. Augur to AGO, 21 February 1874, 488 M 1870, AGO.

28. Interview with John Jefferson, 1941.

Chapter Fifteen: Blood on the Saddle

1. "Record of Engagements," 1933:105; Return of the Fourth Regiment of U.S. Cavalry, December 1873, Returns from Regular Army Cavalry Regiments, 1833–1916, M744, 42/58; Hudson to Post Adjutant, Fort Clark, 15 December 1873, 4997, Records of the Adjutant General Office (AGO), RG94, M666, 135/249–54, NA (hereafter cited as AGO).

2. Interview with Rebecca Wilson, 1943; Swanson, n.d.:25–26.

3. 1870 census, Maverick County, Texas, M593, 1597; Pension files of Lewis White, 804588, and Joseph Ramour (alias Joe Remo), 1252104, Records of the Veterans Administration, RG15, NA; Interview with John Jefferson, 1941. William Miller's mother may have been a Black Seminole. Interview with William "Dub" Warrior, 1994.

4. Muster roll of Seminole Negro Indian Scouts, 30 June–31 August 1874, Records of the AGO, RG94, NA (hereafter cited as Muster Roll); Haley, 1976:170–72; Utley, 1984:214–23; Nohl, 1962:102–7; Leckie, 1963:185–207; Leckie, 1986:1; Pate, 1976:263–75.

5. Strong, n.d.:53; Hatfield, n.d.; Hunter 1944:178–79; Wallace, 1968:193; Neal, n.d.

6. Leckie, 1986:74; Carter, 1961:485–87; Carter, 1982:105; Nohl, 1962:115–18.

7. Haley, 1989:196–97; Carter, 1961:494–95; Carter, 1982:107–9.

8. Woodhull, 1937:125–26; Jones, 1976:455.

9. Wallace, 1968:157, 174.

10. Pate, 1976:263–75; Utley, 1984:226–33; Leckie, 1986:2.

11. Bullis to Smith, 27 April 1875, General Orders no. 10, Department of Texas, 12 May 1875, 2696, M666, 217/359–61, AGO; Crimmins, 1926:20–21; Shipman, 1926:58–63; Woodhull, 1937:121–22.

12. Crimmins, 1933:83–84; Leckie, 1967:144–45; Carlson, 1989:80; Muster Roll, 31 August and 31 October 1875.

13. Atkinson to Smith, 16 November 1874, A1085; Bullis to Smith, 14 May 1875, B791, Records of the Bureau of Indian Affairs (BIA), RG75, M234, 805/no frames, NA (hereafter cited as BIA).

14. Fisher and Dykes, 1966:57; Bonnet, 1926:36–37; Letter from John Jefferson, 27 May 1949; Interview with Julia Payne, 1944. John Creaton, a resident of Eagle Pass, mentioned in his unpublished autobiography that King Fisher killed another Black Seminole. According to Creaton, the unarmed scout hit Fisher with his quirt during

an argument in front of a saloon. The outlaw then fatally shot the scout. Creaton, n.d.:32–33.

15. Bullis to Assistant Adjutant General, Texas, 28 May 1875, 2959; Hatch to Assistant Adjutant General, Texas, 9 August 1875, 4643, Special File, 1872–76, Records of Army Continental Commands, RG393, NA (hereafter cited as Special File); *Annual Report of the Commissioner of Indian Affairs (ARCIA)*, 1875:30.

16. Elizey Danuel [*sic*] to Genuel [*sic*], 7 March 1876; Endorsements by Mackenzie, 20 April 1876, and Sheridan, 29 April 1876, 2397, Special File.

17. Schofield to Adjutant General, 8 February 1877, 37, Letters Sent, Fort Duncan, March 1875–May 1877, Records of Army Continental Commands, RG393, NA; Interviews with John Jefferson, 1941, 1943.

18. Dorst to Adjutant General, Department of Texas, 14 April 1909, 28985, Correspondence Relating to Various Subjects, Records of Army Continental Commands, RG393, NA; Petition signed by thirty-four Kinney County residents, 24 April 1876, 4377, Special File; Crimmins, 1926:19.

19. Ord to Williams, 15 June 1876, S448, M234, 805/no frames, BIA; Ord's endorsement on Gregg to Assistant Adjutant General, Department of Texas, 25 May 1876, 2880, Special File.

20. Utley, 1984:344–50; Carlson, 1989:50–51, 88–107; Rippy, 1926:282–95; Clendenen, 1969:61–84; Pate, 1976:175–94; Mason, 1970:1; Muster Roll, 31 December 1875–29 February 1876.

21. Rodenbough and Haskin, 1896:295; Woodhull, 1937:122; Butler, 1935:360; Leckie, 1967:150–51; Crimmins, 1926:19; Rippy, 1926:294–95; Porter and Wallace, 1961:85; Muster Roll, 30 June–31 August 1876.

22. Interviews with Rebecca Wilson and Molly Perryman, 1941.

23. Interview with Curly Jefferson, 1941; Neal, 1990:16; Letter from Charles Neal, Jr., to Alcione M. Amos, 6 February 1993.

24. Interviews with Curly Jefferson, John Jefferson, 1941; Penny Factor, 1943; Neal, 1990:17.

25. Neal, 1990:18.

26. Swanson, n.d.:13, 30, 38; Interviews with John Jefferson, Curly Jefferson, 1941; Julia Payne, 1942.

27. Leckie, 1967:152; Wallace, 1951:83; Muster Roll, 28 February–30 April 1877.

28. 45th Cong., 2d Sess., H.D. 64:31; 45th Cong., 1st Sess., H.D. 13:171, 189; Raht, 1963:205; Telegram from Shafter to Ord, 7 July 1877, 3813; and Bullis to Dodt, 9 July 1877, 4079, both filed with 1653, M666, 200/159–64, AGO.

29. Muster Roll, 31 August–31 October 1877; Shafter to Adjutant General, Department of Texas, 5 October 1877, 1653; Bullis to Dodt, 12 October 1877, 1653; Shafter to Assistant Adjutant General, Department of Texas, 24 December 1877, 1653, M666, 203/396–403, 410–13, 389–95, AGO.

30. Reeve, 1950:203.

31. 45th Cong, 2d Sess., H.D. 64:85–86; Reeve, 1950:206–7; Rister, 1928:187–88; Bullis to Dodt, 22 December 1877, 1653, M666, 203/335–41, AGO.

32. Crimmins, 1926:21.

33. 45th Cong. 2d Sess., H.D. 64:169; Rister, 1928:187–89; Rodenbough and Haskin, 1896:275; Reeve, 1950:214; Bullis to Dodt, 22 December 1877, 1653; Young to Acting Assistant Adjutant General, District of the Nueces, 18 December 1877; Itinerary of a scout under Captain S. B. M. Young, November and December 1877, M666, 203/335–41, 444–59, 460–79, AGO.

Chapter Sixteen: The End of the Scouts

1. Swanson, n.d.:21; Haley, 1989:196; Muster roll of Seminole Negro Indian Scouts, 31 October–31 December 1878, Records of the Adjutant General Office (AGO), RG94, NA. Swanson compiled an alphabetical list of all the men who served in the Detachment of Seminole Negro Indian Scouts with a summary record of their enlistments.

2. Sweet and Knox, 1883:520–21; Butler, 1935:358–62; Rister, 1928:188–89; Woodhull, 1937:124–25.

3. Woolford, 1962:491, 497.

4. Crimmins, 1926:20; Rister, 1928:267–68; Woodhull, 1937:121–22; Fenley, 1939: 32–33; Sowell, 1947; Wallace, 1951:84; Interviews with Julia Payne, 1942, 1944.

5. Interview with John Jefferson, 1941; "Notes by Gen'l John L. Bullis, U.S. Army, retired commanded the scouts from 72 to 81, 9 yrs," Records of Cards and Correspondence Relating to Various Subjects, 1909–12, 28985, Records of the Department of Texas, 1870–1913, Records of Army Continental Commands, RG393, NA; Crimmins, 1926:21; Wallace, 1951:85; Butler, 1935:358–62; Raht, 1963:198. Not all the Black Seminoles were fond of Bullis. One of them, Dan Johnson, was sent to prison for pulling a gun on the officer; Johnson also called Bullis a "white S.O.B.": Case 223, 1876; Case 247, Kinney County, Texas District Court Records.

6. Swanson, n.d.:27, 9; Discharge certificate, 21 November 1876, in pension file of Elijah Daniels, 1346837, Records of the Veterans Administration, RG15, NA (hereafter cited as VA); Telegram from Assistant Adjutant General, Department of Texas, to Shafter, 21 December 1876; Bullis to Post Adjutant, Fort Clark, 31 December 1876; Unsigned and undated endorsement to Bullis to Post Adjutant, 47 DT 77, Letters Received, Department of Texas, 1876–77, Records of Army Continental Commands, RG393, NA.

7. Bullis to Assistant Adjutant General, Department of Texas, 14 June 1880; Stanley to Adjutant General, Department of Texas, 19 May 1882, 488 M 1870, Records of the AGO, RG94, M619, NA (hereafter cited as AGO).

8. Stanley to Adjutant General, Department of Texas, 19 May, 19 June 1882; Sheridan's endorsement of 1 June 1882 to telegram from Stanley to Assistant Adjutant General, 488 M 1870, AGO; Interviews with Molly Perryman, 1942, 1943; Rebecca

Wilson, 1943; Affidavits by Jack Bruner, 14 January 1913, and August Bruner, 18 January 1913, in pension file of James Bruner, 1361661, VA.

9. Jumper to Tufts, March 1884, 3139–85 encl. to 8582–84; Tufts to Price, 26 March 1884, 8582–84; Choctaw and Chickasaw freedmen, Cherokee freedmen, Indian Division, Records of the Department of the Interior, RG48, NA; Commissioner of Indian Affairs to Tufts, 18 February 1885, Letterbook 134, 134–35, Letters Sent, Bureau of Indian Affairs (BIA), RG75, NA; Interview with George Noble, 1942.

10. French to Adjutant General, Department of Texas, 23 May 1883; Jumper to Tufts, 17 September 1883; Sheridan to Secretary of War, 27 October 1883, 488 M 1870, AGO; French, n.d.

11. Bliss to Adjutant General, Department of Texas, 26 August 1884; Ives to Adjutant General, Department of Texas, 24 August 1884; Headquarters, Department of Texas, Special Order 104, 18 August 1884, 488 M 1870, AGO.

12. Endorsement by Stanley dated 16 May 1885 to Smith to Adjutant General, Department of Texas, 24 August 1884; Headquarters, Department of Texas, Special Order 104, 18 August 1884, 488 M 1870, AGO; Papers handed to Kibbit [sic], 17 March 1886 (the papers Kibbitts presented to the commissioner were returned to him; only the wrapper remains on file), 7024–86; Dawes to Secretary of the Interior, 20 March 1886, 8066–86; Kellogg to Atkins, 25 March 1886, Atkins to Kellogg, 25 March 1886, 8574–86; Sheridan to Commissioner of Indian Affairs, 14 February 1887, 4313–87, Letters Received, BIA; Acting Commissioner of Indian Affairs to John Jumper, 17 March 1886, Letterbook 146, 8–9; Atkins to Secretary of the Interior, 22 March 1886, Letterbook 156, 457–58, Letters Sent, BIA, RG75, NA.

13. Petition of Florida Seminole Negroes who ask for legislation in their behalf, January 1888, 3565–88, Letters Received, BIA.

14. Post Return, Fort Ringgold, Texas, October 1892, Returns, U.S. Military Posts, 1800–1916, M617, 1022/no frames, RG94, NA (hereafter cited as Post Return).

15. 53d Cong., 2d Sess., H.D. 1, part 2, 1:141; Post Return Ft. Ringgold, Texas, November 1892, M617, 1022/no frames; Gregg, 1937:169–73, esp. n81.

16. Return of Third Regiment of U.S. Cavalry, December 1892, Returns from Regular Army Cavalry Regiments, 1833–1916, M744, 32/no frames, RG94, NA; Post Return, Fort Ringgold, Texas, December 1892, M617, 1022/no frames; Keyes to Assistant Adjutant General, Texas, 25 and 28 December 1892; William to Commanding General, Department of Texas, 30 December 1892, Letters and Reports Received Relating to Garza Revolution, 1891–93, Records of Army Continental Commands, RG393, NA (hereafter cited as Garza Revolution Letters); and 53d Cong., 2d Sess., H.D. 1, part 2, 1:142.

17. Post Return, Fort Ringgold, Texas, January–February 1893, M617 1022/no frames; Chase to Adjutant General, Department of Texas, 12 March 1893; Encl. D to Chase to Adjutant General Department of Texas, 31 May 1893, Garza Revolution

Letters; 53d Cong., 2d Sess., H.D. 1, part 2, 1:143; Wheaton to Adjutant General, Department of Texas, 26 September 1894, 6779, General Correspondence, AGO, RG94, NA (hereafter cited as General Correspondence).

18. Colonel E. Z. Steever, Fourth Cavalry, Annual Report Covering Operations of the Department of Texas for Fiscal Year 1912, 10 October 1912, 1961997, General Correspondence.

19. Telegram from surgeon, Fort Sam Houston, San Antonio, Texas, 26 May 1911, B191-CB-70, Letters Received by the Commission Branch, AGO, 1863–70, M1064, 459/852, RG94, NA; Interviews with John Jefferson, 1941, 1950; Letter from John Jefferson to Porter, 12 July 1946; McCright, 1981:19.

20. Brooks to Commissioner of Indian Affairs, 18 August 1912, 14308-1914-123, Classified Files of the BIA, RG75, NA (hereafter cited as Classified Files); Sibley to Commanding General, Southern Department, 2 June 1913, 2036921; Assistant Secretary of War to Garner, 22 July 1914, 2189177H, General Correspondence.

21. Breckinridge to Secretary of the Interior, 18 May 1914, 14308-1914-123, Classified Files; To whom it may concern, 10 July 1914, 2189177H, General Correspondence; Interview with Miss Charles Emily Wilson, 1992.

Chapter Seventeen: Farewell to John Horse

1. Interviews with Bill Daniels, 1943; Dolly July, 1941.

2. Interviews with Rosa Fay, Julia Payne, 1942; Dolly July, 1941; Jane Phillips, 1943.

3. Interviews with Dolly July 1941, 1943; Rosa Fay, Julia Payne, 1942; Jane Phillips, Penny Factor, Rena July, 1943.

4. Interview with Jane Phillips, 1943.

5. Interviews with Dindie Factor, Rena July, and Bill Daniels, 1943.

6. Interview with John Jefferson, 1943.

7. Parmes, 1872:425.

8. Interviews with Julia Payne, 1932, 1942, 1944.

9. Interview with William (Bill) Warrior, 1943.

10. 34th Cong., 1st Sess., H.D. 135:86. For more on the San Carlos situation from the point of view of a Mexican who lived there, see Raht, 1963:81–82.

11. Interview with Joaquin Belloc Cuellar, 1943. A similar episode, with Don José Garza Galán as one of the characters but without mentioning John Horse, is cited in ca. 1878, Guajardo Papers.

12. Interview with Rosa Fay, 1942. Román Galán Castillón worked as supervisor for Nacimiento from 1875 to 1910. Fabila, 1945:31.

13. Interviews with Rosa Fay, 1942; Molly Perryman, 1943.

14. 60th Cong., 1st Sess., S.D. 215, part 3:2202; Declaration by John Willett, 17 June 1895; El Nacimiento, anexo num. 5, informe primera parte, 93–95, 98–103,

Departamento Agrario (hereafter cited as El Nacimiento); Interview with John Jefferson, 1941.

15. Andrés to C. Gobernador del Estado, 21 March 1882, Archivo General del Estado de Coahuila, Saltillo (hereafter cited as Archivo de Coahuila).

16. Se comunico a los interesados y al Presidente municipal de Múzquiz, 22 March 1882, Archivo de Coahuila.

17. 60th Cong., 1st Sess., S.D. 215, part 3:2202.

18. Interview with Dolly July, 1941.

19. Interviews with John Jefferson, 1941; Molly Perryman, Sarah Daniels, 1942; Jane Phillips, Fred Fletcher, 1943; Letter from John Jefferson to Porter, 1948.

20. Interviews with Dolly July, 1944; Julia Payne, Jane Phillips, 1943.

21. Interviews with Dolly July, 1941; Jane Phillips, 1943, Dindie Factor, 1942; John Jefferson, 1941, 1943.

22. Interview with Riley Aiken, 1942.

23. Interview with Curly Jefferson, 1941.

24. Death certificate of Juan Caballo, Porter Papers, Schomburg Center for Research in Black Culture (hereafter cited as Porter Papers). For a discussion of the controversy surrounding John Horse's death, see "Freedom Over Me: A Folk-History of the Wild Cat-John Horse Band of Seminole Negroes, 1848–1882," Porter Papers.

25. El Nacimiento, anexo num. 5, informe primera parte, 107–11, 113.

26. Interviews with Molly Perryman, 1942; Jane Phillips, 1943.

27. Interview with John Jefferson, 1941; Letter from John Jefferson to Porter, 1948; Interview with Rosa Fay, 1942. Joe Coon left two sons: Henry Thompson, whose mother was Mary Warrior, and John Jefferson, whose mother was Phyllis Bruner. He also fathered a girl named Annie, born around 1867 to a woman named Hannah. 1870 U.S. census, Cameron County, Texas, M593/1578:115.

28. El Nacimiento, informe resumen, primera parte, derecho, 62, 75.

29. Garza Galán to C. Oficial Mayor, Encargado de la Secretaria de Fomento, 16 October 1891, num. 44-12-60, Acervo Histórico Diplomático, Secretaria de Relaciones Exteriores.

30. "Lista de los negros de la tribu Mascogo agraciada por el gobierno general con terrenos de la Colonia del Nacimiento," Porter Papers.

31. Acuerdo de Reconocimiento que los Terrenos Cedidos a la Colonia "El Nacimiento" Jurisdicción de Músquiz, Estado de Coahuila; han salido del dominio de la Nación, 30 October 1919.

32. *Diário Oficial*, 30 November 1938, 17–20.

◪ Bibliography

Published Sources

Adams, George R. 1970. "The Caloosahatchee Massacre: Its Significance in the Second Seminole War." *Florida Historical Quarterly* 48:368–80.

Alessio Robles, Vito. 1938. *Bosquejos históricos* [Historical sketches]. Mexico City: Editorial Polis.

American State Papers: Documents, Legislative and Executive, of the Congress of the United States. 38 vols. 1832–61. Washington, D.C.: Gales and Seaton.

Anderson, William Marshall. 1959. *An American in Maximilian's Mexico, 1865–1866: The Diaries of William Marshall Anderson.* San Marino, Calif.: Huntington Library.

Annual Report of the Commissioner of Indian Affairs. Washington, D.C.: A. O. P. Nicholson.

Banta, William M. 1933. *Twenty-Seven Years on the Texas Frontier.* Council Hill, Okla.

Barr, James. 1836. *A Correct and Authentic Narrative of the Indian War in Florida with a Description of Major Dade's Massacre.* New York: J. Narine.

Bemrose, John. 1966. *Reminiscences of the Second Seminole War.* Edited by John K. Mahon. Gainesville: University Press of Florida.

Bonnet, W. A. 1926. "King Fisher, a Noted Character." *Frontier Times* 3:36–37.

Botkin, B. A., ed. 1989. *Lay My Burden Down.* Athens: University of Georgia Press.

Box, Michael James. 1869. *Adventures and Explorations in New and Old Mexico, Being the Record of Ten Years of Travel and Research by Capt. Michael James Box of the Texas Rangers.* New York: James Miller.

Boyd, Mark F. 1951. *Florida Aflame: Background and Onset of the Seminole War, 1835.* Tallahassee. Reprinted from *Florida Historical Quarterly* 30:1–115.

———. 1958. "Horatio S. Dexter and Events Leading to the Treaty of Moultrie Creek with the Seminole Indians." *Florida Anthropologist* 11:65–95.

Boyd, Orsemus B. 1982. *Cavalry Life in Tent and Field.* Lincoln: University of Nebraska Press.

Brevard, Carolyn Mays. 1924. *A History of Florida: From the Treaty of 1763 to Our Times*. 2 vols. Edited by James Alexander Robinson. DeLand: Florida State Historical Society.

Brown, Thomas Elton. 1973. "Seminole Indian Agents, 1842–1874." *Chronicles of Oklahoma* 51:59–83.

Buchanan, Robert C. 1950. "A Journal of Lt. Robert C. Buchanan During the Seminole War." Edited by Frank R. White. *Florida Historical Quarterly* 29:132–51.

Butler, Grace L. 1935. "General Bullis: Friend of the Frontier." *Frontier Times* 12:358–62.

Carlson, Paul H. 1989. *"Pecos Bill": A Military Biography of William R. Shafter*. College Station: Texas A&M University Press.

Carroll, John M., ed. 1971. *The Black Military Experience in the American West*. New York: Liveright.

Carter, Robert G. [1935] 1961. *On the Border with Mackenzie: Or Winning West Texas from the Comanches*. New York, N.Y.: Antiquarian Press.

———. [1926] 1982. *The Old Sergeant's Story: Fighting Indians and Bad Men in Texas from 1870 to 1876*. Mattituck, N.Y. and Bryan, Tex.: J. M. Carroll.

Childs, Thomas. 1873. "General Childs, U.S.A.: Extracts from his Correspondence with his Family." *Historical Magazine*, 3d Series, 2:299–304, 371–74; 3:169–71, 280–84.

Clendenen, Clarence C. 1969. *Blood on the Border: The United States Army and the Mexican Irregulars*. New York: Macmillan.

Cohen, Myer M. [1836] 1964. *Notices of Florida and the Campaigns*. Gainesville: University of Florida Press.

A Concise Narrative of the Seminole Campaign. 1819. Nashville: M'Lean and Tunstall.

Covington, James W. 1968. "Migration of the Seminoles into Florida." *Florida Historical Quarterly* 46:340–57.

———. 1982. *The Billy Bowlegs War, 1855–1858: The Final Stand of the Seminoles Against the Whites*. Cluluota, Fla.: Mickler House.

Cox, Isaac J. 1925. "The Border Missions of General George Mathews." *Mississippi Valley Historical Review* 12:309–33.

Crimmins, Martin L. 1926. "The Border Command-Camp Bullis." *Army and Navy Courier* 2:18–21.

———, ed. 1933. "Shafter's Explorations in West Texas." *West Texas Historical Association Yearbook* 9:83–96.

Dabbs, Jack A. 1963. *The French Army in Mexico, 1861–1867: A Study in Military Government*. The Hague: Mouton.

Davis, T. Frederick. 1930–31. "United States Troops in Spanish East Florida, 1812–1813." *Florida Historical Quarterly* 9:3–23, 96–116, 135–55, 259–78; 10:24–34.

Doherty, Herbert J. 1961. *Richard Keith Call, Southern Unionist*. Gainesville: University of Florida Press.

Downey, Fairfax, and Jacques Noel Jacobsen, Jr. 1973. *The Red Bluecoats: The Indian Scouts U.S. Army.* N.p.: Old Army Press.

"East Florida Documents." 1929. *Georgia Historical Quarterly* 13:154–58.

Elton, James Frederick. 1867. *With the French in Mexico.* London: Chapman and Hall.

Fabila, Alfonso. 1945. *La Tribu Kikapoo de Coahuila* [The Kickapoo tribe of Coahuila]. Mexico City: Secretaria de Educación Pública.

Fehrenbach, T. R. 1974. *Comanches: The Destruction of a People.* New York: Knopf.

Fenley, Florence. 1939. *Oldtimers: Their Own Stories.* Uvalde, Tex.: Hornby Press.

Festival of American Folklife. 1993. Washington, D.C.: Smithsonian Institution.

Fisher, Ovie Clark, with J. C. Dykes. 1966. *King Fisher: His Life and Times.* Norman: University of Oklahoma Press.

Flores Tapia, Oscar. 1980. *Coahuila: La reforma, la intervención y el imperio, 1854–1867* [Coahuila: The reform, the intervention, and the empire, 1854–1867]. Saltillo, Coahuila: Biblioteca de la Universidad Autónoma de Coahuila.

Forbes, James Grant. 1821. *Sketches, Historical and Topographical, of the Floridas.* New York: C. S. Van Winkle.

Ford, John Salmon. 1963. *Rip Ford's Texas.* Edited by Stephen B. Oates. Austin: University of Texas Press.

Foreman, Grant, ed. 1931. "Report of the Cherokee Deputation into Florida." *Chronicles of Oklahoma* 9:423–38.

———. 1972a. *The Five Civilized Tribes.* Norman: University of Oklahoma Press.

———. 1972b. *Indian Removal: The Emigration of the Five Civilized Tribes.* Norman: University of Oklahoma Press.

Fornell, Earl W. 1956. "Texans and Filibusters in the 1850's." *Southwestern Historical Quarterly* 59:411–18.

Forry, Samuel. 1928. "Letters of Samuel Forry, Surgeon U.S. Army, 1837–1838." *Florida Historical Quarterly* 6:133–48, 206–219; 7:88–105.

Foster, Laurence. [1935] 1978. *Negro Indian Relationships in the Southeast.* New York: AMS Press.

Froebel, Julius. 1859 *Seven Years' Travel in Central America, Northern Mexico, and the Far West of the United States.* London: Richard Bentley.

Gadsden, James. 1937. "The Defences of the Floridas: A Report of Captain James Gadsden, Aide-de-Camp to General Andrew Jackson." *Florida Historical Quarterly* 15:242–48.

Gentry, William Richard. 1937. *Full Justice: The Story of Richard Gentry and His Missouri Volunteers in the Seminole War.* St. Louis.

Gibson, A. M. 1963. *The Kickapoos: Lords of the Middle Border.* Norman: University of Oklahoma Press.

Giddings, Joshua R. [1858] 1964. *The Exiles of Florida; or, The Crimes Committed by Our Government against the Maroons Who Fled from South Carolina and Other Slave States,*

Seeking Protection under Spanish Laws. Gainesville: University of Florida Press. Facsimile.

Glisan, Rodney. 1874. *Journal of Army Life*. San Francisco: A. L. Bancroft.

Godfrey, Mary. [1836] 1977. *An Authentic Narrative of the Seminole War*. New York: Garland.

Goggin, John M. 1939. "An Anthropological Reconnaissance of Andros Islands, Bahamas." *American Antiquity* 5:21–26.

———. 1946. "The Seminole Negroes of Andros Island, Bahamas." *Florida Historical Quarterly* 24:201–6.

Grant, Ulysses S. 1990. *Memoirs and Selected Letters: Personal Memoirs of U.S. Grant, Selected Letters, 1839–1865*. New York: Library of America.

Gregg, Robert D. 1937. *The Influence of Border Troubles on Relations between the United States and Mexico, 1876–1910*. Baltimore: Johns Hopkins University Press.

Guajardo, Alberto. 1940. "Horse Sense: Liston and the Lipan Indians." *Publications of the Texas Folklore Society* 16:343–46.

Guild, Josephus C. [1878] 1971. *Old Times in Tennessee*. Knoxville: Tenase.

Haley, James Evetts. [1936] 1989. *Charles Goodnight: Cowman and Plainsman*. Norman: University of Oklahoma Press.

Haley, James L. 1976. *The Buffalo War: The History of the Red River Indian Uprising of 1874*. Garden City, N.Y.: Doubleday.

Hammond, E. Ashbury, ed. 1969. "Bemrose's Medical Case Notes from the Second Seminole War." *Florida Historical Quarterly* 47:401–13.

Hancock, Ian. 1975. *Creole Features in the Afro-Seminole Speech of Brackettville, Texas*. St. Augustine, Trinidad: Caribbean Linguistic Society.

———. 1980. *The Texas Seminoles and Their Language*. Austin: African and Afro-American Studies and Research Center, University of Texas at Austin.

Hanna, Alfred J. 1936. *Fort Maitland: Its Origin and History*. Maitland, Fla.: Fort Maitland Committee.

Harris, N. Sayre. 1932. "Journal of a Tour in the Indian Territory." *Chronicles of Oklahoma* 10:219–56.

Hartley, William B., and Ellen Hartley. 1973. *Osceola, the Unconquered Indian*. New York: Hawthorn.

Heitman, Francis Bernard. 1903. *Historical Register and Dictionary of the United States Army, From Its Organization September 29, 1789 to March 2, 1903*. 2 vols. Washington, D.C.: U.S. Government Printing Office.

Hitchcock, Ethan Allen. [1909] 1971. *Fifty Years in Camp and Field: Diary of Major-General Ethan Hitchcock*. Freeport, N.Y.: Books for Libraries Press.

Hodge, Frederick Webb. [1905] 1960. *Handbook of American Indians North of Mexico*. New York: Pageant Books.

Hollingsworth, Henry. 1942–43. "Tennessee Volunteers in the Seminole Campaign: The Diary of Henry Hollingsworth." Edited by Stanley F. Horn. *Tennessee Historical Quarterly* 1:269–74, 344–66; 2:61–73, 163–78, 236–56.

Hughes, W. J. 1964. *Rebellious Ranger: Rip Ford and the Old Southwest.* Norman: University of Oklahoma Press.

"'I'm in the Wewoka Switch': Heard in the Oil Fields over the World." 1963. *Chronicles of Oklahoma* 41:455–58.

"Jacksonville and the Seminole War, 1835, 36. Part III. Indian Hostilities. Latest Intelligence." 1925. *Florida Historical Quarterly* 4:22–30.

Jarvis, Nathan S. 1906–7. "An Army's Surgeon Notes of Frontier Service, 1833–48." *Journal of the Military Service Institution* 39:130–35, 275–86, 451–66; 40:269–77.

Jones, H. Conger. 1976. "Seminole Scouts, Old Enemy of Indians, Still Thrive on Border." In *La Hacienda.* Del Rio, Tex.: Whitehall Memorial Museum.

Kappler, Charles J., comp. 1903–41. *Indian Affairs: Laws and Treaties.* Washington, D.C.: U.S. Government Printing Office.

Kennedy, William. 1925. *Texas: The Rise, Progress, and Prospects of the Republic of Texas.* Fort Worth, Tex.: Molyneaux Craftsmen.

Kieffer, Chester L. 1979. *Maligned General: The Biography of Thomas Sidney Jesup.* San Rafael, Calif.: Presidio Press.

Latorre, Felipe A., and Dolores L. Latorre. 1976. *The Mexican Kickapoo Indians.* Austin: University of Texas Press.

Leckie, William H. 1963. *The Military Conquest of the Southern Plains.* Norman: University of Oklahoma Press.

———. 1967. *The Buffalo Soldiers: A Narrative of the Negro Cavalry in the West.* Norman: University of Oklahoma Press.

———, ed. 1986. *Indian Wars of the Red River Valley.* Sacramento, Calif.: Sierra Oaks Publishing Co.

"Letters of John Innerarity and A. H. Gordon." 1933. *Florida Historical Quarterly* 12:[37]–41.

Littlefield, Daniel F. 1977. *Africans and Seminoles: From Removal to Emancipation.* Westport, Conn.: Greenwood Press.

Lundy, Benjamin. [1847] 1969. *The Life, Travels, and Opinions of Benjamin Lundy Including His Journeys to Texas and Mexico, with a Sketch of Contemporary Events, and a Notice of the Revolution in Hayti.* New York: Negro Universities Press.

Mahon, John K. 1962a. "The Treaty of Moultrie Creek, 1823." *Florida Historical Quarterly* 40:350–72.

———. 1962b. "Two Seminole Treaties: Payne's Landing, 1832, and Ft. Gibson, 1833." *Florida Historical Quarterly* 41:1–21.

———. 1985. *History of the Second Seminole War, 1835–1842.* Revised edition. Gainesville: University Press of Florida.

Manero, Vicente E. 1878. *Documentos interesantes sobre colonización* [Interesting documents about colonization]. Mexico City: Imprenta de la V. e Hijos de Murguia.

Marcy, Randolph B., and George B. McClellan. [1853] 1961. *Exploration of the Red River of Louisiana in the Year 1852*. Dallas: Highlands Historical Press. Facsimile.

Marcy, Randolph B. 1866. *Thirty Years of Army Life on the Border.* New York: Harper and Row.

Martin, Sidney Walter. 1943. "Richard Keith Call, Florida Territorial Leader." *Florida Historical Quarterly* 21:332–51.

Maza, Francisco F. de la. 1893. *Codigo de colonización y terrenos baldios de la República Mexicana, 1451–1892* [Law of colonization and uncultivated land in the Republic of Mexico, 1451–1892]. Mexico City: Oficina Tipográfica de la Secretaria de Fomento.

McCall, George A. [1868] 1974. *Letters from the Frontiers.* Gainesville: University Press of Florida. Facsimile.

McCright, Grady E. 1981. "John Bullis: Chief Scout." *True West,* 12–19.

Memoria [Memorandum]. 1852. Mexico. Ministerio de Guerra y Marina. Mexico City: Imprenta de Vicente y Torres.

A Memorial and Biographical History of McLennan Falls, Bell, and Coryell Counties, Texas, Containing a History of This Important Section of the Great State of Texas, From the Earliest Period of Its Occupancy to the Present Time, Together with Glimpses of Its Future Prospects; Also Biographical Mention of Many of the Pioneers and Prominent Citizens of the Present Time, and Full-Page Portraits of Some of the Most Eminent Men of This Section. 1893. Chicago: Lewis Publishing Co.

Meyer, Michael C., and William L. Sherman. 1991. *The Course of Mexican History.* 4th ed. New York: Oxford University Press.

Miller, Robert R. 1985. *Mexico: A History.* Norman: University of Oklahoma Press.

Monk, J. Floyd. 1978. "Christmas Day in Florida, 1837." *Tequesta* 38:5–38.

Montgomery, Cora. 1852. *Eagle Pass; or, Life on the Border.* New York: G. P. Putnam.

Morse, Jedidiah. [1822] 1972. *A Report of the Secretary of War of the United States on Indian Affairs.* St. Clair Shores, Mich.: Scholarly Press.

Motte, Jacob R. 1953. *Journey into Wilderness: An Army Surgeon's Account of Life in Camp and Field During the Creek and Seminole Wars, 1836–1838.* Edited by James F. Sunderman. Gainesville: University Press of Florida.

Myers, Sandra L. 1971. "The Lipan Apaches." In *Indian Tribes of Texas.* Waco, Tex.: Texian Press.

Neal, Charles M. Jr. 1990. "Incident on Las Moras Creek." *Annals: Official Publication of the Medal of Honor Historical Society* 13:16–19.

Newcomb, James R. 1863. *History of Secession Times in Texas and Journal of Travel from Texas Through Mexico to California.* San Francisco.

Newcomb, W. W., Jr. 1961. *The Indians of Texas: From Prehistoric to Modern Times.* Austin: University of Texas Press.

Niox, Gustave Leon. 1874. *Expédition du Mexique, 1861–1867*. Paris: J. Dumaine.

Official Opinions of the Attorneys General of the United States Advising the President and Heads of Departments, in Relation to Their Official Duties. 1852–70. Washington, D.C.: R. Farham.

Owsley, Frank L., Jr. 1985. "Ambrister and Arbuthnot: Adventurers or Martyrs for British Honor?" *Journal of the Early Republic* 5:289–308.

Parmes, Enrique. 1872. "Among the Mexican Mines." *Southern Magazine* 10:416–26.

Pate, J'Nell. 1976. "The Red River War of 1874: An Enlisted Man's Contribution." *Chronicles of Oklahoma* 54:263–75.

Patrick, Rembert W. 1954. *Florida Fiasco: Rampant Rebels on the Georgia Florida Border, 1810–1815*. Athens: University of Georgia Press.

Phelps, John W. 1927. "Letters of Lieutenant John W. Phelps, U.S.A., 1837–1838." *Florida Historical Quarterly* 6:67–84.

Porter, Kenneth W. 1943a. "Davy Crockett and John Horse: A Possible Origin of the Cookskin Story." *American Literature* 15:10–15.

———. 1943b. "The Early Life of Luis Pacheco n'e Fatio." *Negro History Bulletin* 7:52, 54, 62, 64.

———. 1943c. "Farewell to John Horse: An Episode of Seminole Negro Folk History." *Phylon* 8:265–73.

———. 1943d. "Louis Pacheco: The Man and the Myth." *Journal of Negro History* 28:65–72.

———. 1943e. "Wild Cat's Death and Burial." *Chronicles of Oklahoma* 21:41–43.

———. 1944. "Seminole Flight from Fort Marion." *Florida Historical Quarterly* 22:113–33.

———. 1945. "Notes on Seminole Negroes in the Bahamas." *Florida Historical Quarterly* 24:56–60.

———. 1946a. "The Hawkins' Negroes go to Mexico." *Chronicles of Oklahoma* 24:55–58.

———. 1946b. "The Legend of the Biloxi." *Journal of American Folklore* 59:168–73.

———. 1947. "The Episode of Osceola's Wife: Fact or Fiction?" *Florida Historical Quarterly* 26:92–98.

———. 1949. "The Founder of the 'Seminole Nation' Secoffee or Cowkeeper?" *Florida Historical Quarterly* 27:362–84.

———. 1950. "Negro Guides and Interpreters in the Early Stages of the Seminole War, Dec. 28, 1835–Mar. 6, 1837." *Florida Historical Quarterly* 35:174–82.

———. 1951. "The Seminole in Mexico, 1850–1861." *Chronicles of Oklahoma* 29:153–68.

———. 1952. "The Cowkeeper Dynasty of the Seminole Nation." *Florida Historical Quarterly* 30:341–49.

———. 1955. "Osceola and the Negroes." *Florida Historical Quarterly* 33:235–39.

———. 1960. "Thlonoto-sassa: A Note on an Obscure Seminole Village of the Early 1820's." *Florida Anthropologist* 13:115–19.

————. 1971. *The Negro on the American Frontier.* New York: Arno Press.

Porter, Kenneth W., and Edward S. Wallace. 1961. "Thunderbolt of the Frontier." *Westerners New York Posse Brand Book* 8:73–75.

Potter, Woodburne. [1836]. 1966. *The War in Florida.* N.p.: Readex Microprint.

Raht, Carlysle G. [1919] 1963. *The Romance of Davis Mountains and the Big Bend Country: A History.* Odessa, Tex.: Rahtbooks Co.

"Record of Engagements with Hostile Indians in Texas 1868 to 1882." 1933. *West Texas Historical Association Yearbook* 9:101–18.

Reeve, Frank D., ed. 1950. "Frederick E. Phelps: A Soldier's Memoirs." *New Mexico Historical Review* 25:187–221.

Reports of the Committee of Investigation Sent in 1873 by the Mexican Government to the Frontier of Texas. 1875. New York: Baker and Goodwin.

Rerick, Rowland H. 1902. *Memoirs of Florida; Embracing a General History of the Province, Territory and State; and Special Chapters Devoted to Finances and Banking, the Bench and Bar, Medical Profession, Railways and Navigation, and Industrial Interests.* 2 vols. Atlanta: Southern Historical Association.

Revere, Joseph Warren. 1872. *Keel and Saddle : A Retrospect of Forty Years of Military and Naval Service.* Boston: J. R. Osgood and Co.

Rippy, James Fred. 1919. "Border Troubles Along the Rio Grande, 1848–1860." *Southwestern Historical Quarterly* 23:91–111.

————. 1922. "Anglo-American Filibusters and the Gadsden Treaty." *Hispanic American Historical Review* 5:155–80.

————. 1926. *The United States and Mexico.* New York: Knopf.

————. [1929] 1964. *Rivalry of the United States and Great Britain Over Latin America, 1808–1830.* New York: Octagon Books.

Rister, Carl C. 1928. *The Southwestern Frontier, 1865–1881.* Cleveland: Arthur H. Clark Co.

Rodenbough, Theophilus F. 1875. *From Everglade to Canon with the Second Dragoons, (Second United States Cavalry); An Authentic Account of Service in Florida, Mexico, Virginia, and the Indian Country, Including the Personal Recollections of Prominent Officers, With an Appendix Containing Orders, Reports and Correspondence, Military Records, etc., etc., 1836–1875.* New York: Van Nostrand.

Rodenbough, Theophilus F., and William L. Haskin. 1896. *The Army of the United States: Historical Sketches of Staff and Line with Portraits of Generals-in-Chief.* New York: Maynard, Merrill.

Root, George A., ed. 1931. "No-ko-aht's Talk, May 31, 1867." *Kansas Historical Quarterly* 1:153–59.

Schoen, Harold. 1936. "The Negro in the Republic of Texas." *Southwestern Historical Quarterly* 19:292–326.

Scholes, Walter Vinton. 1969. *Mexican Politics during the Juarez Regime, 1855–1872*. Columbia: University of Missouri Press.

Shearer, Ernest C. 1951a. "The Callahan Expedition, 1855." *Southwestern Historical Quarterly* 55:430–51.

———. 1951b. "The Carvajal Disturbances." *Southwestern Historical Quarterly* 55:201–30.

Shipman, O. L. 1926. *Taming the Big Bend: A History of the Extreme Western Portion of Texas from Fort Clark to El Paso*. N.p.

Silver, James W. 1949. *Edmund Pendleton Gaines: Frontier General*. Baton Rouge: Louisiana State University Press.

Simmons, James W. 1837. "Recollections of the Late Campaign in East Florida." *Atkinson's Casket*, 542–47.

Simmons, William Hayne. [1822] 1973. *Notices of East Florida*. Gainesville: University Press of Florida. Facsimile.

Sinkin, Richard N. 1979. *The Mexican Reform, 1855–1876: A Study in Liberal Nation-Building*. Austin: Institute of Latin American Studies, University of Texas at Austin.

Smith, Ralph A. 1963. "The Mamelukes of West Texas and Mexico." *West Texas Historical Association Yearbook* 39:65–88.

Sonnichsen, C. L. 1986. *The Mescalero Apaches*. 2d edition. Norman: University of Oklahoma Press.

Sowell, A. J. 1947. "Last Indian Raid in Frio Canyon." *Frontier Times* 24:500–503.

Sprague, John T. [1848] 1964. *The Origin, Progress, and Conclusion of the Florida War*. Gainesville: University Press of Florida. Facsimile.

State Papers and Publick Documents of the United States, from the Accession of George Washington to the Presidency, Exhibiting a Complete View of Our Foreign Relations Since that Time. 1817. 10 vols. Boston: T. B. Wait and Sons.

Strong, Henry. n.d. *My Frontier Days and Indian Fights on the Plains of Texas*. N.p.

Sturtevant, William C. 1962. "Spanish-Indian Relations in Southeastern North America." *Ethnohistory* 9:41–94.

———. 1971. "Creek into Seminole." In *North American Indians in Historical Perspective*. Edited by Eleanor Burke Leacock and Nancy Oestreich Lurie. New York: Random House.

Sumpter, Jesse. 1969. *Paso del Aguila: A Chronicle of Frontier Days on the Texas Border as Recorded in the Memoirs of Jesse Sumpter*. Compiled by Harry Warren and edited by Ben Pingenot. Austin: Encino Press.

Swanson, Donald A., ed. n.d. *Enlistment Record of Indian Scouts Texas Who Served in One of the Scout Detachments at Fort Clark, Texas. 1. Seminole Negro-Indian Detachment August 1872–September 1914. 2. Lipan Indian Scout Detachment December 1878–December 1879. 3. Lipan Indian Scout Detachment November 1880–June 1881*. Bronte, Tex.: Ames-American Printing Co.

Swanton, John Reed. [1922] 1970. *Early History of the Creek Indians and Their Neighbors*. New York: Johnson Reprint Co.

Sweet, Alexander E., and J. Amory Knox. 1883. *On a Mexican Mustang: Through Texas from the Gulf to the Rio Grande*. Hartford, Conn.: S. S. Scranton and Co.

The Territorial Papers of the United States. 1934. Washington, D.C.: U.S. Government Printing Office.

Texas Indian Papers. 1959–66. 5 vols. Edited by Dorman H. Winfrey. Austin: Texas State Library.

Thompson, Richard A. 1986. *Crossing the Border with the 4th Cavalry: MacKenzie's Raid into Mexico, 1873*. Waco, Tex.: Texian Press.

Trout, Ireaneous. 1909. "The Seminole and Their Country." *Florida Review* 1:83–84.

Tyler, Ronnie C. 1967. "The Callahan Expedition of 1855: Indians or Negroes?" *Southwestern Historical Quarterly* 70:574–85.

———. 1968. "Exploring the Rio Grande: Lt. Duff C. Green's Report of 1852." *Arizona and the West* 10:43–60.

———. 1972. "Fugitive Slaves in Mexico." *Journal of Negro History* 57:1–12.

Utley, Robert M. 1984. *Frontier Regulars: The United States Army and the Indian, 1866–1891*. Lincoln: University of Nebraska Press.

Vignoles, Charles Blacker. [1823] 1977. *Observations upon the Floridas*. Gainesville: University Press of Florida. Facsimile.

Wallace, Edward S. 1951. "General John Lapham Bullis, the Thunderbolt of the Texas Frontier." *Southwestern Historical Quarterly* 54:542–62; 55:77–85.

Wallace, Ernest. 1964. *Ranald S. Mackenzie on the Texas Frontier*. Lubbock: West Texas Museum Association.

———, ed. 1967. *Ranald S. Mackenzie's Official Correspondence Relating to Texas, 1871–1873*. Lubbock: West Texas Museum Association.

———, ed. 1968. *Ranald S. Mackenzie's Official Correspondence Relating to Texas, 1873–1879*. Lubbock: West Texas Museum Association.

Wallace, Ernest, and Adrian S. Anderson. 1965. "R. S. Mackenzie and the Kickapoos: The Raid into Mexico in 1873." *Arizona and the West* 7:105–26.

Wallace, Ernest, and E. Adamson Hoebel, eds. 1952. *The Comanches: Lords of the South Plains*. Norman: University of Oklahoma Press.

The War of the Rebellion: A Compilation of the Official Records of the Union and Confederate Armies. [1880–1900] 1971–72. Gettysburg, Pa.: National Historical Society.

The Washington Directory and National Register for 1846. Washington, D.C.: Gather and Addison.

Washburn, Wilcomb, comp. 1973. *The American Indian and the United States: A Documentary History*. 4 vols. New York: Random House.

Webb, Walter Prescott. 1965. *The Texas Rangers: A Century of Frontier Defense*. 2d edition. Austin: University of Texas Press.

Welch, Andrew. [1841] 1977. *A Narrative of the Early Days and Remembrances of Oceola Nikkanochee, Prince of Econchatti*. Gainesville: University Press of Florida. Facsimile.

Wilhelm, Thomas. 1873. *History of the Eighth U.S. Infantry* 2 vols. N.p.: Headquarters of the Eighth U.S. Infantry.

Williams, John Lee. [1837] 1962. *The Territory of Florida*. Gainesville: University Press of Florida. Facsimile.

———. [1827] 1976. *A View of West Florida*. Gainesville: University Press of Florida. Facsimile.

Woodhull, Frost. 1937. "Seminole Indian Scouts on the Border." *Frontier Times* 15:118–27.

Woodward, Thomas S. [1859] 1939. *Woodward's Reminiscences of the Creek or Muscogee Indians, Contained in Letters to Friends in Georgia and Alabama*. Birmingham: Alabama Bookstore and Birmingham Book Exchange.

Woolford, Sam, ed. 1962. "The Burr G. Duval Diary." *Southwestern Historical Quarterly* 65:487–511.

Wright, Irene A. 1924. "Dispatches of Spanish Officials Bearing on the Free Negro Settlement of Gracia Real de Santa Teresa de Mose, Florida." *Journal of Negro History* 9:144–95.

Wright, J. Leitch, Jr. 1968. "A Note on the First Seminole War as Seen by the Indians, Negroes, and Their British Advisers." *Journal of Southern History* 34:565–75.

Wyllys, Rufus Kay. 1929. "The East Florida Revolution of 1812–1814." *Hispanic American Historical Review* 9:415–45.

Young, Hugh. 1934–35. "A Topographical Memoir on East and West Florida with Itineraries." *Florida Historical Quarterly* 13:16–50, 82–104, 129–64.

Additional Reading

Alexander, J. H. 1977. "The Ambush of Captain John Williams, U.S.M.C.: Failure of the East Florida Invasion, 1812–1813." *Florida Historical Quarterly* 56:280–96.

Amos, Alcione M. 1977. "Captain Hugh Young's Map of Jackson's 1818 Seminole Campaign in Florida." *Florida Historical Quarterly* 55:336–46.

Amos, Preston E. 1974. *Above and Beyond in the West: Black Medal of Honor Winners, 1870–1890*. Washington, D.C.: Potomac Corral, The Westerners.

Bittle, George C. 1964. "Richard Keith Call's 1836 Campaign." *Tequesta* 29:67–72.

———. 1966. "The Florida Militia's Role in the Battle of Withlacoochee." *Florida Historical Quarterly*, 44:303–11.

Boyd, Mark F. 1937. "Events at Prospect Bluff on the Apalachicola River, 1808–1818: An Introduction to Twelve Letters of Edmund Doyle, Trader." *Florida Historical Quarterly* 16:55–96.

Buker, George E. 1975. *Swamp Sailors: Riverine Warfare in the Everglades, 1835–1842*. Gainesville: University Press of Florida.

Craig, Alan K., and Christopher S. Peebles. 1969. "Captain Young's Sketch Map, 1818." *Florida Historical Quarterly* 48:176–79.

———. 1974. "Ethnoecologic Change among the Seminoles, 1740–1840." In *Man and Cultural Heritage: Essays in Honor of Fred B. Kniffer.* Edited by H. J. Walker and William G. Haag. Baton Rouge: Louisiana State University Press.

Dunlay, Thomas W. 1982. *Wolves for the Blue Soldiers: Indian Scouts and Auxiliaries with the United States Army, 1860–90.* Lincoln: University of Nebraska Press.

Elliott, Charles Winslow. [1937] 1979. *Winfield Scott: The Soldier and the Man.* New York: Arno Press.

Faulk, Odie B. 1968. "Projected Mexican Military Colonies for the Borderlands, 1848." *Journal of Arizona History* 9:39–47.

———. 1969. "Projected Mexican Colonies in the Borderlands, 1852." *Journal of Arizona History* 10:115–28.

Fenton, Jim. 1990. "John L. Bullis: 'Farsighted and Keen' Trans-Pecos Land Speculator." *Journal of Big Bend Studies* 2:73–86.

Gifford, John C. 1944. "Five Plants Essential to the Indians and Early Settlers of Florida." *Tequesta* 4:36–44.

Gómez, Arthur R. 1990. *A Most Singular Country: A History of the Occupation in the Big Bend Country.* Provo, Utah: Charles Redd Center for Western Studies, Brigham Young University.

Halbert, Henry S., and T. H. Ball. [1895] 1969. *The Creek War of 1813 and 1814.* Tuscaloosa: University of Alabama Press.

Hamilton, Holman. 1941. *Zachary Taylor: Soldier of the Republic.* New York: Bobbs-Merrill.

Hancock, Ian. 1980. "Texan Gullah: The Creole English of the Brackettville Afro-Seminoles." In *Perspectives on American English.* Edited by J. Dillard. The Hague: Mouton.

———. 1986. "On the Classification of Afro-Seminole Creole." In *Language Variety in the South: Perspectives in Black and White.* Edited by Michael B. Montgomery and Guy Bailey. Tuscaloosa: University of Alabama Press.

———. 1992. *The Texas Seminoles and Their Language.* Brackettville and Austin, Tex.: Seminole Scout Historical Association.

Johnson, John Allen. 1970. "The Medal of Honor and Sergeant John Ward and Private Pompey Factor." *Arkansas Historical Quarterly* 29:361–75.

Johnson, Michael. 1981. "Runaway Slaves and the Slave Communities in South Carolina, 1799–1830." *William and Mary College Quarterly Historical Magazine* 38:418–41.

Kersey, Harry A., Jr. 1981. "The Seminole Negroes of Andros Island Revisited: Some New Pieces to an Old Puzzle." *Florida Anthropologist* 34:169–76.

Klos, George. 1989. "Blacks and the Seminole Removal Debate, 1821–1835." *Florida Historical Quarterly* 68:55–78.

Koerper, Phillip F., and David T. Childress. 1984. "The Alabama Volunteers in the Second Seminole War, 1836." *Alabama Review* 37:4–12.

Landers, Jane. 1984. "Spanish Sanctuary: Fugitives in Florida, 1687–1790." *Florida Historical Quarterly* 62:296–313.

Laumer, Frank. 1968a. "Encounter by the River." *Florida Historical Quarterly*, 46: 322–39.

———. 1968b. *Massacre!* Gainesville: University Press of Florida.

Littlefield, Daniel F. 1979. *Africans and Creeks: From the Colonial Period to the Civil War.* Westport, Conn.: Greenwood Press.

Mahon, John K. 1966. "British Strategy and Southern Indians: War of 1812." *Florida Historical Quarterly* 45:285–302.

McReynolds, Edwin C. 1957. *The Seminoles.* Norman: University of Oklahoma Press.

Milligan, John D. 1974. "Slave Rebelliousness and the Florida Maroon." *Prologue* 6: 5–18.

Mulroy, Kevin. 1993. *Freedom on the Border: The Seminole Maroons in Florida, the Indian Territory, Coahuila, and Texas.* Lubbock, Tex.: Texas Tech University Press.

Murdoch, Richard K. 1959. "The Return of Runaway Slaves, 1790–1794." *Florida Historical Quarterly* 38:96–113.

Opala, Joseph. 1981. "Seminole-African Relations on the Florida Frontier." *Papers in Anthropology* 22:11–51.

Owsley, Frank L., Jr. 1967. "British and Indian Activities in Spanish West Florida During the War of 1812." *Florida Historical Quarterly* 46:111–23.

———. 1981. *Struggle for the Gulf Borderlands: The Creek War and the Battle of New Orleans, 1812–1815.* Gainesville: University Press of Florida.

Patrick, Rembert W. 1963. *Aristocrat in Uniform: General Duncan L. Clinch.* Gainesville: University Press of Florida.

Pierce, Michael D. 1993. *The Most Promising Young Officer: A Life of Ranald S. Mackenzie.* Norman: University of Oklahoma Press.

Pratt, Julius William. 1925. *Expansionists of 1812.* New York: Macmillan.

Price, Richard, ed. 1979. *Maroon Societies: Rebel Slave Communities in the Americas.* Baltimore: Johns Hopkins University Press.

Prucha, Francis Paul. 1969. *The Sword of the Republic: The United States Army on the Frontier, 1783–1846.* New York: Macmillan.

———. 1981. *Indian Policy in the United States, Historical Essays.* Lincoln: University of Nebraska Press.

Remini, Robert V. 1977. *Andrew Jackson and the Course of American Empire, 1767–1821.* New York: Harper and Row.

Richards, Brigadier General George. 1932. "Captain John Williams, U.S. Marine Corps: A Tradition." *Marine Corps Gazette*, 17:11–14.

Rippy, James Fred. 1919. "The Indians of the Southwest and the Diplomacy of the United States and Mexico, 1848–1853." *Hispanic American Historical Review* 2: 363–96.

Robson, Lucia St. Clair. 1988. *Light a Distant Fire*. New York: Ballantine Books.

Robinson, Charles M., III. 1993. *Bad Hand: A Biography of General Ranald S. Mackenzie*. Austin, Tex.: State House Press.

Sarkesian, Sam C. 1984. *America's Forgotten Wars*. Westport, Conn.: Greenwood Press.

Sleight, Frederick W. 1953. "Kunti, a Food Staple of Florida Indians." *Florida Anthropologist* 6:46–52.

Te Paske, John. 1975. "The Fugitive Slave: Intercolonial Rivalry and Spanish Slave Policy, 1687–1764." In *Eighteenth-Century Florida and Its Borderlands* Edited by Samuel Proctor. Gainesville: University Press of Florida.

Thurman, Melburn D. 1977. "Seminoles, Creeks, Delawares and Shawnees: Indian Auxiliaries in the Second Seminole War, 1836–8." *Florida Anthropologist* 30: 144–65.

Valliere, Kenneth L. 1979. "The Creek War of 1836, A Military History." *Chronicles of Oklahoma* 57:463–85.

Watts, Jill M. 1986. "'We Do Not Live for Ourselves Only': Seminole Black Perspectives and the Second Seminole War." *UCLA Historical Journal* 7:5–28.

Weisman, Brent Richards. 1989. *Like Beads on a String: A Culture History of the Seminole Indians in North Peninsular Florida*. Tuscaloosa: University of Alabama Press.

Wickman, Patricia R. 1991. *Osceola's Legacy*. Tuscalosa: University of Alabama Press.

Wright, J. Leitch, Jr. 1976. "Blacks in British East Florida." *Florida Historical Quarterly* 54:425–42.

———. 1981. *The Only Land They Knew: The Tragic Story of the American Indian in the Old South*. New York: Free Press.

———. 1986. *Creeks & Seminoles: The Destruction and Regeneration of the Muscogulge People*. Lincoln: University of Nebraska Press.

Theses and Unpublished Material

Abraham. Abraham's manuscript. Typescript at the P. K. Yonge Memorial Library of Florida History, University of Florida, Gainesville.

"Acuerdo de reconocimiento que los terrenos cedidos a la Colonia 'El Nacimiento' jurisdicción de Músquiz, Estado de Coahuila, han salido del dominio de la Nación" [Agreement recognizing that the lands given to El Nacimiento colony, in the jurisdiction of Musquiz, Coahuila, are no more under the Nation's domain]. 30 October 1919. Typescript in the personal collection of Alcione M. Amos. Courtesy of Dolores L. Latorre.

Agreement between president of Mexico and Wild Cat and Papicua, 26 July 1852 (in Spanish). Photocopy in the personal collection of Alcione M. Amos.

Bliss, Zenas R. n.d. "Reminiscences." Typescript at the Barker Texas History Center, University of Texas at Austin.

Cooper, Mark. 1894. "Memoirs of Major A. Cooper." Typescript at P. K. Yonge Memorial Library of Florida History, University of Florida, Gainesville.

Creaton, John. n.d. "John Creaton: An Autobiography, 1856–1932." John Creaton Collection, Barker Texas History Center, University of Texas at Austin.

French, Major General Francis H. "Diary While Serving as 2nd Lt. at 'E' Co, 19th Infy at Fort Clark, 1883." Photocopy in the personal collection of Thomas P. Senter. Courtesy of Bill Haenn and the Vinton Trust.

"El Gobiernador Interino del Estado de Coahuila a todos sus habitantes, Septiembre 25, 1850" [From the interim governor of the state of Coahuila to all its inhabitants, September 25, 1850]. Photocopy in the personal collection of Alcione M. Amos.

Hatfield, Charles G. 1925. Papers. Order of the Indian Wars Collection, Archives, U.S. Military History Research Center, Carlisle Barracks, Pa.

Lancaster, Jane Fairchild. 1986. "The First Decades: The Western Seminoles from Removal to Reconstruction, 1836–1866." Ph.D. diss., Mississippi State University.

Mason, Joyce Evelyn. 1970. "The Use of Indian Scouts in the Apache Wars, 1870–1886." Ph.D. diss., Indiana University, Bloomington.

McClellan, Major Edwin N. 1931. "Indian Fights, 1807–1813." Material and sources of chapter 19, volume 1. History of the United States Marine Corps. First edition, revised. Typescript in the Library of the U.S. Marine Corps Historical Center and Museum, Washington, D.C.

Miller, Susan A. 1988. "Wild Cat and the Origins of the Seminole Migration to Mexico." Master's thesis, University of Oklahoma, Norman.

Moseley, Edward H. 1963. "The Public Career of Santiago Vidaurri, 1855–1858." Ph.D. diss., University of Alabama, Montgomery.

Neal, Charles M., Jr. n.d. "For Habitual Courage." n.p.

———. n.d. "The Owl Medicine Death Curse of Maman-ti." n.p.

Newton, Bertram A. n.d. "A History of Red Bays, Andros." Typescript in the personal collection of Alcione M. Amos. Courtesy of Reverend Bertram A. Newton.

Nohl, Lessing H., Jr. 1962. "Bad Hand: The Military Career of Randal Slidell Mackenzie, 1871–1889." Ph.D. diss., University of New Mexico, Albuquerque.

Prince, Lieutenant Henry. n.d. "Diary of Henry Prince." Typescript in the personal collection of Thomas P. Senter. Courtesy of Frank Laumer.

Schwartz, Rosalie. 1974. "Runaway Negroes: Mexico as an Alternative for United States Blacks (1825–1860)." Ph.D. diss., California State University, San Diego.

Sprague, John T. n.d. "Journal of a Wagon Train Expedition from Ft. Inge to El Paso del Norte, 1850 by Captain and Brevet Major John T. Sprague." Original in the collection of Ben E. Pingenot, Brackettville, Tex.

Thompson, Richard A. 1992. "The Night the Dog Talked." n.p.

Willett, John. "Declaration, June 17, 1895." Typescript in the personal collection of Alcione M. Amos. Courtesy of Dolores L. Latorre.

Congressional Documents

SERIAL SET

15th Congress, 2d Sess., H.D. 14.
15th Congress, 2d Sess., H.D. 122.
25th Congress, 2d Sess., H.D. 78.
25th Congress, 2d Sess., H.D. 219.
25th Congress, 2d Sess., H.D. 327.
25th Congress, 2d Sess., S.D. 507.
25th Congress, 3d Sess., H.D. 225.
26th Congress, 1st Sess., S.D. 278.
27th Congress, 2d Sess., H.R. 723.
31st Congress, 1st Sess., S.D. 49.
33d Congress, 2d Sess., H.D. 15.
34th Congress, 1st Sess., H.D. 135.
43d Congress, 1st Sess., H.D. 257.
45th Congress, 1st Sess., H.D. 13.
45th Congress, 2d Sess., H.D. 64.
53d Congress, 2d Sess., H.D. 1.
60th Congress, 1st Sess., S.D. 215.

Newspapers

Cherokee Advocate
Diário Oficial (Mexico)
Fort Smith Herald
La Patria (Mexico)
San Antonio Texan
El Siglo Diez y Nueve (Mexico)
Texas Monument
Texas Republican
Texas State Gazette
Texas State Times
Western Texan

Archival Material

Uɴɪᴛᴇᴅ Sᴛᴀᴛᴇs Oғғɪᴄɪᴀʟ Sᴏᴜʀᴄᴇs

Records of the Veterans Administration, RG15, NA
  Pension Files
Records of the District Courts of the United States, RG21, Washington National
  Records Center, Suitland, Md.
  Records of the Circuit Court, District of Columbia
Records of the Bureau of the Census, RG29, NA
  1870, Census of Cameron, Maverick, and Uvalde Counties, Tex. Microfilm Publi-
    cation, 593
  1910, Census of Kinney County, Tex., Microfilm Publication, T624
Naval Records Collection of the Office of Naval Records and Library, RG 45, NA
  Subject File HJ—1816
Records of the Department of the Interior, RG48, NA
  Records of the Indian Division
Records of the Department of State, RG59, NA
  Despatches from U.S. Consuls in Piedras Negras, 1868–1906, Microfilm Publica-
    tion, 299
Records of the Bureau of Indian Affairs (BIA), RG75, NA
  Classified Files
  Letters Received, 1824–81, Microfilm Publication, 234
    Creek Agency, Emigration, 1840–49, roll 240
    Florida Superintendency, Emigration, 1839–53, roll 291
    Seminole Agency Emigration, 1827–46, rolls 806–7
    Seminole Agency, 1847–59, rolls 858–61
    Texas Agency, 1847–59, rolls 858–61
    Western Superintendency, 1832–51, roll 924
    Letters Received, 1881–1907
    Letters Sent, Correspondence of the Land Division
    Special Files, 1807–1904, Microfilm Publication, 574
    Special File number 96, roll 13
Records of the Office of the Quartermaster General (QMGO), RG92, NA
  Consolidated Correspondence File, 1794–1915
    Fort Gibson
    Gopher John
    Jesup, General Thomas

John Cowaya

Kirkham, R. W.

Seminole War 1837

Letters Sent by the Office of the Quartermaster General, 1818–70, Microfilm Publication, 745

Records of the Adjutant General Office (AGO), RG94, NA

General Correspondence File

General Thomas S. Jesup Papers

Letters Received by the AGO, 1822–60, Microfilm Publication, 567

Letters Received by the AGO, 1861–70, Microfilm Publication, 619

Letters Received by the Commission Branch of the AGO, Microfilm Publication, 1064

Letters Sent by the AGO, Microfilm Publication, 565

Record of Medical History of Post, Fort Duncan, Texas

Regular Army Muster Rolls, Seminole Negro Indian Scouts, Texas

Returns from Regular Army Cavalry Regiments, 1833–1916, Microfilm Publication, 744

Returns from U.S. Military Posts, 1800–1916, Microfilm Publication, 617

Records of the Office of the Secretary of War, RG107, NA

Letters Sent by the Secretary of War Relating to Military Affairs, 1800–89, Microfilm Publication, 6

Records of the U.S. Army Continental Commands, RG393, NA

Department of Texas

Letters and Reports Received Relating to the Garza Revolution, 1891–93

Letters Received, 1876–77

Letters Received Related to Difficulties with Indians (Indian File), 1870–1913.

Records of Cards and Correspondence Relating to Various Subjects, 1909–12, file 28985 (Seminole Negroes)

Headquarters Army of the Southwestern Frontier, Microfilm Publication, 1202

Headquarters Records, Fort Duncan, Texas

Letters Sent

Letters Received

Headquarters Records, Fort Gibson, Indian Affairs, 1844–51, Microfilm Publication, 1466

Headquarters Records, Fort McKavett, Reports of Expeditions and Scouts, December 1870–May 1875

Military Division of the Missouri, Special File, Seminole Negro Indians, 1872–76.

Ninth Military Department, Letters Sent, 1840–45

Second Military Department, Letters Sent

Kinney County, Texas, District Court Records

UNITED STATES ARCHIVAL COLLECTIONS

Archivo de la Secretaria de Gobierno, Saltillo, Coahuila, Bancroft Library, University of California at Berkeley

Governors' Records, Archives Division, Texas State Library, Austin

Guajardo Papers, Beinecke Library, Yale University, New Haven

Muzquiz Records, Beinecke Library, Yale University, New Haven

Porter, Kenneth W. Papers. Schomburg Center for Research in Black Culture, New York

MEXICAN ARCHIVAL COLLECTIONS

Archivo del Departamento Agrario, Mexico City

Archivo General del Estado de Coahuila, Saltillo, Coahuila

Archivo de la Secretaria de la Defensa, Mexico City

Archivo de la Secretaria de Relaciones Exteriores, Mexico City

❧ Index

Arpeika (Sam Jones, chief): and Cherokee
delegation, 87; chiefs abducted by, 80;
description of, 36; and Lake Okeechobee
battle, 88–89, 91; and removal negotiations, 78, 96, 103, 128
Arredondo, José Antonio, 143
Ashby, Maj. John, 84
Asi Yahola. *See* Osceola (Asi Yahola, chief)
assimilation, 6, 27, 148–49
Augur, Brig. Gen. C. C., 188, 189–90
August (Black Seminole chief), 95, 122

Bahamas, resettlement to, 26
Banta, William, 129
Baptist church, 148–49, 191
Barnett, Tony, 87, 115, 120, 122, 128
Bassinger, Lt. William E., 42
battles (Seminole War): Caloosahatchee
River, 99; Hatcheelustee Creek, 69–71;
Jupiter Inlet, 92–93; Lake Okeechobee,
88–93; Lockahatchee River, 92–93; map
of, *38*; Orange Creek, 103–4; Peliklakaha,
54–55, 106; Wahoo Swamp, 40–41, 62–
65, 69. *See also* military; warriors;
Withlacoochee River
Beall, Maj., 100–101
Belknap, W. W., 184
Belknap, Brig. Gen. William G., 125–26
Bell, Gov. Peter H., 134, 143
Ben (Black Seminole), 70–72, 77
Benjamin, Archibald, 153
Benjamin, William, 153
Big Bend area, exploration of, 208
Big Cypress Swamp, 104
"big fight," 164–69
bilingualism, importance of, 6, 29, 63
Billy (guide), 56, 59–60
Biloxi Indians, 150
Black Creeks: in Mexico, 163–64; removal
of, 211; as scouts, 182, 207; status of,
152–53
Black Dirt (chief), removal of, 112. *See also*
Crazy Black Dirt
blacks: among Upper Creeks, 14; classes of
among Seminoles, 77; control of, 74; as
plunder, 61. *See also* Black Creeks; Black
Seminoles; slaves
Black Seminoles: advocate for, 116–18;
attitudes toward, 4, 11; censuses of, 28,
197, 226–27; conditions for, 6–7;

definition of, 229n. 10; description of, 95;
divisions in, 187; emancipation for, 95–96,
106, 113, 115–25; eviction from Fort
Clark of, 210, 211, 216; hostility toward,
198–99, 200–202; integration of, 6, 27;
kidnapping of, 117–18, 121–23, 126, 134,
140, 143; land grants for, 179, 186–88,
211–16; language of, 6, 29, 63, 148, 243n.
25; leaders of, 27, 80, 81, 88, 121, 187,
211; migrations of, 2, 29; military service
of, 98–105; and removal negotiations, 31,
72–73, 75, 77, 95; returned to slavery,
117–26; rights guaranteed for, 77, 95, 113;
settlements of, 62, *190*, 198, 215; and
Spanish rule, 4–5; surrender of, 87–88. *See
also* emigration; Mascogos (Black
Seminoles in Mexico); removal; Seminole
Negro Indian Scouts
Bliss, Maj. Zenas R., 179–81, 212
Boehm's Canyon (Texas), action near, 193
Bonaparte, Louis Napoleon, 169
Bonneville, Maj. B. L., 123, 124–25
Boone, Capt. Nathan, 114
Bowlegs, Aleck, 171
Bowlegs, Billy (chief): attack by, 99; and
removal negotiations, 103, 128, 132; slaves
of, 125; and Third Seminole War, 107
Bowlegs, Sgt. David, 170, 208, 211
Bowlegs, Dolly, 191, 211
Bowlegs, Friday, 164, 171
Bowlegs, Harriet (Seminole), 125
Bowlegs, Jack, 164
Bowlegs, Jacob, 171
Bowlegs, Jim, 115, 128, 132–33
Bowlegs, Julio, 171
Bowlegs (chief): attitudes toward, 4; death of,
26; Jackson's attack on, 21–23; as leader,
18; migration of, 25; Newnan's attack on,
10
Boyd, Capt. Orsemus Bronson, 181
Brackettville (Texas): encampment near, 130;
scouts at, 182–83; settlements at, *190*
Bradley, Pvt. John, 201
Brazos River, winter quarters at, 128
British Post, 15–16. *See also* Fort Gadsden;
Negro Fort
Brooke, Lt. Col. George M., 28, 30, 76, 129,
134, 141
Brownsville (Texas): scouts recruited from,
182; settlement at, 171

interpreters: as counselors, 6, 27; and removal negotiations, 75; as targets, 106; wages for, 112

Ives, 2d Lt. Edward B., 212–13

Izard, Lt. James F., 48. *See also* Camp Izard, seige of

Jackson, Andrew: appointments for, 20; associates of, 59; attitudes toward, 24; Florida campaign of, 11, 14–16, 20–23, 26; presidential administration of, 31

Jefferson, Curly, 133–34, 187

Jefferson, John, 220–21, 254n. 27

Jesup, Gen. Thomas Sidney: and capture of Seminoles, 82–85, 96; and Cherokee delegation, 85–87; emancipation offered by, 95–96, 106, 115–25; Florida campaign of, 66–75, 92–93; John Horse's request to, 115–18; negotiations by, 75–78, 81–84; on removal, 94–96; and runaways, 78–82; and Seminole delegation, 113

Johnson, Dan, 251n. 5

Johnson, Dick, 171

Johnson, Kitty, 128–30, 153, 171, 182

Jones, Adj. Gen. Roger, 84, 98

Jones, Sam. *See* Arpeika (Sam Jones, chief)

Juan (Black Seminole interpreter), 6

Juana (John Horse's half-sister): children of, 120–22; description of, 29, 182; and emigration to Mexico, 128, 132; marriage of, 224; and removal, 87

Juárez, Benito, 161, 169–70, 173, 223

Juaristas, 169–71

Judge, Thomas L., 113, 115, 116, 121

July, Cpl. Billy, 214–15

July, Carolina, 189

July, Charles, 189

July, Dembo, 128

July, Dolly, 219, 224

July, John, 189

July, Sgt. Sampson, 128, 189, 211, 213, 222

July, Thomas, 128

July (Black Seminole chief), 95, 100, 115, 189

Jumper, Jim, 126

Jumper, John, 212

Jumper (chief): abduction of, 80; agreement signed by, 77; and Dade's massacre, 41, 43; death of, 97; description of, 35; and Gaines's attack, 48, 52; and Jesup's

campaign, 71, 73, 75–76; locale for, 67–68; and removal, 32, 34; representative of, 83–84; surrender of, 87; treaty signed by, 28

Jupiter Inlet, action near, 92–93

Kenhadjo (chief), 19, 25

Kerr, Capt., 106

Keyes, Maj. Alexander S. B., 202, 214

Kibbitts, John: complaints by, 173, 177; death of, 210; family of, 128, 153, 226; as leader, 171, 187–88, 219; in Mexico, 145, 154; name of, 148; and relocation to United States, 178–80

Kibbitts, Nancy, 171

Kibbitts, Sgt. Robert: attack by, 201–2; requests by, 213; as scout, 180–81; visits to Indian Territory by, 177, 211; visit to Washington, D.C., 213

Kibbitts, Roselle, 153

Kickapoo Indians: attacks on, 172, 184–86; defection of, 141–42; emigration by, 131, 134, 171–73; eviction of, 222; land grants for, 140–41, 145–46, 224–26; Mascogo relations with, 177; in Nacimiento, 171–73, 177; possible relocation of, 178, 180, 186; recruitment of, 128–29

Kickapoo Springs (Texas), action near, 189

King Payne (chief), 4, 6, 10, 25, 126

King Philip. *See* Emathla, King Philip (chief)

Kiowa Indians, 181, 189

Kirby, Maj. Reynold M., 53–54

Kirkham, Lt. R. W., 120, 122

Kissimmee River, 88

koonti (root), as food, 13, 71

Laguna Cuarto, action near, 194

Laguna de Jaco (Chihuahua), campaign in, 145–46, 150

Laguna de Parras: emigrants relocated to, 161; French destruction of, 170–71

Laguna Sabinas (now Cedar Lake), Apache camp at, 196

Lake Monroe, battle at, 74

Lake Okeechobee: battle at, 88–93; Seminole meeting near, 103

Lake Tohopekaliga, cattle seized near, 76

land turtles, as food, 30

Langberg, Col. Emilio, 145, 154

language: of Black Seminoles, 148, 243n. 25;
and importance of bilingualism, 6, 29, 63
Las Moras Creek (Texas), emigrants'
quarters at, 130; settlement on, *190*, 198,
215
Leitner, Frederick, 92
Léon (Lion, Seminole leader), 157
Lindsay, Col. William, 54
Lipans. *See* Apache Indians
Little River, Seminole land near, 116, 118
Livingston (steamer), 97
Llano River, blacks' stay at, 129
Lockahatchee River, battle at, 92–93
Lone Wolf (Kiowa chief), 189
Loomis, Maj., 100
Loomis, Lt. Col. Gustavus, 119, 122–23
Louisiana, militia from, 47, 53, 56
Lowe, Lt. Percival G., 214–15
Lower Creeks, alliances of, 4–5, 17

Mackenzie, Col. Ranald S.: appointment for,
184; campaigns of, 185–86, 191–95;
recommendations by, 197–98, 207, 212
Macomb, Maj. Gen. Alexander, 98–99
Madison, James, 3, 7
Mad Panther. *See* Coa Hadjo (Mad Panther,
chief)
Magruder, J. A., 191
Mahon, John K., 232n. 1
Maldonado, Col. Juan Manuel, 131, 140,
144
Mangas de Agua, 214–15
Marcy, Randolph B., 134, 178
Marcy, William L., 117, 124
Mariscal, Trinidad, 191
marriage: among different groups, 150, 152;
customs for, 149; of Mexicans to Black
Seminoles, 189; of Seminoles to Black
Seminoles, 6
Martinez, Eusebio, 214–15
Mascogos (Black Seminoles in Mexico):
alliances of, 221; assimilation of, 148–49;
attacks on, 145–46, 164–70; census of,
226–27; complaints against, 151–52, 155–
56, 158; description of, 131, 152–53;
eviction of, 222; land grants for, 140–41,
145–46, 173, 177, 222–27; leadership for,
155–56, 164; locale of, *138*; name changes
for, 148, 243n. 26; as professional
warriors, 163–64; religion of, 148–49,

155; retaliation on hostiles by, 164–69;
return to Nacimiento by, 171–73, 177;
versus Seminoles, 158–59; skills of, 164,
177–78; threats to, 139–40, 145; transfer
to Laguna de Parras of, 161–64; U.S. fears
of, 141, 147, 177
Mason, John T., 116–17
Mason, John Y., 124–25
Mason, Lt. Col. Richard B., 115
Matamoros (Mexico), settlement at, 171, 201
material culture, changes in, 148–49
Mathews, Gen. George, 3–4, 7–8
Maximilian (emperor of Mexico), 170–71
May, Jonathan, 201
McCallip, Pleasant, 202
McIntosh, John H., 4, 11
McIntosh, Gen. Roly, 120
McIntosh, Capt. William, 17–18, 20
McKee, John, 111
McQueen, Peter, 13–14, 20
medicines, 220
Mellon, Capt. Charles, 74
Menchaca, Don José Antonio, 132
Merritt, Joe, 74
Mescaleros. *See* Apache Indians
Mexican Revolution, 162, 213–14, 221
Mexico: administration of, 161; American
campaigns in, 184–85, 199–200, 202–6,
209; emigrants supported by, 139–41,
161, 173; land grants in, 140–41, 145–46,
173, 222–27; Mascogo emigration from,
179; Mascogos in, *138*; military support
for, 141–45, 154–55, 157–59, 161;
negotiations with, 131–32; religion in,
148–49; revolution in, 162, 213–14, 221;
slave hunters in, 139, 142–44, 153–55,
160; slavery outlawed in, 127; wars in,
156, 161, 169–71, 177
Micanopy (chief): abduction of, 80;
agreement signed by, 77; associates of,
27–28, 33–36, 112; capture of, 87; and
Cherokee delegation, 86–87; and Dade's
massacre, 41–42, 44; death of, 125;
description of, 26; family of, 31, 35–36;
and Gaines's attack, 48; locale for, 68;
power of, 35, 67; and removal negotiations, 34, 75, 83; removal of, 78, 97, 112;
representative of, 77, 83–84; Scott's attack
on, 55–56; treaty signed by, 28; and
Washington delegation, 113